Rethinking Peace and Conflict Studies

Titles include:

Roland Bleiker
AESTHETICS AND WORLD POLITICS

Claire Duncanson
FORCES FOR GOOD?
Military Masculinities and Peacebuilding in Afghanistan and Iraq

Kirsten J. Fisher
TRANSITIONAL JUSTICE FOR CHILD SOLDIERS
Accountability and Social Reconstruction in Post-Conflict Contexts

Daria Isachenko
THE MAKING OF INFORMAL STATES
Statebuilding in Northern Cyprus and Transdniestria

Roger Mac Ginty
INTERNATIONAL PEACEBUILDING AND LOCAL RESISTANCE
Hybrid Forms of Peace

SM Farid Mirbagheri
WAR AND PEACE IN ISLAM
A Critique of Islamic/ist Political Discourses

Audra L. Mitchell
LOST IN TRANSFORMATION
Violent Peace and Peaceful Conflict in Northern Ireland

Frank Möller
VISUAL PEACE
Images, Spectatorship and the Politics of Violence

Chavanne L. Peercy
LOCAL LEADERSHIP IN DEMOCRATIC TRANSITION

Michael Pugh
LIBERAL INTERNATIONALISM
The Interwar Movement for Peace in Britain

Oliver P. Richmond and Audra Mitchell (*editors*)
HYBRID FORMS OF PEACE
From Everyday Agency to Post-Liberalism

Emil Souleimanov
UNDERSTANDING ETHNOPOLITICAL CONFLICT
Karabakh, South Ossetia and Abkhazia Wars Reconsidered

Lynn M. Tesser
ETHNIC CLEANSING AND THE EUROPEAN UNION
An Interdisciplinary Approach to Security, Memory, and Ethnography

---

Rethinking Peace and Conflict Studies
Series Standing Order ISBN 978–1–403–99575–9 (hardback) & 978–1–403–99576–6 (paperback)
(*outside North America only*)

You can receive future titles in this series as they are published by placing a standing order. Please contact your bookseller or, in case of difficulty, write to us at the address below with your name and address, the title of the series and one of the ISBNs quoted above.

Customer Services Department, Macmillan Distribution Ltd, Houndmills, Basingstoke, Hampshire RG21 6XS, England

---

Transitional Justice for Child Soldiers

Accountability and Social Reconstruction in Post-Conflict Contexts

Kirsten J. Fisher
Research Fellow, Human Rights Research and Education Centre, University of Ottawa

palgrave
macmillan

First published 2013 by
PALGRAVE MACMILLAN

Palgrave Macmillan in the UK is an imprint of Macmillan Publishers Limited, registered in England, company number 785998, of Houndmills, Basingstoke, Hampshire RG21 6XS.

Palgrave Macmillan in the US is a division of St Martin's Press LLC, 175 Fifth Avenue, New York, NY 10010.

Palgrave Macmillan is the global academic imprint of the above companies and has companies and representatives throughout the world.

Palgrave® and Macmillan® are registered trademarks in the United States, the United Kingdom, Europe and other countries.

ISBN 978–1–137–03049–8

This book is printed on paper suitable for recycling and made from fully managed and sustained forest sources. Logging, pulping and manufacturing processes are expected to conform to the environmental regulations of the country of origin.

A catalogue record for this book is available from the British Library.

A catalog record for this book is available from the Library of Congress.

Contents

Acknowledgements

For their support of this project – financial, intellectual, and emotional – I owe a great deal of gratitude to many individuals and institutions. Some of them are listed here.

For their generous financial support of my research, I thank the Social Sciences and Humanities Research Council of Canada (SSHRC), the Canadian Consortium on Human Security (CCHS), the Human Security Program of the Department of Foreign Affairs and International Trade (DFAIT), the Academy of Finland through its support of the Centre of Excellence in Global Governance Research at the University of Helsinki, and the University of Ottawa's Human Rights Research and Education Centre (HRREC).

This book has benefited immeasurably from the intellectual input of many people. Special appreciation is extended to Matthew Grellette, Stephen Lamony, Jeremy Levitt, Pacifique Manirakiza, Valerie Oosterveld, Darryl Robinson, Elisa Romano, Richard Vernon, and Stephanie Vieille, whose insight and critical comments on parts or the whole of earlier versions of the manuscript were instrumental in helping me struggle through very tricky legal, political, social, and theoretical terrain. I owe a very special note of thanks to Caitlin Hayward, who spent considerable time and effort discussing and debating the arguments of this book, reading different drafts of chapters, helping me shape my thoughts into intelligible prose, and generally supporting me and the project, going well beyond the call of friendship. Naturally, any mistakes are my own.

Additionally, I want to express thanks to the Uganda Human Rights Commission and its commissioners who always opened their doors to me to answer any questions I had; to Erin Baines of the Liu Institute for Global Justice and to the staff of the Justice and Reconciliation Project (JRP) in Gulu for helping me to access some more remote interviews at an Internally Displaced Persons (IDP) camp in Amuru; to Lino Owor Ogora; to Grace Akello of Gulu University; and to William Odur and Ayoo Paska of Gulu Regional Referral Hospital's Mental Health Unit, who spent considerable time facilitating and translating interviews in the communities in and around Gulu.

The situation in northern Uganda is highlighted in this book because it is a particularly good example of the challenges of reintegrating large numbers of former child soldiers into communities that were victims of the brutality committed by an armed group that (forcibly) recruited children. It demonstrates the conflicting needs of a community to reintegrate suspected perpetrators of atrocity for peace and the dissatisfaction that community members feel with being instructed to welcome home suspected perpetrators as innocent victims. In the aftermath of two decades of violent conflict and terror, an entire community struggles to reconstitute itself and come to terms with atrocity. Fieldwork conducted in Uganda between 2007 and 2013 serves as a basis for this book. The research includes interviews with former child soldiers, victims of the conflict who had not been soldiers, clan chiefs and elders, academics, NGO and Ugandan civil society representatives, and government officials. To everyone who contributed to my understanding of the conflict and post-conflict situation in northern Uganda, I offer my appreciation for your sharing your time, opinions, and experiences with me so that we can work towards a better means of pursuing transitional justice for situations in which children both perpetrated and were themselves victims of atrocity.

The following pages incorporate some restructured, updated, and reworked previously published material. Contributing to the arguments of Chapters 4 and 5 is revisited material from various discussions found throughout my first book, *Moral Accountability and International Criminal Law* (Routledge 2012). I thank the Taylor and Francis Group for permission to re-use this material.

Finally, I owe recognition to my family for its enduring support and encouragement, and special thanks to my mother for her invaluable help in copy-editing my words. And to Jason.

It is impossible not to fall short of properly addressing all aspects of the subject of child soldiers around the world or to offer a definitive framework with which to deal with child soldier perpetrators of severe harm. My aim with this book is to illuminate the situation of the child soldier, both in armed conflict and in the reintegration experience, to dispel the unhelpful and deceptive universalized non-responsible child narrative, and to offer some suggestions for a framework of thinking about and addressing the responsibility of child soldiers that can help ease reintegration of child soldiers and facilitate social reconstruction of the society affected by violent conflict and mass human rights violations. I hope I am at least successful in inspiring new critical thinking.

Abbreviations

AFDL	Alliance des Forces Démocratiques pour la Libération du Congo-Zaïre (DRC)
AFRC	Armed Forces Revolutionary Council (Sierra Leone)
AUC	Auto-defensas Unidas de Colombia (Colombia)
CAR	Central African Republic
CBT	Cognitive Behavioural Therapy
CDF	Civil Defence Forces (Sierra Leone)
CDR	Coalition pour la Défense de la République (Rwanda)
CRC	Convention on the Rights of the Child (United Nations)
DDR	Disarmament, Demobilization, and Reconciliation
DRC	Democratic Republic of the Congo
ELN	Ejército de Liberación Nacional (Colombia)
FAC	Forces Armees Congolaises (DRC)
FAP	Formerly Abducted Person
FARC	Fuerzas Armadas Revolucionarias de Colombia (Colombia)
ICC	International Criminal Court
ICD	International Crimes Division (of Uganda's High Court)
ICL	International Criminal Law
ICTR	International Criminal Tribunal for Rwanda
ICTY	International Criminal Tribunal for the former Yugoslavia
IDP	Internally Displaced Person
IHL	International Humanitarian Law
LLTE	Liberation Tigers of Tamil Eelam (Tamil Tigers)
LRA/M	Lord's Resistance Army/Movement
MRND	Mouvement Républicain National pour la Démocratie et le Développement (Rwanda)
NGO	Non-Governmental Organization
PTS	Post Traumatic Stress
PTSD	Post Traumatic Stress Disorder
RENAMO	Resistência Nacional Moçambicana (Mozambique)
RLP	Refugee Law Project (Uganda)
RSLAF	Republic of Sierra Leone Armed Forces
RUF	Revolutionary United Front (Sierra Leone)
SC	Security Council (United Nations)
SCSL	Special Court for Sierra Leone

STD	Sexually Transmitted Disease
TELO	Tamil Eelam Liberation Organization (Sri Lanka)
TRC	Truth and Reconciliation Commission
UN	United Nations
UNAMIR	United Nations Assistance Mission for Rwanda
UPDF	Uganda People's Defence Force

Introduction

'Is a child still a child when pressing the barrel of a gun to your chest?' asks Lieutenant-General (Ret'd) Roméo Dallaire (Dallaire 2010: 2). Dallaire served as Force Commander of the peacekeeping United Nations Assistance Mission for Rwanda (UNAMIR), where he was first confronted with child soldiers during the genocide of 1994. He then went on to found the Roméo Dallaire Child Soldiers Initiative to end the use of child soldiers in conflict. Children should not know or be involved in war. With his question, however, Dallaire points to an important and disturbing concern in conflict and in post-conflict social reconstruction: child soldiers are a paradox that confuses our understanding of terms like childhood, perpetrator, and innocence. This paradox makes the issue of post-conflict justice even more complex: when children do participate in conflict, when they commit horrific acts of violence, when they later come face to face with the victims of their violence, when they themselves are likely victims of abuse and violence, when they need to reintegrate into a peaceful and well-ordered society, and when they are needed to contribute to its rebuilding and to flourish as members of the society's future, how should child soldier perpetrators of abuses be perceived and treated?

Millions of the world's children are caught up in armed conflicts – as witnesses, victims, and even targets. In numerous conflicts around the world, children are also participants in war. Many of the conflicts in which children fight are characterized by violent cruelty. Some of these children are causal perpetrators of some of the worst acts of depraved murder, disfigurement, and terrorism imaginable. Civilians suffer at their hands – amputations, mutilations, agonizing death (Amann 2001: 169). In some cases, children commit atrocities against their own families and communities (United Nations 2011: 10).

This book explores how child perpetrators of atrocity should be conceived and addressed. What is the best approach to understanding and addressing harmful acts committed by child soldiers to support positive peace and social reconstruction in the aftermath of mass atrocity? This book questions whether, from the perspective of both moral and practical consideration, child members of armed groups or armed forces that commit grave acts of atrocity should be held accountable for the harm they commit. Can persons under the age of 18 be responsible for acts of atrocity they commit in war? And if so, how should they be held accountable to properly address their personal responsibility and to help the post-conflict society move forward in a healthy manner?

The use of children or youths as active participants in armed conflict is a global phenomenon with a long history (Rosen 2005; Litvak 2006). Recent years have seen growing awareness of child soldiering, increased international will to support and advance children's rights, and the development of international criminal law and the global fight against impunity for atrocity crimes, which draw new attention to child perpetrators of shocking violations of human rights. Traditionally, in battle, as in other areas of life, children were employed as small adults capable of performing critical tasks and contributing to the job at hand. In combat, a child's role was generally supportive to the war effort; for example, children assumed roles as charioteers, armour bearers for adult soldiers, buglers, aides or squires, and 'porters, drummers, cooks, and... other non-combatant roles' (Dallaire 2010: 105). What distinguishes the present from the past is not the use of child soldiers in itself, but the continued recruitment of child soldiers despite a growing robust prohibition against the use of children in armed conflict. It is also that in contemporary battles around the world children are recruited to be agents of great atrocity; some of the world's most horrific fighting groups that perpetrate grave abuses and acts of terrorism against civilians are comprised primarily of young people and soldiers who were recruited young.

As the 20th century progressed, there arose a presumption that children should not be exploited as workers, especially in dangerous jobs, and that children were not particularly valuable in warfare (Mann 1987: 35). Despite these presumptions, persons under the age of 18 never really disappeared from the arena of armed conflict. By the end of the Second World War, youths were participating both in the Third Reich army and in some campaigns against the Nazis (Rosen 2005). This use of children in the 20th century, though, was seen as an aberration, a deviation from the accepted norms, 'which did not disturb the pre-existing assumption' that children were incapable of contributing to the war effort (Mann 1987: 35).

The pre-existing modern assumption against the contribution of children to armed conflict, whether it really exists or not, has also not been effective in shielding young persons from combat in the latter half of the 20th century or the beginning of the 21st. In many contemporary conflicts around the world young persons are targeted for participation precisely for the fact that they are young. The phenomenon of children at war attracts attention not only because they are young, but also because of the conditions of their recruitment and the combat experiences of most. Their participation is often not voluntary, even if you can consider young persons capable of such decisions. And their continued participation is usually ensured by physical and psychological abuse and the infliction of terror. Although national protection for children against exploitation and physical harm has increased over the last century, there is the incompatible prevalence of the use of youths in hostilities. It is estimated that at any point in the contemporary post-Cold War world, about 250,000–300,000 children under the age of 18 are serving as soldiers, guerrilla fighters, or in support roles in more than 25 countries globally, in the Americas, Africa, Asia, Europe, and the former Soviet Union (Derluyn et al. 2004: 861; Sendabo 2004: 12; Boothby et al. 2006: 88; Betancourt et al. 2010: 17; Flock 2012).

International legal instruments have not been effective in eradicating the use of children and youths in war. Such attempts also have a fairly lengthy history. As early as 1924, the League of Nations adopted the Geneva Declaration of the Rights of the Child, which claimed for every child the right to survival, nutrition, shelter, health care, humanitarian relief, protection from exploitation, and the right to grow up in an environment that fosters the child's development (Geneva Declaration of the Rights of the Child 1924). The United Nations' Declaration of the Rights of the Child was adopted in 1959 (Declaration of the Rights of the Child 1959). Since then, there have been increasing efforts on the part of the international community to limit the use of children in war through international conventions. The 1977 Additional Protocols to the Geneva Conventions request the adherence to restrictions on the participation of children in war, at least for those under the age of 15. Additional Protocol I stipulates in Article 77 that 'the parties to the conflict shall take all feasible measures in order that children who have not attained the age of fifteen years do not take a direct part in hostilities', and that if a party to conflict must resort to recruiting among those aged 15–18, priority should be given to those who are oldest

(ICRC 1977a: 77(2)). Additional Protocol II reiterates these sentiments, aiming to protect victims of non-international armed conflict (ICRC 1977b: Part II 4(3)). The United Nations Convention on the Rights of the Child (CRC), Article 38 (1989) goes further and prohibits state parties 'from recruiting any person who has not attained the age of fifteen years into their armed forces' and promotes prioritizing older candidates over younger ones when recruiting persons between the ages of 15 and 18. These obligations were then further clarified by the Optional Protocol to this convention which entered into force in 2002 and concerned specifically the involvement of children in armed conflict. The Optional Protocol limits direct participation in hostilities to members of the armed forces who have attained the age of 18 (Article 1), limits compulsory recruitment to persons who have attained the age of 18 (Article 2), and demands special protection for volunteer recruits under the age of 18, ensuring that recruitment is genuinely voluntary, and that such recruitment is carried out with the informed consent of the person's parents or legal guardians (Article 3).

In 2007, the United Nations Children's Fund (UNICEF) developed the Paris Principles, an update of the decade-old Cape Town Principles, that were to inform the development of international norms and shifts in policy at the national, regional, and international levels and prevent the recruitment of child soldiers. This update was prompted by the rapid changes in knowledge regarding children in conflict and changes in international law, such as the inclusion of the recruitment of children under the age of 15 as a war crime in the Rome Statute (Paris Principles: 1.3). According to the Paris Principles, a child soldier is

> any person below 18 years of age who is or who has been recruited or used by an armed force or armed group in any capacity, including but not limited to children, boys, and girls used as fighters, cooks, porters, messengers, spies or for sexual purposes. It does not only refer to a child who is taking or has taken a direct part in hostilities.
> (Paris Principles: 2.1)

Importantly, the Paris Principles do not refer to child soldiers but to children associated with an armed force or armed group.

Over the past 20 years, the international community has made significant strides forward in its aims to construct and enforce new international norms and laws against conscripting and enlisting children to participate in armed conflict. As mentioned, in addition to the conventions mentioned above, the Rome Statute of the International Criminal

Court (ICC) strengthens the international legal norms prohibiting the use of children in war by listing as a war crime 'conscripting or enlisting children under the age of fifteen years into the national armed forces or using them to participate actively in hostilities' (Rome Statute, Article 8(b)(xxvi)). As of the writing of this book, a number of high-profile international trials have centred around the charges of child recruitment. The Special Court for Sierra Leone (SCSL) was the first United Nations (UN) backed tribunal to deliver a guilty verdict for the military conscription of children with its conviction of three former leaders of Sierra Leone's former Armed Forces Revolutionary Council (AFRC) (SCSL 2007). The SCSL also found Charles Taylor, former President of Liberia, guilty of 'other serious violation of international humanitarian law' including 'conscripting or enlisting children under the age of 15 years into armed forces or groups, or using them to participate actively in hostilities'.[1] He was convicted in April 2012, and was sentenced to 50 years in prison in May of that year.[2] The very first case to go to trial at the ICC was that of Thomas Lubanga Dyilo (hereafter Lubanga), who was charged under Articles 8(2)(e)(vii) and 25(3)(a) of the Statute with the war crimes of conscripting and enlisting children under the age of 15 years into an armed group and using them to participate actively in hostilities.[3] On 14 March 2012, he was convicted of these crimes as a co-perpetrator.[4] In July of the same year he was sentenced to 14 years in prison.[5] In a relatively short period of time, the international prohibition against the use of child soldiers has grown considerable teeth with which it can be enforced.

And yet, the effects of the prosecution of recruiters of child soldiers and the attempts to create new international norms are as of yet unseen. There is little evidence that the moral campaign prohibiting using children in war has been effective, especially in regards to non-state armed groups (Boothby et al. 2006: 87). There are currently many active child soldiers in combat and there is no evidence to support a belief that the use of child soldiers is in a significant decline (Gates and Reich 2010: 4; Flock 2012). There are many reasons that armies turn to children to fill their ranks. Characteristics such as their malleability, eagerness to satisfy those in charge, and their less mature moral identities make child and youth recruits more attractive than adults to some military leaders (Grover 2008: 54). They are cheaper, often working for little other than subsistence and promises of wealth or power in the future regime. They are trainable, easily manipulated (Wessells 2006: 35), and can be easy to indoctrinate, and since they can be desirous of approval from their superiors, they can aim to do as asked to the best of their abilities. They lack fully formed and internalized moral codes, and they are often seen as more ferocious (Singer 2005: 106).

Usually, children are seen by the military leaders as more expendable than adults (Dallaire 2010: 3). They also offer certain strategic advantages such as being smaller and more capable of manoeuvring undetected, often being ignored as potential threats, and being more likely to generate reluctance in the enemy to fire, as adults are more liable to hesitate before firing at a child or are less willing to fire at all simply because it is a child (Wessells 2006: 34–36). And so, arguably, 'It is no coincidence that 60 per cent of the nonstate armed forces in the world today deliberately make use of child soldiers. For rebel groups, using the child soldier doctrine is a way to overcome their weak starting point as far as recruiting, organization, and other state-centered systemic barriers to their growth' (Singer 2005: 95).

The phenomenon of child soldiers, despite the international legal provisions that aim to end the active involvement of children in violent conflict, is a pervasive and persistent one. Much of the work that has developed out of the recent increased attention to the phenomenon focuses on promoting awareness, examining the recruitment of child soldiers and advancing the cessation of the use of youths in this way, and on their rehabilitation and post-traumatic healing (see: Singer 2004; Honwana 2006; Wessells 2006; Dallaire 2010; Johnson et al. 2012; Whitman 2012). The aim of such valuable work is the strengthening of protection for children from the effects of armed conflict. This book acknowledges that such work is crucial to the advancement of a just world. The human rights, and commonly the basic dignity, of these children are violated in their recruitment and/or abduction, and child soldiers risk permanent physical and mental disabilities and their lives in fighting (Sendabo 2004: 12). This book also recognizes, however, that in the meantime, before the use of child soldiers is halted entirely or there is only the exceptional negligible example of child and youth recruitment, young soldiers are still participating in armed conflicts in which they commit violent acts and contribute to widespread assaults on civilian populations. This fact generates some important moral and practical questions and challenges, especially in regards to establishing post-conflict justice and generating social reconstruction. These former soldiers who contributed to the devastation of the communities to which they may return often arrive back into civilian life to face ambiguous and confusing reception that reflects their complex moral and legal situations. These agents of atrocity, who are both victims and perpetrators, occupy a unique space along the spectrum of responsibility, and the difficult questions facing every post-conflict society grappling with how to pursue transitional justice are compounded with the need to conceptualize and appropriately address these victim-perpetrators.

For example, a large number of children and youths from northern Uganda were abducted by the Lord's Resistance Army (LRA) and forced to participate in violent conflict against their own people and the government of Uganda. Over a period of 20 years, an estimated 30,000–60,000 children and youths were abducted to fill the ranks of this rebel group as fighters and in support roles (Baines 2010: 409). These children and youths were transformed almost instantly into victims and perpetrators of shocking horrors. Aside from the brutal abductions and cruel life as forced soldiers that these children endured, reintegration back into community life after escape, rescue, or being surrendered presents additional challenges for them as they attempt to rejoin communities that were victimized by the rebel army of which they were soldiers, find employment without education or skills, and deal with the emotional scars of their captivity and the harm they perpetrated.

Part of the reason that their reception back into society is difficult is that many returning LRA soldiers are burdened with the acts they committed in the bush and their identities as former fighters that they cannot shake. Uganda's treatment of formerly abducted persons (FAPs) is sensitive to their victimization: granting amnesty for returnees, and welcoming instruments of support for their reintegration. And yet, while many Ugandans profess to forgive all wrongdoing, forgiveness seems an intellectual exercise that is considered by some inconsistent with the dictates of justice and their emotional capabilities (Veale and Stavrou 2007: 288). In the villages there is often resentment and aggression towards returnees for their part in the victimization of civilians. Even when they are not faced with outright hostility, they are regularly ostracized and marginalized (Akello et al. 2006: 234–235). In a way, the response that some returning LRA soldiers face is tantamount to retaliation or informal community-based punishment.

In other cases around the world, young former fighters are faced with more formal mechanisms of retribution. Some are treated as adult participants, and are held responsible for their participation in the conflict in the same manner as are adults.

> Contrary to the [often advanced] principle that child soldiers should be treated first and foremost as victims in need of support and

> assistance for reintegration, some have been detained solely on the basis of their alleged association with armed groups, or for desertion and other military offences while in armed forces (Global Report 2008).

In the aftermath of the Rwandan genocide, there were over 1,000 children imprisoned and awaiting trial, accused of participating in the genocide (Reis 1997). Colombia's judicial system has also been seen to criminalize the actions of young combatants, making reintegration for freed former child soldiers difficult (Sendabo 2004: 16). Also, despite criticism from Amnesty International and other international human rights protection organizations, the US imprisoned young persons during its war on terror in Guantánamo Bay, a facility that does not conform to juvenile justice or fair trial standards (Human Rights Watch 2008).[6] Given the hardships that these participants in conflict face, there is much to be said for their compassionate treatment and sensitive rehabilitation and reintegration into civilian life.

There is much more to be said on the very broad topic of child soldiers than can be covered in the pages of any one book. The scope of this text concentrates on one important aspect among many. This text is interested primarily in young persons who contribute to mass atrocity, and most specifically in conflicts internal to a state. While there are many conflicts world-wide in which persons under the age of 18 play a role in fighting forces, this book is particularly interested in societies that must rebuild in the wake of widespread, systematic, and violent violations of human rights by reintegrating young agents of atrocity. Reintegration of child soldiers into the societies that were victimized by their actions is acutely difficult. 'Unlike disarmament and demobilization, reintegration cannot be imposed or centralized. It is a slow and complex process... [and] it is usually the weakest link in the DDR chain' (Faltas 2005: 1).

The discussion in this book is limited to the moral and practical goals of justice and social reconstruction in societies that have been shattered by civil war; its focus is an exploration of the moral responsibility of a specific subset of children and youths employed in combat situations and the proper response to their responsibility, or lack of responsibility, for effective transitioning of a society. The use of child soldiers in vicious civil armed conflicts is a significant global problem and the use of child soldiers in these conflicts causes particular challenges as societies attempt, post-conflict, to rebuild and restore social harmony. Although definitely not all, 'Many conflicts within the present international system are protracted civil conflicts that have become internationalized; costs have been incurred and the parties are struggling for survival' (Bercovitch 2011: 179), and young persons are forced into these groups to then later be returned often to the same people who were victimized by the harmful actions to which the children and youths contributed. Child soldiers return to communities that have been affected by the conflict in which they participated, to communities which have been victimized by them or others like them in their capacity as causal agents of atrocity, to communities that bore the brunt of their violence. In the aftermath of the violence, victims, perpetrators, and victim-perpetrators must live side by side. The importance of the successful reintegration of returnees to the project of post-conflict social reconstruction is tremendous.

With an eye to justice, reintegration, and social reconstruction, this book questions the right response to acts that, if committed by adults, would be eligible to be judged as acts of genocide, crimes against humanity, or war crimes, but that, because they are committed by persons under the age of 18, do not fall within the jurisdiction of the ICC and are generally discounted by most domestic criminal law systems that attempt to conform with an emergent interpretation of international law. The general policy of international law thus far has been to criminalize the recruitment of these young persons and to treat the young fighters as victims or tools of the adult recruiters. While it might seem right and reasonable to hold adults accountable for their recruitment of young fighters, particularly forceful recruitment, doing so does not resolve questions regarding the moral and legal standing of these young fighters or affirm that rightness requires them to be treated only as victims or tools.

The issue of conceptualizing and addressing the responsibility of these participants in combat is important for reasons both theoretical and practical. Part of what this text aims to do is to explore the range of moral responsibility that attaches to young perpetrators of atrocity. In many cases, young perpetrators have committed acts that, if committed by a different agent, could be considered under international criminal law to be 'the most serious crimes of concern to the international community' (Rome Statute, Preamble). The unique conditions that each individual child soldier faces as well as the conditions common to most (forceful recruitment, coercive wartime experiences, and their immaturity) influence the degree of agency they can exercise and therefore their moral responsibility. A comprehensive evaluation of responsibility that takes into account features that diminish responsibility is necessary to assure proper post-conflict accountability. Even if practical considerations demand that responsible agents are not brought to account for their wrongdoing, such decisions ought to be made under full comprehension of the moral responsibility of agents and to whom immunity is to be granted.

Practically, attention needs to be directed towards facilitating social reconstruction and the successful transition of these young agents back to civilian life. Cases in which this is most difficult and for which successful reintegration is most critical are cases in which children have been recruited to participate in the widespread and violent atrocity of an intrastate conflict. These children, who are often violently abducted or lured away without having a true understanding of the conflict or their role in it, are often indoctrinated and are frequently forced into committing wrongful actions or they are victimized so that their loyalty is misdirected and maintained by the fighting group which they have joined (Blattman and Annan 2010). In such cases, former child soldiers present challenges to the society's successful reconstruction both in their role as casualties of war who were wounded, if not physically then psychologically, by their wartime experiences, and also as executors of violence who, upon returning home can be ostracized, condemned, and feared for their participation in the conflict.

Successful reintegration of young fighters is a significant worldwide concern. Absent successful reintegration of ex-soldiers, a society can be left fragmented, wounded, and mired in internal discord, and is therefore hampered in its ability to move beyond the conflict. Returnees not properly reintegrated and found a space and purpose in the community can be dangerous in and of themselves (Sendabo 2004: 15; IRIN 2008). The detriments of children and youths engaged in war have a much longer life than simply the duration of the conflict.

> [T]he doctrine's implications do not stop at the conflict's termination. Rather, the use of underage combatants lays the groundwork for future violence and instability. The experiences that children come away with from participating in war can have a devastating effect both for them and for the broader society. The cumulative effect of these traumatic experiences will color and inform their choices, opinions, and perspectives for the rest of their lives.
>
> (Singer 2005: 108)

Therefore, transitional justice processes must be designed with awareness of the unique challenges that face child soldiers and of the needs of the post-conflict society that must reintegrate child soldiers successfully.

Transitional justice is not a term that refers to any particular approach to justice; rather, the term refers to a strategy, a way of thinking about justice after atrocity. It is 'a convenient way of describing the search for a just society in the wake of undemocratic, often oppressive and even violent systems' that offers 'a deeper, richer and broader vision of justice which seeks to confront perpetrators, address the needs of victims and assist in the start of a process of reconciliation and transformation' (Boraine 2006: 18). This book argues that an approach to transitional justice that takes seriously the agency of child soldier participants in violent conflict as responsible moral entities is necessary in order to appropriately address the responsibility of, and harm caused by, these unique actors, promote the best interests of the children, and advance post-conflict social reconstruction. It argues that there is particular value in accountability that must not be overlooked in misguided attempts to make easy work of reintegration. Needed are creative solutions to context-specific social reconstruction problems.

This book takes issue with what will be called the 'non-responsible child narrative': the claim that no person under the age of 18 can possess the capacity to be responsible for acts of atrocity they commit as a member of an armed force or armed group.[7] The non-responsible child narrative grounds the general policy of post-atrocity justice processes that criminalizes the recruitment of these young persons by adults and treats the young fighters universally only as victims or as tools of the adults. This book argues that the non-responsible child narrative and the resultant policy are problematic in two ways: morally and practically. Conceptually, treating child soldiers in this manner might be flawed in that transitional justice processes might be dismissing significant contributors to mass atrocity as nothing more than tools when doing so might not be reflective of their true roles and responsibility. And practically, treating them as such might be a hindrance to the child soldiers in the already difficult process of reintegration and might be an impediment to the broader project of social reconstruction.

Chapter 1 of this book aims to satisfy two goals: it aims to familiarize readers with some of the varied experiences that child soldiers face in different contexts around the world, and it reviews some aspects of the broader study of child soldiers, including terms used and how they will be used in this text. This chapter grounds the rest of the book by demonstrating that great generalizations about the child soldier experience, as reflected in the non-responsible child narrative, inaccurately miss the significant variety of experiences and actions of child soldiers.

Chapter 2 explores the poor reception that many child soldiers face in their attempts to reintegrate into civilian life. Child soldiers face a number of real challenges that hinder reintegration, such as physical wounds and psychological trauma and a lack of income-generating skills because of missed opportunities for education and skills-training. These personal challenges can be compounded because they can affect how a society perceives and receives a returnee. Community members also receive former young fighters with a certain amount of ambiguity regarding their possible past actions and responsibility for them. An imposed non-responsible child narrative can encourage negative reception as the only outlet for weighing up responsibility, and greatly hamper the success of reintegration. Therefore, the chapter argues, more of an effort to address society's perceptions and conceptions of responsibility and agency and to represent them in transitional justice mechanisms is required.

Chapter 3 explores the concept of responsibility and examines the difficulties that obstruct the task of easily assigning or denying moral or legal responsibility to these young perpetrators of atrocity. The task of determining responsibility hinges on appropriately evaluating their participation in collective action and the atrocity environment which influences behaviour and colours moral judgement and views about social norms, their psychological immaturity, and also the means by which they were recruited into violence. This chapter argues that none of these factors denies absolutely any responsibility for the commission of atrocity. It also suggests that while factors such as coercion and the youthfulness of the soldiers are given significant attention, the influence of collective action in atrocity contexts should also be better acknowledged and addressed in transitional justice processes.

Chapter 4 examines the value of accountability and defends the pursuit of accountability as the right and just response to wrongs committed according to a retributive-expressive justification. The objective of accountability cannot be the deterrence of potential future wrongdoers out of fear of prosecution or other processes of accountability, rehabilitation, or incapacitation of perpetrators so they will not reoffend; however, accountability is indispensable as a means of communication and confirmation of values and, where applicable, the corresponding transformation of norms.

Chapter 5 questions whether there is a need for accountability to foster social reconstruction in post-conflict societies. Is a means of dealing with the past that asks causal perpetrators to account for their actions, accept responsibility when appropriate, and disclose the results of actions taken required? This chapter argues that some means of adequately addressing the agency and responsibility of former participants is needed for the successful reintegration of these participants, for proper respect for human rights, and for the society's transition from a condition of violence to one of positive peace.

Chapter 6 argues that accountability is important also in order to avoid the risks associated with avoidance and suppression that can harm both individuals and societies. The wellbeing of individuals and the society can be threatened by attempts to avoid and suppress the past as a way to quickly and easily move beyond the harm. This chapter argues that acknowledging and addressing harms of the past are critical to successfully moving forward.

Chapter 7 evaluates possible options for addressing harms perpetrated by former child soldiers. It argues that transitional justice in post-conflict contexts that must deal with child soldiers should consider making use of a variety of accountability mechanisms that can include international and national criminal trials that respect juvenile justice standards. Persons under the age of 18 should not be universally shielded from formal criminal accountability in post-atrocity contexts based only on a strict division between 17 and 18, but prosecutions are not suitable to address questions of responsibility for most child soldiers. This chapter also introduces a distinctive process of truth-telling and mediation as a means to address the actions of some child soldiers.

The final chapter of this book highlights some of the distinct challenges that females face as members of fighting groups and the difficulties they encounter when they attempt to leave behind their participation in war and resume their lives within the communities. The stigmatization of girls is often different from that of boys in these communities, and there is more of a sense of shame associated with their victimization. Special attention must be paid to gender-specific experiences pre- and post-demobilization. This chapter argues that both crimes committed against female child soldiers as well as wrongdoing committed by female child soldiers need a new focus. Accountability for all of the variety of crimes associated with female child soldiers is important to their successful reintegration and for community healing.

The questions that these chapters address are significant to a world in which there are so many young perpetrators of violence for whom there is a distinct lack of formal and consistent means of addressing their actions. As will be further elaborated in the following pages, accountability takes many forms. Accountability is not only the limited and narrow processes of criminal justice systems. Accountability, more broadly, is a process of asking individuals or collectives to offer a description or report of and a reason for their actions, accept responsibility and penalty when appropriate, and disclose the results of actions taken. Such a process, as clarified in the following pages, does not necessarily assume wrongdoing. It does, however, take seriously the moral agency of perpetrators of atrocity, and also expresses the importance of acknowledging the harms suffered by the victims. A variety of accountability mechanisms should be employed by transitional justice schemes and young perpetrators of atrocity should be incorporated in processes of accountability as appropriate.

This book argues that a general policy of viewing all children associated with fighting groups uniformly as not capable of responsibility for acts of atrocity they commit is misleading and unhelpful. Neither treating child soldiers harshly as adult enemies or monsters, nor whitewashing all agents under the age of 18 with the non-responsible child narrative is effective or just. This book argues that there is no reason to reject outright the possibility that a person under the age of 18 who was a member of an armed group or armed force that commits atrocities could bear moral or legal responsibility for his or her actions. It also argues that accountability in the aftermath of mass atrocity is important for its expressive significance and its ability to communicate respect for human rights, equality, and balance within the community. Legal punishment is a powerful condemnation of harmful actions in violation of promulgated law. Nevertheless, criminal legal systems and the resultant legal punishment of wrongdoers are not the only form of accountability that generates expressive significance. Some child soldier perpetrators might warrant juvenile criminal prosecutions and legal punishment for their acts, but more may deserve an alternative process of accountability, perhaps a modified mediation process, that will allow individuals to explore events, account for actions, take responsibility when appropriate, disclose results of acts, accept penalty if suitable, and expose factors that negate or diminish responsibility.

Accountability is a critical component of post-conflict social rebuilding. In a post-conflict context, accountability should be far-reaching, denying impunity for all categories of individuals who bear responsibility for serious and unwarranted harms committed during the hostilities. All persons under the age of 18 should not be eliminated from the domain of responsible agents of atrocity simply for their age. Absolving all persons under the age of 18 of any responsibility can have negative effects on the social reconstruction process and negative repercussions for individual former child soldiers. Absolving individuals under the age of 18 of any responsibility denies the community the chance to fully explore past harms and the effects of the harms; it groups together all causal agents under the age of 18 (child soldiers), therefore, not distinguishing those who bear personal responsibility from those who do not, consequently stigmatizing them all the same; and it conceptually rejects the robust agency that young persons possess and regard themselves as possessing.

1
Child Soldiering

Consider these three accounts:

> They are forcing to kill people. And they killed many. Not only me, they are in the group, and they will give four people, ten people. They will say 'kill this one'. When you refuse, then they kill you. So, we've been doing that – to kill, and to keep your own self.
>
> (Formerly Abducted Soldier, Uganda, Interview with author)[1]

> 'I joined the FARC in a rage,' she says, referring to the Revolutionary Armed Forces of Colombia, Latin America's longest-standing rebel army. 'I wanted to get revenge on the people who killed my father.'
>
> (Biderman 2012)

> 'I was going to liberate my country.'
>
> (Former Child Soldier, in what is now newly established South Sudan, quoted in Green 2013)

The stories are not as uncommon as they ought to be: all over the world, children and youths are drawn or abducted from lives of poverty, uneasiness, or insecurity to ones even more perilous, as active members of armed fighting groups. Worldwide, at any point in the contemporary post-Cold War era, hundreds of thousands of persons under the age of 18 are associated with armed fighting groups – either armed forces or armed groups. As mentioned in the introductory chapter of this book, it is estimated that about 250,000–300,000 children are serving as soldiers, guerrilla fighters, or in support roles in combat in more than 25 countries globally, in the Americas, Africa, Asia, Europe, and the former Soviet Union.[2] For many, the reality of child soldiering is intimidation, pressure, brutalization, and the commission of violent and cruel actions against civilians and enemy combatants, and against other recruits.

Despite different media attempts to portray one or other of a few fairly uniform depictions of child soldiering,[3] the concept and the individual experiences of child soldiers are far from consistent or standardized. The manner of recruitment, the level of identification with the cause and the fighting group, and what it means to be a child soldier differ drastically from context to context and from individual to individual within the same environment. While there are some commonalities in the experiences of child soldiers globally, there are also significant distinctions based not only on the nature of the conflict or on geographical considerations, but also on personal temperaments, individual goals, and personal manners of interpreting alternatives and the choices of the child soldiers themselves. So emotionally charged are the issues of atrocity and child soldiers that extreme positions and solutions surface. One extreme regards child soldiers as included in a despised group of illegal actors and enemies who deserve unique treatment that can abandon even basic human rights standards and protections usually afforded criminals (see: Singer 2005: 154; Jamison 2008); the other extreme views all children active in violent conflict, regardless of age or circumstances and without exception, as lacking any capacity for moral responsibility. To truly grapple with the scope of the problem of child soldiering for post-conflict social reconstruction, the very rudimentary depictions of child soldiers as monsters or unconditionally as pure innocents must be abandoned for a more nuanced understanding of the variety of actors who are child soldiers. For transitional justice to be effective, it must acknowledge the distinctions, and, it will be argued in the following chapters, offer a wide range of mechanisms for accounting for harms of which child soldiers were causal agents.

This chapter offers a varied picture of the child soldiering experience, drawing primarily from the experiences of boys and girls who are or were associated with fighting groups in Colombia, Sri Lanka, the Democratic Republic of the Congo (DRC), Sierra Leone, and Uganda. According to the strict 18 principle that defines a child soldier as anyone who is associated with a fighting force and who is below the age of 18, included in the many states that recruit child soldiers are North American and European states in which child soldiers are, or have been, associated with national armies, including the UK, the US, and Canada. The recruitment and use of these military personnel is, depending on individual stances, either considered acceptable if the minor individual freely volunteers and his or her involvement is parentally supported, or it is seen as morally reprehensible and at odds with international conventions and the law that 'is moving, albeit somewhat unevenly, towards eighteen as the threshold age of permissible military service' (Drumbl 2012: 135). This is an issue for another book.

Despite the variety of experiences of child soldiers formally defined, there is a common, particularly troubling, problem: many child soldiers globally engage in the commission of atrocious harms against their fellow human beings, often fellow citizens – harms that fall well outside the parameters of behaviour permissible during war. There are two strands of international law that govern aspects of international and intrastate armed conflict. International humanitarian law (IHL) and international criminal law (ICL) define acceptable and non-permissible conduct. Many fighting forces that engage in the illegal recruitment of child soldiers also engage in other conduct not permissible under international law, including acts of war crime and crimes against humanity. Many child soldiers associated with these groups engage in these actions.

Part of transitional justice is the more limited *jus post bellum* (justice after war), the pursuit of accountability, and the denial of impunity, for those who commit serious human rights abuses in armed conflict. *Jus post bellum* concerns the principled approaches to achieving justice after conflict and helping a society transition well from conflict to peace (Orend 2002; DiMeglio 2006; Stahn and Kleffner 2008; May and Forcehimes 2012; May 2012). Access to formal justice to address such crimes is considered an essential element in ensuring transition to peace and democracy after mass violations of human rights (UNDP 2004), and the promotion of rule of law and the end to impunity are increasingly regarded as imperatives (Rome Statute; UN Human Rights Council 2009), both theoretically and as a matter of law. This book is above all interested in how to best assess and address the actions of child soldiers who perpetrate acts of atrocity but who, as a category of perpetrator, are generally treated according to extremes – either overlooked as responsible agents or punished harshly for their contribution to one side of a conflict.

Understanding the basic experiences of an assortment of child soldiers allows us to better assess the range of responsibility that child soldiers might bear for their individual contribution to harms committed and also acknowledge the fact that the homogeneous picture of child soldiers as young boys wielding automatic weapons too large for their small frames is unrepresentative and unhelpful in many ways. The category of child soldier is much more diverse and deserves a more nuanced approach to transitional justice than the non-responsible child narrative suggests. The aim of this chapter is to assuage vagueness and conflation of concepts and impressions in order to better understand the experiences and needs of (former) child soldiers. First, it offers definitions of the terms used in order to render the arguments in this book clear and accessible. Then it examines some of the different experiences that child soldiers face, demonstrating that recruitment, treatment and activity, and post-conflict demobilization and response vary across conflicts and geography. It then engages with the claim that no person under the age of 18 can voluntarily join a fighting force, arguing that this general position, espoused by much of the humanitarian discourse, is itself unhelpful and potentially detrimental to the social reconstruction process.

Definitions

Despite the growing legal norms surrounding the conception of a child soldier, it is a label that has surprisingly ambiguous and broad meaning, referring to a range of experiences and therefore often conveying different things to different audiences. What constitutes a child soldier is the topic of considerable historic and contemporary debate. Despite heated deliberation to reach their decision (Renteln n.d.), the drafters of the Convention on the Rights of the Child (CRC), in which much relevant international law is grounded, settled on 15 years of age as the minimum acceptable age for the recruitment of young persons into war (CRC: Article 38). Some states, however, dissatisfied with the outcome of the difficult negotiations of 1989 that led to the age of 15 being stipulated in the CRC manifestly expressed their discontent in reservations to the treaty, to the extent that some self-imposed the minimum age of 18.[4] Eventually, the Optional Protocol for the United Nations Convention on the Rights of the Child (Article 3) officially clarified that 18 was the minimum age of compulsory recruitment and 15 the minimum age of voluntary recruitment (United Nations 2002). Some critics, however, argue that a child (a person under the age of 18) does not have the capacity to volunteer for military activity.[5]

This book employs the definition of a child soldier provided by the Paris Principles, the most current internationally recognized definition of a child implicated in war: 'a child associated with an armed force or armed group'

> refers to any person below 18 years of age who is or who has been recruited or used by an armed force or armed group in any capacity, including but not limited to children, boys, and girls used as fighters,

> cooks, porters, messengers, spies or for sexual purposes. It does not only refer to a child who is taking or has taken a direct part in hostilities (Paris Principles).

By this definition, then, a child soldier is anyone who was recruited, abducted, or conscripted under the age of 18 to contribute to armed conflict. This definition does not take into account the method by which the child was recruited, and says nothing about whether a child is capable or incapable of volunteering for soldiering. It is important to note that the designation 'child soldier' is not equivalent to that of 'child combatant', which would refer to young 'combatants' as defined under international law, denoting someone who is not a protected civilian and who has an unqualified right to directly participate in hostilities and whose participation is therefore lawful (ICRC 1977a: Article 43). 'The term "*child soldier*", in contrast, as defined under the Cape Town Principles (1977) [and also the Paris Principles], reveals nothing about whether the child's involvement is, or is not, in accord with international law provisions regarding the involvement of children in armed conflict' (Grover 2008: 54 emphasis original).

A challenge to defining child soldiers for theory and the practice of law and transitional justice is the question of what is the consequence of an individual's 18th birthday. Childhood is generally regarded as a period when children, still dependent on caregivers, are afforded the opportunity to grow and develop into moral human beings and productive members of their communities; it is generally conceived of as a period that 'implies a safe space in which children can grow, play and develop' (Angucia 2009: 79). Despite arguments that childhood is a social construction and one that primarily reflects Western conceptions of developmental stages according to age (Denov 2010: 2), it is reasonably compatible with universal understandings of human development and human freedom to argue that persons who were abducted as children or youths to engage in armed conflict have lost, or have had negatively impacted, an important developmental stage, the loss or impact of which is likely to affect them greatly. For the purposes of this book, an ex-fighter who is over the age of 18 when he or she departs from the conflict is considered to be, and referred to, as a child soldier if recruitment, initiation into warfare, and the commission of acts of serious harm happened before he or she reached the age of 18.

In this text, the terms 'child' and 'young person' are used broadly, and 'adolescent' and 'youth' are used somewhat interchangeably throughout. In international law and treaties, there is considerable inconsistency and overlap in respect to defining these stages.[6] While adolescents and youths are generally considered to be young people who are older than 'children' and younger than 'adults' (Barber 2009:6), therefore assigning the title of 'children' to persons younger than adolescents, this text generally regards 'children' as does the Convention on the Rights of the Child (CRC), as 'every human being below the age of eighteen' (CRC: Article 1). This text, then, makes no distinction, unless explicit, between older children (who might elsewhere be referred to as 'youths') and younger children. The titles 'adolescent' and 'youth' are used when making specific distinctions between older child soldiers and those who are younger.

The use of the term 'child soldier' is contentious for another reason, in that it suggests and can produce stigmatization for the use of the title 'soldier'. Margaret Angucia claims to prefer the term 'war-affected children' since the term 'child soldiers' 'has an ambiguous representation in terms of soldiering as a chosen profession and children who do not have the capacity to make the choice of soldiering as their profession' (Angucia 2009: 78). Angucia's explanation of the terms highlights a significant debate in the discourse regarding children in conflict; with her choice of term, she underscores her position that no child (person under the age of 18) has the capacity to decide to contribute to armed conflict.[7] However, the more common term 'child soldier' denotes distinctions between the ways children can be affected by war. The term 'child soldier' represents one way among many in which children are affected by war by denoting involvement in the armed conflict and the likelihood of being implicated in the commission of violent acts against other human beings. This effect of war on children is different from others, such as displacement, the trauma that comes from living in the midst of war, insecurity, poverty, loss of education, the disruption of health or other social services, or being orphaned. The category of child soldier is not a homogeneous group, but it is a unique subset of a broader group of children affected by conflict.

The Paris Principles also shy away from the term 'child soldier', using instead the term 'a child associated with an armed force or armed group' (Paris Principles 2007). This definition might better reflect a more nuanced understanding of the roles of young persons who contribute to and support the fighting group. Not all child soldiers are fighters; as mentioned, many engage in supportive roles such as porters or cooks. This book uses the term 'child soldier' because it is the label that is most widely understood to refer to persons under the age of 18 who have participated in the activities of a fighting group. This book is most interested in the phenomenon of young persons implicated in collective violent action. While it will reference peripherally the responsibility of those who only participate in supportive roles, the focus of this discussion is on those young persons who played, or are suspected of playing, an active role in the commission of atrocity.

Other terms used in this book that require attention are 'returnee', 'victim', and 'perpetrator'. 'Accountability' is also defined here for use in this book. For the purposes of this text, a returnee is an ex-soldier who has returned to civilian life. This could be because the conflict has ended, or because the returnee has voluntarily left, escaped, been released, or been rescued. The use of the word 'returnee' to refer to ex-soldiers is not to be confused with civilians who were displaced because of the conflict and are returning home.

For the purposes of this book, the term 'victim' is used to refer to any person who was directly wounded (physically, mentally, psychologically) or harmed emotionally or psychologically by wounds inflicted on a loved one due to the conflict. To reflect reality, this text will refer to civilians who were targeted and harmed by the armed group or armed force as victims, and it will also refer to child soldiers as victims.

A 'perpetrator', for the purposes of this text, is any person who was a causal agent of an injury suffered by another. This label is devoid of any judgement of the criminal or moral responsibility of the perpetrator for his or her actions; it simply denotes the fact that the individual committed an action that resulted in harm to another.

'Accountability' takes many forms; and for the purposes of this text, accountability refers to a process of acknowledgement and explanation of actions taken that involves the actor assuming responsibility when appropriate. Accountability means that the agent accepts the consequences of his or her actions. A process of accountability must allow for the possibility of penalty for wrongful acts when suitable.

Experiences

Child soldiers are active in a variety of roles as members of fighting groups around the world. Each experience is unique. The aims, cultures, and compositions of fighting groups differ across wars and geography. The experiences of individual child soldiers are not homogeneous across the conflicts, or even within particular contexts. The following subsections of this chapter are meant to reveal some of the variety of experiences that child soldiers live in some conflicts, as a way to both offer a glimpse into life as a child soldier and to highlight the fact that broad generalities that ground the strict 18 tenet miss important distinctions that demand consideration.

The conflicts

As mentioned in the introductory chapter, there are different reasons for why child soldiers are attractive to architects of war and atrocity. Children can be appealing in some cases because their size, pliability, and desire to please (among other reasons) can render them easy recruits who are easily manipulated. They may also be in good supply when there is a need to compensate for a dearth of adult soldiers because in a protracted war adult numbers are reduced due to conflict-related death and/or because the conflict, or one side of the conflict, is unpopular. Children make up the majority demographic in many conflict-affected countries resulting in a constant supply of potential recruits (War Child n.d.).

Many of these conflicts originated out of genuine attempts to correct injustices or perceived injustices, but the parties to the conflicts grew over time to lose sight of the original goals and/or to use unjust tactics in pursuit of their aims. Colombia is a good example of a protracted conflict that developed over time to rely on child soldiering that involves activities outside the parameters of generally accepted conduct during war. The armed conflict in Colombia, which began in the mid-1960s, is an intractable low-intensity, multi-party conflict between the government of Colombia and peasant guerrilla groups, such as the Ejército de Liberación Nacional (ELN) and the Fuerzas Armadas Revolucionarias de Colombia (FARC), and also includes the involvement of other paramilitary groups such as the pro-government, Auto-defensas Unidas de Colombia (AUC). What is sometimes viewed as a war solely about drugs, is also about class, economics, and power; and FARC and ELN were created, in 1964 and 1965, respectively, by communist insurgents to fight against wealthy landowners and the conservative government (Briggs 2005: 41). In Colombia, child soldiers being members of the guerrilla and paramilitary groups was a relatively late phenomenon that did not exist until the 1990s (Human Rights Watch 2003: 19).

Sri Lanka's civil war between the Sri Lankan government and the Liberation Tigers of Tamil Eelam (LTTE, also called Tamil Tigers) was also a long conflict that relied on child soldiering. The LTTE was a separatist militant group that sprung from tensions between Sri Lanka's two largest ethnic groups, the Sinhalese and the Tamils. Since Sri Lanka gained independence from Britain in 1948, the Tamil minority has felt increasingly marginalized and politically disenfranchised. Created in 1975, the LTTE has two wings – the political and the military wings. For almost 30 years, between 1983 and 2009, the Tamil Tigers fought a civil war for the creation of an independent state for the Tamil people (Wang 2011). Initially founded partly from student discontent, the Tamil Tigers always had a predominantly young base, and the recruitment of children and females to 'make up for the heavy shortfall in [adult] male combatants killed in battle' was a pronounced characteristic of this group (Krishnan 2011: 138). The LTTE was considered one of the most organized, effective, and brutal terrorist groups in the world (Pickert 2009; Wang 2011: 100).

African child soldiers represent to most the general practice of child soldiering. Most media depictions of child soldiers present an image of a young African boy with a large weapon.[8] Children have participated in violent conflict in Angola, Burundi, the Central African Republic (CAR), Chad, Cote d'Ivoire, the DRC, Mozambique, Rwanda, Sierra Leone, Somalia, Sudan, Uganda, and Zimbabwe. In many of these conflicts, the majority of children were kidnapped and forced into fighting.

In Sierra Leone, corruption, poor governance and mismanagement, high unemployment, and the gradual erosion of civil society 'led to mounting disillusionment, particularly among the young, and were a recipe for rebellion and an eventual brutal civil war' (Denov 2010: 49). Interestingly, while Myriam Denov includes a rebellious youth culture in her list of factors contributing to the civil war (Denov 2010: 50), she points out that

> the initial recruitment drive did not involve children... [but that] as the rate of attrition among adult RUF combatants increased, with factors such as the prolongation of the war, the horrible conditions of service, the lack of salary (whereby many soldiers augmented their pay through looting or mining), the high death toll and the overall senselessness and brutality of the war, the RUF needed to devise another recruitment strategy.
>
> Denov (2010: 63)

In the end, as was the case with the guerrilla FARC and ELN in Colombia and the Tamil Tigers in Sri Lanka, the predominance of children in the fighting force became a conspicuous characteristic of the Revolutionary United Front (RUF).

In Uganda, the latest period in a long history of brutal human rights abuses is the recent conflict in the north of the country. A run of successive deposed leaderships ended in 1986 with current President Yoweri Museveni assuming power in a coup. Uganda has a history of ethnic conflict and when Museveni took power he dismissed the Ugandan army that at the time consisted primarily of soldiers from the north of the country. Northerners became fearful for their safety and their rights (Branch 2010: 30–31). In response, a number of rebel groups rose to the challenge of fighting Museveni's reign (Finnström 2008: 69; Green 2008: 39–40; Esuruku 2012: 146–147). Over time, all but one – Joseph Kony's Lord's Resistance Army (LRA) – disappeared. As Joseph Kony and his LRA lost popular support in northern Uganda in the early 1990s, they began to commit atrocities against the civilian population (Baines and Stewart 2011: 250). Until 2006, Joseph Kony and his LRA terrorized northern Uganda, abducting up to 60,000 children into its fighting group (Finnström 2008; Allen and Vlassenroot 2010).

In both the First Congo War, 1986–1987, and the Second Congo War (also known as the Great War of Africa) that began in 1998 and officially ended in 2003, the recruitment of child soldiers was rampant in the DRC. In the First Congo War, Laurent Kabila, leader of the Alliance des Forces Démocratiques pour la Libération du Congo-Zaïre (AFDL), offered employment with his rebel army that would overthrow the Mobutu dictatorship and 'hundreds of street children, unemployed youths, and pupils heeded Kabila's call' (Stearns 2012: 144). The AFDL were successful and the First Congo War brought Kabila to power. The AFDL then fell apart when Kabila and his Rwandan and Ugandan backers turned on each other, beginning the Second Congo War. In 1998, the Rwandan Hutu rebels, known as Interahmwe, joined forces with the Zairian army to launch an offensive against the Congolese Tutsis in the east of the country. The war and the hostilities that have continued since the war was officially ended in 2003 have been extremely complex, with numerous rebel groups fighting each other, many swapping sides. Children have been frequently kidnapped from their families by rebel groups to become soldiers who commit atrocious acts of brutality and murder.

'Rebels without a cause' is a term that could perhaps represent many child soldiers, but especially certain child soldiers fighting in Africa. For example, both the RUF and the LRA endeavoured to instil widespread terror in the same civilian population for which they professed to fight and from which their child soldiers were recruited. These communities were themselves the targeted victims of most of the rebels' terrorist propaganda and physical assaults.

Soldiers in some fighting groups identify more with the group and the cause than do soldiers in other conflicts. Putting aside for the moment the debate regarding whether persons under the age of 18 can truly volunteer for active duty in armed conflict, it is important to recognize that some child soldiers are recruited more forcefully than others. In each of these conflicts, children have been recruited both voluntarily and forcefully, but fighting groups differ according to how the majority of soldiers join the group and how much they identify with the group. In Colombia, it is reported that many, perhaps as many as nearly 83 per cent of children, enlisted voluntarily in the illegal armed groups (Briggs 2005: 43; Singer 2005: 61; Theidon 2007: 75; Bjørkhaug 2010: 3).

In Sri Lanka, many Tamil Tiger child soldiers joined of their own volition and saw themselves as fighting for liberation, honour, and glory (de Soyza 2011; Mapp 2011: 76). They identified with the cause for which they fought, and 'joined the Tamil separatist movement out of altruistic reasons to save their group identity from being eclipsed' (Somasundaram 2002: 1268). In her memoir of her experiences as a child Tamil Tiger, Niromi de Soyza presents her motivation to join based on a sense of oppression and fear of the Sri Lankan government, her identification with the cause, and her respect for the LTTE (de Soyza 2011). In his book, *Innocents Lost*, journalist Jimmie Briggs recounts the story of Ida Carmelita who witnessed the murder of two of her teenaged brothers by members of the paramilitary government-aligned Tamil group known as Tamil Eelam Liberation Organization (TELO). One of her other brothers joined the Tamil Tigers. 'Learning of her brothers' fate, the local LTTE enticed her to join them in fighting to avenge their deaths. So in 1996, seventeen-year-old Ida Carmelita left her family to spend the next three years as a guerrilla soldier for the Tamil Tigers' (Briggs 2005: 82). Like Colombian child soldiers, Tamil youths were drawn to the propaganda machine of the fighting force: speeches and videos, public displays of war paraphernalia, funerals and posters of fallen heroes, and heroic, melodious songs and stories that serve to draw out feelings of patriotism and a 'martyr cult' (Somasundaram 2002: 1269). Of course, not all child soldiers in the Tamil Tigers' ranks or fighting in Colombia identified with the groups' causes or eagerly volunteered to fight. It is important to remember that even in fighting groups in which there is a high level of initial identification with the cause of the fight, many of the fighters were also kidnapped and coerced to fight.

For the most part, child soldiers in the DRC, Sierra Leone, and Uganda were forcefully recruited. In Sierra Leone, children fought on all sides of the conflict, for the RUF, the AFRC (Armed Forces Revolutionary Council, a military group that overthrew the government in 1997 but was not supported by the people of Sierra Leone), the CDF (Civil Defence Forces, a paramilitary organization that supported the elected government of Ahmed Tejan Kabbah against the RUF and AFRC), and the Republic of Sierra Leone Armed Forces (RSLAF), the Sierra Leonean army. The RUF and AFRC, however, were responsible for most of the forced recruitment that happened (Truth and Reconciliation Report, Sierra Leone, 2003: 41). Uganda's LRA is notorious for its abductions. By far the majority of the child soldiers of the LRA ranks were forcefully abducted to the extent that it almost seems nonsensical to talk about the voluntary recruitment of LRA child soldiers. And yet, some free ex-soldiers voluntarily rejoined the conflict, either as LRA or government soldiers, to continue committing atrocities (Akello et al. 2006: 234).

Entry into fighting forces takes many forms. A child can volunteer out of ideological identification with a cause, seek employment and respect or adventure, be abducted, or be born to mothers who are in the force. Some are driven to participate in the conflict out of desperate living situations, such as 'poverty and crises in their communities; some may be seduced by promises of glory or excitement' (Honwana 2006: 1). As mentioned, in Africa, many, but not all, children become associated with a fighting force by abduction or coercion. Although the majority of child soldiers fighting in Colombia, on either side of the conflict, joined of their own volition, others in Colombia were recruited forcibly. Many former LTTE child soldiers report having been forcefully taken from their families, while others claim to have identified with the cause and volunteered. Human Rights Watch claims the 'sophisticated LTTE propaganda machine' is to blame for some of the volunteers, as is the witnessing or suffering of abuses by the Sri Lankan government and security forces by children who then felt 'driven to join' and sought to protect their families and avenge real or perceived abuse (Human Rights Watch 2004: 5). Another of the LTTE's principle recruitment strategies was coercion, to visit Tamil homes to inform parents that they must provide a child for the cause, and families that resisted were harassed and threatened (Human Rights Watch 2004: 2). De Soyza claims in her memoir that she volunteered, and even persisted in her attempts to join the LTTE after her initial attempts to volunteer were rejected (de Soyza 2011).

Conflicts in which child soldiers fight are not essentially different from other conflicts, nor are they homogeneous in origin or viciousness. Conflicts in which child soldiers fight and commit atrocity are exceptional in their use and abuse of the children who become the causal agents of devastation. In an attempt to promote the rights of the child globally and consistency in the way that children are treated in post-conflict contexts, however, unsophisticated narratives have been produced that can, despite their objective to simplify post-conflict justice, generate problems and a lack of confidence in transitional justice by the post-conflict population.

Life as a child soldier

Despite their differences, fighting groups that include large numbers of children have commonalities: children can assume the full range of roles necessary for the functioning of the fighting group, and life for a child in a fighting group can be both dangerous and difficult to escape. Children are considered by some atrocity leaders to be cheap, easy to recruit, and 'expendable' (Dallaire 2010: 117–118). They can be sent into battle as scouts or decoys, drawing the enemy's fire. Breaking free from the group can be both a physical and a psychological challenge. The fighting group is itself its own reality that consists of an exclusive lifestyle and social order. Children are generally cut off from their families, friends, and communities. Traditional family structures are replaced by militarized ones, according to which, rigid military hierarchies are imposed and 'new values of detachment, cruelty, terror, group solidarity and cohesion' are propagated (Denov 2010: 102).

In Colombia, it is estimated that '30 per cent of some guerrilla units were made up of children [and in] urban militias, the majority of recruits, 85 per cent, were believed to be under eighteen' (Human Rights Watch 2003: 21). Children in Colombia have been associated with all parties to the conflict and have played all roles. The conflict has been accompanied by widespread human rights abuses and breaches of international humanitarian law (IHL) by and against children (Coalition to Stop the Use of Child Soldiers 2008: Colombia). Children associated with fighting groups in Colombia are used as combatants, spies, guards, messengers, 'to lay mines and explosives and to carry out other military tasks' (Coalition to Stop the Use of Child Soldiers 2008: Colombia).

Participation in a fighting group in Colombia, like in the vast majority of groups that recruit children, is an enforced commitment (Bjørkhaug 2010: 17). Although child soldiers may have joined freely according to different motivations, once a member of a fighting group, it is very difficult for a soldier to leave the group and regain civilian status. Soldiers who are caught attempting to leave face severe punishment or execution (Briggs 2005: 42; Bjørkhaug 2010: 19). Like that of child soldiers in other fighting groups around the world, the life of a child soldier in

Colombia is harsh. Each armed group has strict rules and regulations and stiff penalties, including corporal punishment, for disobedience or mistakes. Training is rigorous, food and comfort is limited, and day-to-day experiences can be dangerous. Human Rights Watch describes the FARC as:

> Show[ing] no leniency to children because of their age, assigning children the same duties as adults. Those who break minor disciplinary rules are sent off to dig trenches or latrines, clear forest, cut and carry firewood, or do kitchen duties. If they lose a weapon, they may be forced to enter combat without one until they are able to recover a replacement from the enemy. To deal with serious breaches, a 'war council' is held. Combatants hear the charges and the defence. A death sentence may be passed by a show of hands.
>
> Children who desert are often shot, especially if they take their weapons with them. The same fate awaits suspected informers, infiltrators, or children who fall asleep on guard duty. The commander handpicks a group to carry out the sentence. The child, hand tied by nylon cord, is taken beyond the camp's perimeter and made to wait while the squad digs a grave.
>
> (Human Rights Watch 2003: 7)

Likewise, in Sierra Leone, child soldiers were treated as slaves, and if they tried to escape, they risked torture or death, and some children were 'branded with scars that spelled the letters of the armed group' with which they fought (Truth and Reconciliation Report, Sierra Leone, 2003: 23). The civil war in Sierra Leone was not as long-lasting as some conflicts in Africa (or elsewhere), but it is considered by some to be one of the most brutal (Whitman n.d.: 4), and children played a leading role in the commission of atrocity. Thousands of children were abducted and participated in horrible acts such as amputations, beheading, rape, and burning people alive (Whitman n.d.: 5). Similarly, child soldiers in Uganda's LRA participated in horrific atrocities, including killing family members or fellow community members (Crane: 2008; Blattman 2009: 234; Eichstaedt 2009). Part of the initiation process for some armed groups, such as the LRA, is that the child or youth is forced to commit a violent act of mutilation or murder against a community member or family member before he or she is ushered away to life as a soldier as a way to sever ties between the young person and the community (Lomo and Hovil 2004: 32; Parmar et al. 2010: 233).

Abuses committed against child soldiers are employed to train them, to instil loyalty to the group, and to inspire fear of disobedience. In his book, Jason Stearns depicts how Congolese child soldier Kizito's excitement as he voluntarily joined the AFDL in the First Congo War quickly waned in light of the difficult living conditions that included fleas, a poor diet that made many of the children suffer from diarrhoea, and harsh and exhausting and sometimes bizarre training that included the summary execution of prisoners (Stearns 2012: 146–149). Likewise, child soldiers in Uganda were beaten to harden them for battle and made to participate in the killing of someone quickly upon joining the LRA. As Faith McDonnell writes in the book she co-authored with formerly abducted LRA soldier, Grace Akallo, 'A cycle of fear and guilt keeps the children captive until it is no longer needed' (McDonnell and Akallo 2007: 118).

The experience of child soldiering as a member of the Tamil Tigers was similar in many ways to that of other armed groups, but quite different in the prominent role that the prospect of suicide played in the conflict. The Tamil Tigers were well trained and equipped to die. Prior to engaging in armed combat, young recruits were trained for a number of months by the Tigers, including training in weapons and explosives (Briggs 2005: 86). Unique to the Tamil Tigers was the use of cyanide capsules that hung around the neck of each child soldier. If captured, the soldier was expected to swallow the capsule. The Tigers were also cited as the world leader in suicide terrorism (Pape 2003).

Ishmael Beah describes in his memoir of his experiences as a child soldier in Sierra Leone the callousness of some of the young killers, including himself. He relates a memory of a group of rebels with blood on their clothes 'laughing and giving each other high fives' and bragging about what they had done that day; one carrying 'the head of a man, which he held by the hair' (Beah 2007: 96). Early in his soldiering experience Beah competed for a promotion in the fighting group's ranks by engaging in a race to kill prisoners:

> I had already begun staring at my prisoner. His face was swollen from the beating he had received, and his eyes looked as if they were watching something behind me. His jaws were the only tense part of his facial expression; everything else seemed calm. I didn't feel a thing for him, didn't think that much about what I was doing. I just waited for the corporal's order. The prisoner was simply another rebel

> who was responsible for the death of my family, as I had come to truly believe. The corporal gave the signal with a pistol shot and I grabbed the man's head and slit his throat in one fluid motion. His Adam's apple made way for the sharp knife, and I turned the bayonet on its zigzag edge as I brought it out.... I was proclaimed the winner, and Kanei came second. The boys and the other soldiers who were the audience clapped as if I had just fulfilled one of life's greatest achievements. I was given the rank of junior lieutenant and Kanei was given junior sergeant. We celebrated that day's achievement with more drugs and more war movies.
>
> (Beah 2007: 124)

It is important, however, to recall that not all children associated with armed groups commit atrocities. While many do, some perform only supportive roles, such as cooking, scouting, fetching water, and stealing supplies. While association with certain groups does make it likely that the child committed some atrocity, due to the general composition of the group and its initiation schemes, it is perilous to take for granted that each former soldier participated in atrocity.[9] Another misplaced and hazardous common association suggests that child soldiers are always drugged to be able to commit such brutality (Fegley 2008: 41). Drugs are, in fact, a familiar element in some fighting groups that recruit children, but not in others. Many of the children who fought in the civil war in Sierra Leone were drugged so that their thoughts and fears were numbed, and they developed dependencies on these drugs. Children have described taking 'brown brown' (gunpowder mixed with cocaine) and also having it rubbed into cuts on their bodies (Beah 2007: 121). In Uganda's LRA and Sri Lanka's Tamil Tigers, however, the use of narcotics was not a part of the soldiering experience (Vinci 2005: 371; Schomerus 2010: 95).

The reality of female child soldiers also presents a challenge for generalizations. Either the term 'child soldier' virtually omits the existence of 'female' in the definition, thereby overlooking the distinctive experiences of female child soldiers, or it highlights gender roles and gender-based violence without acknowledging the variety of roles that female child soldiers play. Nevertheless, gender-based violence is a key feature of the experience of many girl soldiers. Girls associated with many armed groups often have the additional hardship of enforced gender roles and sexual violence. 'Girls were subjected to sexual abuse, including rape and forced abortion' (Coalition to Stop the Use of Child Soldiers 2008: Colombia). In Sierra Leone and Uganda as well, the sexual slavery of girls was a common occurrence. The sexual and gender violence committed against female child soldiers will be addressed in much greater detail in Chapter 8.

Female child soldiers in Sri Lanka, however, did not face systemic sexual abuse. Unlike many other fighting groups that recruit child soldiers, the Tamil Tigers demonstrated some semblance of respect for their female soldiers, and female Tigers were treated in many ways similarly to males. Gender identities existed, but gender roles that forced female child soldiers to adopt duties usually reserved for wives (cooking, sex, child care) were not typically part of the Tiger picture (Wang 2011: 103); nor were sexual relationships allowed between soldiers. Sexual violence directed towards a female soldier by a male soldier could be severely punished (Wood 2009: 151). There were even women's brigades (de Soyza 2011), and women were originally referred to as 'Freedom Birds' (Wang 2011). The risk for Tamil females came from their association with the Tigers if they were taken into custody by the Sri Lankan government. Tamil females taken into official custody were vulnerable to torture and sexual abuse by police and military soldiers (Amnesty International 2002). Often, when Tamil Tigers surrendered, they were first jailed before being released either to rehabilitation camps or home.

Life as a child soldier is almost universally often frightening, unpleasant, dangerous, and difficult to escape. For most child soldiers, it is constantly harsh, terrifying, and depraved. Irrespective of how they became associated with the fighting groups, child soldiers must navigate harsh environments that compromise their ability to be autonomous agents. Nonetheless, reports from different child soldiers from different conflicts describe very different experiences. Some live much more comfortable lives than others. Some are forced to commit atrocities, while others are spared. Some identify with the cause and are pleased to exact revenge on the enemy, while others despise the group and only participate out of fear. Some report refusing to obey orders, while others claim that any refusal or expressed dissatisfaction would result in severe punishment or death.

The principle of non-voluntary recruitment

Above, the discussion regarding the use and definition of the term 'child soldier' alluded to a significant debate in international law and human and child rights discourse. It began with a mention of Angucia's claim to prefer the term 'war-affected children' over the term 'child soldier' since the latter makes comparisons with the profession of soldiering which is chosen and entered into freely and, she argues, children do not have the capacity to make the choice of soldiering as their profession. Despite the fact that adult soldiering is not always entered into freely (there are many situations in which citizens must complete some compulsory military training or in which conscription is enforced in times of need), Anguacia draws attention to a noteworthy issue. Her position, common in the discourse regarding children in conflict, claims unequivocally that no person under the age of 18 has the capacity to decide to participate in armed conflict.

Peter Singer claims that the 'rough trend line seems to be that roughly two of every three child soldiers have some sort of initiative in their own recruitment' across the board (Singer 2005: 61). The estimates he cites are 60 per cent of the FARC's child soldiers, 57 per cent in East Asia, and 64 per cent of child soldiers in four African countries surveyed had volunteered to join the fighting force under no threat of violence (Singer 2005: 61). He goes on to argue, however, that,

> To describe this choice as voluntary, however, is greatly misleading. Children are defined, as such, not only because of their lesser physical development, but also because they are judged to be of an age at which they are not capable of making mature decisions. By contrast, to go to war and risk one's life in an act that has societal-wide consequences is one of the most serious decisions a person can make.
>
> (Singer 2005: 62)

Even when child soldiers join purposefully, with some knowledge of the danger, understanding of the cause, and the will to realize the desired result, they are considered not to have voluntarily joined because they are not capable of making serious mature decisions. In its report on child soldiers in the LTTE ranks, Human Rights Watch also reflects this general presumption that children cannot volunteer to participate in armed conflict: 'Under international law, recruitment of children to be soldiers is not only unlawful if the children are forcibly recruited. The LTTE is also violating international law by accepting into its ranks children who join "voluntarily"' (Human Rights Watch 2004: 5). This statement is accurate about the law, but it also reveals the philosophy in which Human Rights Watch is grounded by its use of quotation marks around the word 'voluntarily'. As Catarina Martins sums up, 'Recruitment is never really accepted by the humanitarian discourse as voluntary: when children admit to having chosen to enlist, a number of social explanations present this choice as forceful. Again, there is no room for agency: the child (who may actually be a young adult) is denied freedom and capacity of choice' (Martins 2011: 438).

Without engaging in discussions of child psychology, it is arguably safe to contend that the position that children cannot voluntarily engage in armed conflict is inconsistent with many conceptions of juvenile agency. Children can decide to engage in all manners of harmful activity the consequences of which they may not fully comprehend and from which adults should protect them. Adopting the position that child soldiers cannot voluntarily engage in conflict is a first and necessary step to absolving young persons of any and all responsibility for any wrongdoing that they commit by suggesting that young persons do not have the intellectual and emotional capacity to make such significant decisions, but it could also be untrue and damaging to the recognition of agency of persons under the age of 18. In this position, there is no room for variance or evaluation of individual capacities. It is also not consistent with most common moral codes and parenting techniques that operate according to the assumption that children are capable of making moral judgements and can determine their own desires and act in ways to realize them. It is not consistent with domestic criminal law that maintains that young individuals do, in fact, have the capacity to commit crimes. On the other hand, virtually no common moral code, parenting technique, or domestic criminal law insinuates that all children have the same capacity as the average mature adult. Built into each is a scale that assumes that as individuals grow, learn, and mature, they acquire better decision-making capacities and skills (CRC: Article 5).

Nonetheless, a stark dichotomy between 'voluntariness' and 'coercion' in these cases that equates voluntariness with the freedom to decide between life-peaceful-and-prosperous and life-brutal-and-cruel does point to a lack of voluntariness for most child soldiers. Rather, even in cases where young persons join fighting groups with knowledge, understanding, and will, 'most cases of recruitment takes place in the grey zone between voluntary and coerced recruitment' (Bjørkhaug 2010: 1), based in part on their immaturity and the conditions available to them external to the fighting force. Sometimes those who volunteer are looking for freedom and excitement (Honwana 2006: 1; de Soyza 2011). Sometimes they are hoping to support the cause and defend or fight for the autonomy of their ethnic or social group or to avenge injury inflicted on it (Siegrist 2010: 3; Green 2013). Most often, potential child soldiers have difficult choices to make between separate bad situations and they are not able to fully foresee or understand the long-term consequences of being a child soldier (Bjørkhaug 2010: 8). Ingunn Bjørkhaug refers to child soldiers who were recruited under these conditions as 'voluntary forced'. Their choice to join the fighting group was a response to immediate conditions and life situations and was the selection chosen after consideration of the available options (Bjørkhaug 2010: 10).

Conditions such as coercion and 'voluntary force' affect the degree of responsibility that any person might bear for actions that derive from the circumstances into which he or she was coerced or pushed, but this is not the same as claiming that such individuals are devoid of the requisite agency to make decisions. There is a danger in characterizing and treating young persons as fully lacking agency to make serious choices. Promoting such assumptions can have negative repercussions for social reconstruction and transitional justice enterprises. This will be a recurring thesis in this book.

Conclusion

Transitional justice has a difficult task in devising means of pursuing justice in the wake of mass violations of human rights. There is a temptation to conflate conceptions and agents, especially those which seem most difficult to understand. Misrepresenting or oversimplifying events, contexts and agents, however, risks introducing challenges, even as they might promise to circumvent others. Despite its messiness, transitional justice would be better served by acknowledging the fact that a homogeneous picture of child soldiers is unrepresentative and unhelpful, and understanding the basic experiences of an assortment of child soldiers allows us to better assess the range of responsibility that child soldiers might bear for their individual contribution to harms inflicted. The category of child soldier is much more diverse and deserves a more nuanced approach in transitional justice than it generally receives in the academic literature and in humanitarian circles.

The universalized non-responsible child narrative is neither accurate nor, as will be seen in the following chapter, representative of the conceptions of agency present in most communities to which child soldiers return. An imposed non-responsible child narrative can belie underlying doubts in community members about individual former child soldiers based on the knowledge that many must have contributed to atrocity while not admitting an accurate representation of the variety of experiences of child soldiers. It also belies the uncertainty about the limits of responsibility and agency that exist but cannot be explored if the community's stance is that the relevant questions have been answered by the adoption of the non-responsible child narrative. This book examines these questions again from a starting point that does not assume that all child soldiers should be whitewashed with the same narrative. It might be the case that recognizing that some responsibility for the actions of some is rightfully attributed and that addressing responsibility through accountability processes is necessary for more fulfilling and comprehensive social reconstruction.

The experiences of child soldiers around the world are quite divergent. Causes for civil strife, methods of recruitment, make-up of the fighting forces, level of identification of soldiers with their fighting forces, and level of weapons training and training in military tactics are different from conflict to conflict, between groups in any particular conflict, and between individual experiences. Common among most examples is general isolation of recruits from civilian life, family, friends, and community members, and the fact that once a member, it is often very difficult for soldiers to quit their fighting forces. In each situation, some child soldiers were trained to handle weapons and were taught military tactics, but not all children received such instruction or were provided with weapons. Commonly, harsh corporal punishment was used, and punishment was often administered publicly as an instructive tool. Differences in temperament, desire to please or to advance in the group, fear levels, or personal convictions to avoid harm if at all possible mark differences in experience and possibly in agency and responsibility. Although it is tempting to identify child soldiering with only one narrative and child soldiers with only one character, such simple representation of child soldiering misses important distinctions that must be acknowledged and addressed in transitional justice processes if they are to be truly valuable as instruments of social reconstruction.

2
The Difficult Reintegration

Violent breaches of human rights standards and mass atrocity committed by children are routinely directed at civilian populations. These are often the same civilian populations from which child soldiers were abducted or recruited, and the same civilian populations to which they return when they demobilize. After time spent with the fighting group brutalizing and terrorizing, and being brutalized and terrorized, demobilized child soldiers often have a hard time reintegrating into civilian life. This is true for a number of reasons. This chapter explores the challenges that hamper successful reintegration of child soldiers and social reconstruction enterprises, focusing primarily on the reasons for, and risks of, poor reception of demobilized child soldiers by the community. Reintegration is a social act and societal attitudes can facilitate or obstruct the reintegration of returnees.

Real personal challenges common to returnees who spent time in a fighting force, such as poor psychological and physical health or a lack of valuable skills, can increase the likelihood of a poor reception that can range from ostracism to physical threats and assaults. Poor psychological and physical health is a significant challenge for many demobilized child soldiers. Poor psychological or physical health is a problem in and of itself, but it can also be a significant hindrance to successful social reintegration. As depicted in the previous chapter, during their time with fighting groups, child soldiers typically witness a great deal of violence, they are often made to commit violent acts, and they are often victims of violence and mistreatment. It is often difficult for these young persons to reconcile these traumatic experiences with civilian life. The scars with which former fighters return – psychological, physical, emotional scars – can impede their ability to become productive members of society.

Another reason for demobilized child soldiers to find reintegration challenging is their lack of skills that society regards as beneficial, skills that would be both respected and income-generating. During their time with a fighting group, child soldiers miss opportunities they might have had for formal education and training in vocational skills that could make them employable and stronger contributing members of society. Lack of income-generating skills, and a failure on the part of community members to recognize any of the skills, including decision-making and leadership skills, acquired by many as soldiers, keep former soldiers on the periphery of society.

These factors can contribute to a particular hardship with which many former child soldiers contend in reintegrating into civilian life: the cold reception they receive from society for having been a member of a fighting group. Community members receive fighters, irrespective of age, with a certain amount of ambiguity. Former child soldiers are generally welcomed home as lost children and victims of violence at the same time that they are shunned and reviled. Their immediate families are most often happy and relieved to have them return (although this is not always the case), but they are also often received with a certain amount of fear, distrust, and anger. This anger can originate in response to harms that the child soldier is imagined to have committed. It can also originate in response to harms the child is known to have committed. As mentioned in the previous chapter, part of the initiation process for some armed groups is that the new soldier is forced to commit a violent act of mutilation or murder against a community member or family member before he or she is ushered into the bush to forcibly join the group. This policy, as a means of severing ties between the new soldier and the community, is usually quite effective as it makes young persons believe that they cannot return home and it generates in community members revulsion and anger toward them for their acts (Wessells 2006: 59; Akello et al. 2012: 51).

Each of these factors – trauma, economic and educational concerns, and ambiguous or negative reception – points to different concerns and needs of young persons who return to civilian life after being members of a violent fighting group suspected of committing mass atrocities. And while each factor points to specific distinct challenges that former child soldiers must overcome in their transition from a life of violent conflict that operates according to its own unique rules and moral code to one of relative peaceful order, they are inter-related in that psychological troubles and a lack of income-generating skills can themselves contribute to poor reception, as members of their community regard them as possibly dangerous or a drain on limited resources. The social attitudes towards the considerable needs of these young persons for physical and psychological treatment and for skills training and education compound their reintegration struggles. In the areas of psychology and education, donor communities are actively involved and yet there remain many questions about how best to meet the needs of demobilized child soldiers as well as the broader community that has been devastated by the conflict. Although attention is also given to the reception that former child soldiers face upon re-entry into civilian life and how this reception affects their ability to effectively reintegrate, the attention is insufficient and may originate at the wrong point. What is lacking is a serious consideration of how this reception, especially negative aspects of it, is reflective of principles and convictions held by the local population to which the child soldiers return and how this reception and these convictions affect the society's capacity for social reconstruction in the aftermath of atrocity.

In many post-conflict contexts, there is a tension between conceptions of agency and responsibility that would attribute some responsibility to child soldiers and the non-responsible child narrative that rejects any responsibility for persons under the age of 18. This tension is a serious problem for post-atrocity social reconstruction. However, it should not necessarily be regarded as a challenge to be overcome by educating the society to accept the non-responsible child narrative; rather it should be viewed perhaps as a reflection of healthy conceptions of agency and responsibility consistent with others globally, developed over a long history, little of which was embroiled in war to which child soldiers contribute.

Taking seriously the needs of victims of atrocity means acknowledging their perceptions of what justice dictates and working to reconcile intuitions regarding agency and responsibility with morality, reality, and practice. If the proposed instruments of transitional justice do not accord with the conceptions of agency and responsibility held by the population, problems of irrelevance arise. One solution to this tension is to educate the population in the non-responsible child narrative, thereby eliminating the tension by drawing conceptions of agency and responsibility in line with the international humanitarian community's discourse. Another solution is to re-evaluate the responsibility that child soldiers might bear, thereby giving credence to the local conceptions of agency and responsibility, so long as they reflect reasoned positions that conform to human rights standards and rights of the child. This chapter does not aim to suggest a solution; rather, it draws attention to this tension as a significant and ongoing problem for post-atrocity social rebuilding.

This chapter first examines the concept of reintegration and then focuses on positive social reception as an often lacking requirement of successful reintegration. It illustrates the negative reception that child soldiers often face when they attempt to return home and reintegrate into civilian life. It argues that the negative reception demonstrates that a narrative that depicts all perpetrators of atrocity under the age of 18 as devoid of any responsibility for harms committed is inconsistent with the sentiments and moral codes of many community members. It then examines how international criminal law reflects a blameless conception of child soldiers, laying out the criminalization of conscripting children into armed groups and the corresponding trend to regard persons under the age of 18 as only victims of the crime of juvenile recruitment. The validity of the non-responsible child narrative is the subject of Chapter 3. This chapter deals with practical concerns pertaining to the tension. It shows that policies grounded in an assumed international adoption of the non-responsible child narrative are not prescribed by international law, can cause distress as victims believe some perpetrators are unjustly protected from accountability, and are inconsistently applied, thereby diminishing the credibility of the narrative in the eyes of sceptics. This chapter argues that taking seriously the emotions and perceptions of civilian victims and child soldiers is important to the enterprise of social reconstruction. Entrenched principles and convictions built on conceptions of agency, responsibility, and justice must be acknowledged and incorporated into transitional justice practices.

Reintegration, rehabilitation, and training

Reintegration is a long-term 'process in which former soldiers transition to civilian life, achieving a viable civilian role that offers an alternative to soldiering' (Wessells 2006: 155). Without going into great detail, it is important to highlight the significant physical, psychological, and educational needs of demobilized child soldiers that must be satisfied if they are to successfully reintegrate. Meeting such needs is a long, intense, and complex undertaking and the question of how to meet these needs is beyond the scope of this book. This section outlines the social implications of the physical, psychological, and educational needs of returnees.

The reason that rehabilitation and reintegration is critical in post-conflict contexts is twofold: child soldiers are vulnerable and victims in need of treatment and help, and because not addressing the psychological damage and social grievances of former child soldiers could have the potential to ruin the lives of the society's children and 'lay the groundwork for future conflicts that harm society writ large' (Singer 2005: 183). Successful reintegration of former child soldiers is a key factor in sustainable peace and social reconstruction (Sendabo 2004: 57–66; Grover 2008). If not properly reintegrated, child soldiers 'may continue to use violence to meet their needs, thus blurring the lines between war and peace, and between civilian and aggressor' (Veale and Stavrou 2007: 274). Successful transition can be characterized as a switch from life as a soldier to life as a stable civilian.

Physical health is a primary concern.

> Physically, child soldiers often enter the demobilization camps with many severe health problems. They will frequently be sickly or malnourished. With little concern for public health of cleanliness among child soldier groups in the field, they will also often suffer from high levels of disease, ranging from measles and diarrheal diseases to higher levels of sexual transmitted diseases (STDs)... Children are more likely to enter demobilization programs with debilitating or disabling wounds from fighting. Many of the girl soldiers may also be pregnant or suffer from sexual abuse traumas, which carry added health and disease risks.
>
> (Singer 2005: 193)

Mentioned in the previous chapter is another physical obstacle that some former child soldiers encounter, depending on the conflict in which they were engaged and the side for which they fought: the physical branding or scars inflicted by the fighting group, such as the RUF in Sierra Leone, to mark their property. 'These wounds not only harm the psyche of their victims, but also impede their reintegration into the local society' (Singer 2005: 197). Of course, not only former fighters but also many civilians have enduring physical disorders and complaints from the conflict, but the branding, for those who were marked, is an example of a complaint specific to former child soldiers that distinguishes them from other victims of the violence and stigmatizes them, thereby further affecting social acceptance as well.

Psychological rehabilitation is another critical undertaking. There may be some controversy regarding how psychologically damaged former child soldiers are, but there is little question that most former soldiers experience some form of 'ongoing psycho-social after-effects of the war, such as disturbing memories of violence and abuse, nightmares, anxiety, anger, fear and depression' (Denov 2010: 150). While some argue that a much higher percentage of child soldiers show symptoms of post traumatic stress disorder (PTSD) than do typical civilian children who live in a war zone (Wessells 2006: 132; Kohrt et al. 2008) or adult soldiers (Dickson-Gomez 2003), others argue that the stated post-traumatic disorders and psychological effects of the experiences of child soldiers are exaggerated (Blattman 2009: 231; Drumbl 2012: 53–56). Nonetheless, many demobilized child soldiers suffer from PTSD and difficulties reconciling a life of violence with civilian ordered society as a result of prolonged exposure to violent conflict.[1] As evidence of the interconnectedness of social acceptance and psychological wellbeing, such difficulty is arguably compounded for those who participated in an unpopular conflict or on an unpopular side of a conflict (Summerfield 2001).

It is important not to over-generalize regarding the psychological effects of conflict; not all former child soldiers are traumatized (Paris Principles: Article 7.72.2). Naturally, different agents respond to their experiences differently and different agents have greatly varied experiences to overcome or with which to come to terms. Experiences differ in terms of length of involvement in the fighting force, roles, proximity to violence (if the soldier killed a person and how, or if the soldier saw a person killed and how), and relationship to victims. Former child soldiers also 'differ significantly in their general makeup, temperament, history, and sources of social support', all of which affect how a person deals with events in his or her life (Wessells 2006: 133).

Education, vocational and skills training, and opportunities to support one's own and one's family's livelihoods are seen as other essential elements for successful reintegration (Paris Principles: Article 7.77). They are also factors that can affect reception or acceptance from the community. A lack of ability to support his or her self and family can obstruct a positive attitude towards a returnee. There is little question that youths who have been away from civilian life might have missed possible opportunities for skills training and more formal education that could support their ability to be better viewed as contributing members of society and better able to find gainful employment. Employment is important, both as a means for individuals to provide for themselves economically and also symbolically, since playing a role in the society represents embeddedness and acceptance, both to the former soldier and to other community members (Corbin 2008: 317; Denov 2010: 171).

Successful reintegration demands that focus is directed towards meeting the physical, psychological, and educational needs of demobilized child soldiers; however, meeting these needs is a necessary but not sufficient condition of successful social reintegration. The social dimension to reintegration that consists of the community and its members receiving a former combatant into the group as an accepted member, however, is not only linked to the physical, psychological, and educational needs that might accompany a returnee but also to societal attitudes about actions the returnee might have performed as a participant in the conflict. Many post-conflict reintegration processes, however, ignore or can aggravate a particular tension in the reintegration of former soldiers who are perceived to have committed severe human rights violations. As Angela Veale and Aki Stavrou point out, 'psychosocial rehabilitation and reintegration programs have failed to adequately address issues of impunity' (Veale and Stavrou 2007: 273). Irrespective of whether impunity for these perpetrators is right or wrong, there is a tension between the tendency of some to promote the non-responsible agency portrait of these former fighters and the comfort of community members to accept this portrait and welcome former child soldiers home with impunity. Wellbeing and successful reintegration entail social harmony. Therefore, physical and psychological wellbeing and education will not eliminate the challenges that former child soldiers face in reintegration until the community's principles and convictions built on conceptions of agency, responsibility, and justice are truly acknowledged and addressed by transitional justice practices.

The reception

The communities to which demobilized child soldiers return often have very ambiguous views of the relationship between their victimhood and agency as perpetrators (United States Institute of Peace 2007; Corbin 2008). Tony Wach, a Jesuit Priest in Uganda, asks the question with which many communities must grapple: 'Do you welcome your brother back in your house when he might have killed people in your village or killed people in your family?' (Creighton Backpack Journalism 2012: 5:45 mins). The ambiguous views are often reflective of the tension community members feel between compassion and resentment, between wanting to put the past behind them and wanting past harms acknowledged and addressed, between recognizing the need to allow these young victimized perpetrators to get the help they need to be constructive members of their society and the mistrust and uncertainty some community members feel about the past acts and future tendencies of these former combatants.

To many community members, it seems wrong to regard young causal perpetrators under the age of 18 uniformly as devoid of the capacity for criminal responsibility (Amann 2001; Veale 2006: 104–105; Drumbl 2012: 22). It seems wrong to some to regard them uniformly as purely victims, non-responsible agents, in the same light as one might regard a civilian who was killed or maimed by members of the fighting group but who in no way inflicted any harm on any others. To many, there seems to be something essentially different in these two cases. As already mentioned, the next chapter will investigate the actual moral and legal responsibility that child soldiers might bear for their actions. The purpose of this section is to explore how questions and perceptions about responsibility affect a former child soldier's return and efforts to reintegrate into civilian life.

The perceived difference between the two cases is reflected in the views of community members. Naturally, not all civilians believe there is a difference between these two cases; no civilian population is a homogeneous group. But, there is enough of this sentiment to be salient to a discussion of responsibility and post-conflict social reconstruction. There are those who intellectually buy into the characterization of child soldiers as non-responsible agents but who find it too difficult to feel and react accordingly, especially when faced with a young person who is known to have been active with the fighting group that caused death, mayhem, and terror in the community. There are also those who do not buy into this characterization and who believe that regarding a child soldier in the same way as another victim, a victim who in no way harmed another, is contrary to the dictates of justice as they perceive justice to be. According to Diane Amann, Sierra Leoneans were adamant about wanting former fighters who were suspected of heinous offenses – even children – to be held criminally responsible for their wrongdoing, despite the knowledge that many had been abducted and forced into their brutal actions (Amann 2001: 174). In Rwanda, it was argued that if a child had enough strength to commit the acts and was old enough to know the difference between a Hutu and a Tutsi, he or she should be held responsible for his or her criminal behaviour (Veale 2006: 104). Grace Akello and her fellow researchers recount the story of a former child soldier in northern Uganda who inspired much anger by stating that it was 'inevitable to carry out such acts' (Akello et al. 2012: 51). Mark Drumbl claims, 'Their home communities simply do not accept the suitability of the collectivized faultless passive victim narrative as applied to them as individuals' (Drumbl 2012: 22). Accompanying the 'strong momentum for the protection of conflict-affected children' (Otunnu 2005: 2) is resistance in the hearts and minds of many community members to the universalization of the innocent-child narrative.

The reintegration of child soldiers in Colombia has proved difficult partly because of their status as child soldiers and the accompanying assumptions that they were dangerous and/or criminals. The government-led Disarmament, Demobilization, and Reconciliation (DDR) programme had initially envisaged former child soldiers reunited with their families or placed in foster homes, but the reality of security concerns and the risk of re-recruitment made it impossible for many to return to their families in areas affected by the armed conflict. Also, the stigmatization of child soldiers, regularly perceived as violent and threatening, means that families are reluctant to receive former child soldiers. When demobilized child soldiers are unwelcome or meet poor reception, they face limited options and inadequate guidance.

> Child soldiers from the FARC and ELN, many of whom came from rural areas and enlisted voluntarily for economic reasons, experienced particular difficulties adapting to life in the cities where the centres were located. They were separated from family, friends and community support systems, and faced the additional challenge of stigmatization by the population. Child soldiers demobilizing from the AUC presented greater psychological and behavioural problems, including drug addiction.
>
> (Coalition to Stop the Use of Child Soldiers 2008: Colombia)

For many former soldiers the temptation to return to violence, either by re-joining the fighting force or engaging in gang activity is strong (Moloney 2012), and children continue to be targeted for recruitment into violent conflict in Colombia and elsewhere.

In the DRC, Sierra Leone, and Uganda, many former child soldiers are or were unable to return home to their families for reasons that include having no family to return to or a family that will not welcome them. As is the case in many environments of widespread and persistent conflict, many people were killed and some child soldiers find that they no longer have any immediate family left. Some families refuse to welcome home former child soldiers because of the harm they have perpetrated against others (Eichstaedt 2009: 24; Honwana 2009: 64). And some families discourage children from returning home with the aim 'to protect them from being harmed by members of their community who think those children are responsible for killing or any other bad deeds done in the past' (SOS Children's Village n.d.). Reintegration for former child soldiers is difficult because, despite attempts to teach the population that the children were victims of the war first and foremost, they are often stigmatized for the brutality and destruction the civil war caused. In Sierra Leone, children were accused of the deeds committed by the fighting forces. 'They were banished from their families and their former happy life' (Truth and Reconciliation Report, Sierra Leone, 2003: 23).

For the most part, most demobilized child soldiers may not participate in any process that investigates or addresses responsibility; rather, in Africa they may participate in cleansing ceremonies to wash away the spirits of the dead that might have followed them home (Honwana 2006: 104–134; Baines 2010). Cleansing ceremonies take different forms depending on the community to which the child soldier belongs. In the northern Ugandan Acholi tribe, there is a commonly used traditional cleansing ceremony and a different reconciliation ceremony that requires returnees to ask forgiveness from their victims. Mato Oput, a highly publicized Acholi reconciliation ceremony traditionally performed after a killing, incorporates the guilty acknowledging a wrong committed and asking for forgiveness and then offering compensation. The main objective of Mato Oput and similar reconciliation ceremonies across the country is to restore relationships between the perpetrators and the victims of the crime and reintegrate the perpetrators into their communities.[2] Despite the fact that Mato Oput has been widely explored and publicized in relation to addressing the wrongdoing of the LRA (Baines 2005: iii), the percentage of former rebel soldiers who participate in such ceremonies is low.[3] Predominantly, only cleansing ceremonies are used, such as those used by former LRA child soldiers, the ritual breaking from their violent past by stepping on eggs (Fegley 2008: 45). There are two aspects of the more common ceremonies: the idea of washing away the pollution of death and spirits and the need to break from the past. Neither of these features or goals incorporates accountability for any wrongs committed. In Sudan, 'demobilized children in these ceremonies simply lay down their arms and as a group move forward towards crowds of relatives and neighbors with their backs to the weapons. They are welcomed home, the weapons are often destroyed' (Fegley 2008: 48).

Regardless of the cleansing rituals, former child soldiers are often seen as dangerous to ordered communities. This view, reflecting impressions of the possible trouble caused by child soldiers who are not reintegrated and have nothing constructive to do in society, is reproduced both by Western reports and local populations. Denov highlights the Western reports that claim that

> the violence and disarray embodying the actions of child soldiers during conflict are said to be destined to continue in the war's aftermath. Perceived to be lost in a cycle of unrelenting violence, irrationality and iniquity, children who have participated in armed conflict have generally been assumed to be permanently damaged: 'fluent in the language of violence, but ignorant to the rudiments of living in a civil society... it's often too late to salvage their lives'.
>
> (Denov 2010: 6).

This view regards them as tools or monsters reprogrammed by their experiences.

Despite the prevalence of using cleansing ceremonies, there is in traditional ways and conceptions of justice endorsement of the pursuit of accountability. Significant is the fact that the principle of retributive justice is strong in most of these cultures, despite the reliance on restorative justice mechanisms to reconcile rifts created by harms committed. As I argued to a more comprehensive extent elsewhere, many traditionally used mechanisms of justice (that represent the judicial culture of these African societies) exhibit very sophisticated means of investigating, judging, and punishing (as well as often allowing the individual found guilty to appeal the judgement) that precede practices of restorative justice (Fisher 2012: 144–167). The retributive sentiment is also strong with many members of the local population who voice concern about impunity for harms committed. Michael Wessells reports one elder from Sierra Leone saying, 'Bad crimes must be punished, even when children did the wrong' (Wessells 2006: 218).

Child soldiers often face hostility from their communities of origin or the communities to which they relocate because of harms that they perpetrated or are perceived to have committed (Wessells 2006: 173; Corbin 2008: 323, 328–329; Fegley 2008: 44; Betancourt et al. 2010; Denov 2010: 164–86, 186; Akello et al. 2012: 51, 53). 'Former child soldiers are often blamed and stigmatised for the countless atrocities they committed' (Derluyn et al. 2004: 863). This hostility can manifest as isolation, name-calling, or physical assaults.

> Former child soldiers who attempt to return home enter a difficult terrain awash in unhealed grievances, vigilante justice, and contested

> privileges. The message of one report is that returning former soldiers are generally received well in northern Uganda, but 'more than a quarter of returnees said that they were insulted by community members upon return' and that 'particular youth are targeted and insulted when the community knows or suspects they were involved in raids or killings'.
>
> (Annan et al. 2006: 66).

My own research in Gulu suggests that the percentage of returnees who suffered hostility from community members for being a member of the fighting group is significantly higher (Fisher 2013). Akello asserts that 'affected communities rejected, discriminated and sometimes carried out revengeful acts against former child soldiers' (Akello 2012). 'In some cases, villagers' strong feelings of injustice block child soldiers' attempts to reenter the community' (Wessells 2006: 218). Corbin relates a common story regarding the return of former child soldiers: when someone known to have been a child soldier passes by, community members would complain about the soldier's return to civilian life by saying 'Ah, why has she returned, they've killed so many in the bush, they should have been killed' (Corbin 2008: 329).

A commitment to the principle of fair retribution is also evidenced by the great resentment against former child soldiers for any advantage that they receive in terms of medical care, education, or material resettlement packages. Wessells describes what one elder in Sierra Leone asked him, 'Why should the soldiers who attacked us get all the assistance, when we all have suffered?' (Wessells 2006: 205). Susan Shepler describes a situation, also from Sierra Leone, in which a local population believed it 'not right that former soldiers who inflicted so much suffering on so many innocent people should benefit from the school that the community built' (Shepler 2005: 201). Likewise, in northern Uganda, there is resentment towards the conferring of 'resettlement' resources to former child soldiers (Baines 2005: 35).

Given the general sentiments of the populations, it seems possible that without adequately examining and addressing the agency of returnees, the communities to which they return will have difficulty moving beyond the conflict for a smooth and durable transition and to advance a strong and cohesive society. In fact, Uganda's Refugee Law Project reported, while the conflict in northern Uganda was still heated, that its findings 'indicate that lack of formal mechanisms for the process of truth-telling, or the admittance of guilt on the part of former combatants, is currently hindering the process of reconciliation' (Hovil and Lomo 2005: Report Summary). Under the recent and current formats, there are limited opportunities or demands for former soldiers to report their experiences and actions. Some traditional cleansing rituals allow for the recipient of the cleansing to be asked about his or her war experiences, but, as Alcinda Honwana recounts, 'verbalization is not a fundamental condition for healing' (Honwana 2006: 112). In some cases, giving a report of experiences is required for amnesty, such as was required under Uganda's Amnesty Act, but these statements are not publicly available or created with any concern for individual victims or the broader victim community. Nor is any information garnered for restorative aims from a government military debriefing. There is no information compiled by the reception and rehabilitation centres. There is, therefore, in most cases no process of truth-telling or accountability that aims to deal with the past and asks causal perpetrators to account for their actions, accept responsibility when suitable, disclose the results of actions taken, and assume penalty when appropriate. This lack of accountability is seemingly incompatible with the needs, perceptions, and values of communities to which child soldiers return and into which they must reintegrate.

Non-responsibility under the law

The tension evident in society's reception of former child soldiers is not aided by the 'rhetoric of innocence used by the humanitarian discourse' that is slowly seeping into the practice of international law (Martins 2011: 441). The general inclination of international law and NGOs is to depict child soldiers as non-responsible agents and to promote, through outreach programmes, this characterization within the local populations. This 'not your fault' theme is represented well in Ishmael Beah's memoirs about his experiences as a child soldier in Sierra Leone and the aftermath as he depicts life in a UNICEF rehabilitation centre (Beah 2007). In Sierra Leone, 'NGO workers explained to communities that their children were not responsible for their crimes because of their age and that children had a *right* to be reunified with their family' (Shepler 2005: 200 emphasis original). In northern Uganda also, much work was done to 'educate' the local populations about the non-responsible nature of child soldiers (Corbin 2008: 329; Drumbl 2012: 39–40). Announcements over the radio promoted the non-responsible narrative, and laws threatened anyone who might consider reprisal against former members of the LRA.[4]

As mentioned in the introductory chapter to this book, the current general policy in international criminal law is to criminalize the recruitment of these young persons by adults and to treat the young fighters as victims or tools of the adults.[5] Scarcely a crime a few decades ago,

> the ban on recruiting children took root in the 1990s and has since blossomed into over a dozen indictments in contemporary international criminal courts. Though hundreds of thousands of children still fight in wars across the globe, the age of impunity has finally passed for those who use and recruit child soldiers.
>
> (Webster 2007: 227)

This criminalization of the recruitment of young persons, particularly those under the age of 15, and especially their forceful recruitment, seems reasonable and vital to halting the unwarranted use of young persons in war. However, criminalizing their recruitment and the brutal conditions that many child soldiers face within the fighting group does not necessarily deny some child soldiers any legal or moral responsibility for their own actions. Nonetheless, there is a corresponding trend to regard persons under the age of 18 as only victims of the crime of juvenile recruitment. Whereas criminal law generally conceptualizes the relationship between victim and perpetrator as a dichotomy, with an agent either a victim or a perpetrator, it is possible that the characterization of both victim and perpetrator be assigned to a singular agent. One individual can be both victim and perpetrator, both a victim of the criminal wrongdoing perpetrated by another and also the perpetrator of harms. The simple victim-or-perpetrator dichotomy, however, is realized in the application if not the strict letter of the law when it comes to child soldiers.

The fact that there is no international prohibition against prosecuting persons under the age of 18 for violent crimes is evident in a number of international conventions, including the United Nations Convention on the Rights of the Child (CRC (CRC: Article 40), the Principles and Guidelines on Children Associated with Armed Forces or Armed Groups ('the Paris Principles') (Paris Principles: Articles 3.6–3.7, 3.9 and 8.7–8.11), and the African Charter on the Rights and Welfare of the Child (African Charter: Article 17).[6] Each of these international conventions lays out guidelines for the protection of children's rights and the promotion of children's dignity and reintegration when children are accused of committing crimes. The Paris Principles stipulate that children accused of crimes under international law 'should be considered primarily as victims of offences against international law; not *only* as perpetrators' and that they should be offered 'special protection' (Paris Principles: Article 3.6 emphasis added). Article 3.7 recommends that 'whenever possible, alternatives to judicial proceedings must be sought in line with the Convention on the Rights of the Child and other international standards for juvenile justice (Paris Principles: Article 3.7). The wording of Article 3.7 of the Paris Principles suggests a dissuasion against the use of criminal proceedings for children that is absent from the CRC.

The CRC lays out protections that children accused of criminal acts must be afforded, such as that 'No child shall be alleged as, be accused of, or recognized as having infringed the penal law by reason of acts or omissions that were not prohibited by national or international law at the time they were committed' (Article 40(1)(a)), that every child is guaranteed to 'be presumed innocent until proven guilty according to law' (Article 40(1)(b)(i)) and guaranteed to

> have the matter determined without delay by a competent, independent and impartial authority or judicial body in a fair hearing according to law, in the presence of legal or other appropriate assistance and, unless it is considered not to be in the best interest of the child, in particular, taking into account his or her age or situation, his or her parents or legal guardians.
>
> (Article 40(1)(b)(iii))

Amid a list of protections for children accused of committing criminal acts is the recommendation that states employ 'whenever appropriate and desirable, measures for dealing with such children without resorting to judicial proceedings' (CRC: Article 40(3)(b)). The use of the terms 'appropriate' and 'desirable' suggests something much weaker than is implied in the Paris Principles. In the end, Article 40 in the CRC proposes that, along with rehabilitation support that ought to be available, consideration should be afforded the wellbeing of the child and that response and support should be proportionate to circumstances and offences. Recommendations, therefore, demand special protections for juvenile offenders, including the consideration of alternative mechanisms of accountability, but do not deny the use of prosecutions when the circumstances and offences warrant it.

Under domestic criminal law, age of criminal responsibility is often arranged by degrees such that someone under a certain age (perhaps 10 or 12) is considered too young to be held responsible for acts committed, and someone between the ages of 12 and 18 typically answers to a juvenile criminal system.[7] Sometimes young persons can be prosecuted or sentenced as adults due to the severe nature of their crimes. The age of juvenile criminal liability demarcates the age at which agents are capable of the requisite mental state from the age at which they are too young. The age of majority, at which age a person is an adult under the law and is automatically charged and prosecuted as an adult, is not set globally. The age of majority ranges in Western nations between 16 and 18. In Scotland, it is 16. In many American states it is 18, but in others it is 16 or 17. Juvenile defendants, those under the age of majority, are afforded special protection above the regular rights granted to persons in conflict with the law. Looking to the US one can find a system in which children as young as 7 and as old as 17 can be tried in juvenile court, and increasingly prosecutors were trying children between the ages of 12 and 18 as adults for very serious crimes (Penney and Moretti 2005: 23–25). There are widely divergent notions and legal confirmations regarding the age of criminal responsibility, few of which actually support a strict policy of non-responsibility under the age of 18.

In international law, there is no consensus on the minimum age of criminal responsibility. Taking into account the disparity between countries, international law relating to children merely asks that each state establishes a minimum age of responsibility (Manirakiza 2009: 740). The CRC simply requires that states promote 'the establishment of a minimum age below which children shall be presumed not to have the capacity to infringe penal law' (CRC: Article 40.3). Likewise, the United Nations Standard Minimum Rules for the Administration of Juvenile Justice (also known as the Beijing Rules) notes that age limits will depend on, and are explicitly made dependent on, each respective legal system, thus fully respecting the economic, social, political, cultural, and legal systems of Member States. This makes for a wide variety of ages coming under the definition of 'juvenile', ranging from 7 years to 18 years or above (Beijing Rules 1985: Article 2.2).

The Beijing Rules do recommend that the minimum age not be set too low and that it be fixed, bearing in mind the facts of emotional, mental, and intellectual maturity (Beijing Rules 1985: Article 4.1). The CRC's General Comment No. 10 (2007) regarding children's rights in juvenile justice builds on the recommendation of the Beijing Rules and claims that 'a minimum age of criminal responsibility below the age of 12 years is considered by the Committee not to be internationally acceptable' (Article 32), but that a higher minimum age, such as 14 or 16 ' contributes to a juvenile justice system which, in accordance with article 40 (3) (b) of CRC, deals with children in conflict with the law without resorting to judicial proceedings, providing that the child's human rights and legal safeguards are fully respected' (Article 33). Accordingly, there is a need to set a standard minimum age of criminal responsibility and also to specify how persons under the age of criminal responsibility are dealt with 'when they are recognized as having infringed the penal law, or are alleged as or accused of having done so' (Article 33).

Despite the lack of prohibition against prosecuting young persons, international criminal law, for the most part, regards them as outside its jurisdiction as perpetrators. Neither the International Criminal Tribunal for the former Yugoslavia (ICTY) nor the International Criminal Tribunal for Rwanda (ICTR) prosecuted any person under the age of 18. Young persons have protected status under international humanitarian law and are, therefore, considered by many not liable for any actions they allegedly commit (Crane 2008; Grover 2008). It is interesting that the Special Court for Sierra Leone (SCSL), a hybrid court established through an agreement between the UN and the government of Sierra Leone and of which David Crane was the founding Prosecutor, was created with the authority to bring before the court as perpetrators persons as young as 15 years of age, with the caveat that

> should any person who was at the time of the alleged commission of the crime between 15 and 18 years of age come before the Court, he or she shall be treated with dignity and a sense of worth, taking into account his or her young age and the desirability of promoting his or her rehabilitation, reintegration into and assumption of a constructive role in society.
>
> (Statute of the Special Court for Sierra Leone: Article 7(1))

Crane, however, decided that no person under the age of 18 would be indicted by the SCSL.[8] This decision was based on two lines of reasoning. One was that child soldiers are 'not legally liable for acts committed during the conflict' and should be regarded as victims for whom rehabilitation is the 'appropriate norm under international law' (Crane 2008: 15). The other was that it would be impractical to prosecute even particularly violent children because there were so many (Crane 2008: 15).

His first argument makes a strong normative statement about the possibility of attributing responsibility to young persons. An alternative argument that Crane could have employed might have been that since it was the case that the SCSL was established to prosecute those who bore the greatest responsibility for war crimes and crimes against humanity committed during the civil war in Sierra Leone (Statute of the Special Court for Sierra Leone), no persons under the age of 18 did actually bear sufficient personal responsibility as one of the most responsible and therefore no person under the age of 18 would be prosecuted before the SCSL. Crane decided to make a declaration that would reach much further, claiming that 'no child between 15 and 18 had the sufficiently blameworthy state of mind to commit war crimes in a conflict setting' (Crane 2008: 15).

In a similar move, the jurisdiction of the ICC is limited to persons 18 years of age and older. Article 26 of the Rome Statute is entitled 'Exclusion of jurisdiction over persons under eighteen' and states that 'the Court shall have no jurisdiction over any person who was under the age of 18 at the time of the alleged commission of a crime' (Rome Statute: Article 26). In a UNICEF publication entitled *International Criminal Justice and Children*, only six sentences are dedicated to 'children as perpetrators of crimes under international law', and the message again acts to reinforce the idea that persons under the age of 18 should not be regarded as responsible for any harm they commit:

> While children's experiences of war crimes, crimes against humanity and genocide are first and foremost as victims, children are also sometimes recruited to be active parties to those crimes. In Sierra Leone, children were abducted and made to terrorize the civilian population, including amputating the limbs of civilians. In Rwanda, some children directly participated in killings during the genocide. Children, mostly from poor families, may be coerced into participating in crimes, either threatened, indoctrinated, manipulated or drugged. Forcing children to commit atrocities during an armed conflict is itself a war crime, resulting in severe psychological harm, and is a violation of their rights. Child perpetrators are thus victims of criminal policies for which adults are primarily responsible.
>
> (UNICEF 2002: 33)

This blanket of non-responsibility for agents under the age of 18 can be seen both as potentially a serious problem of not accurately reflecting true responsibility and as a critical gap in the jurisdiction of international criminal law. Persons between the age of 15 and 18 can be conscripted or enlisted to participate in war but the Court has no jurisdiction over these persons. 'Thus, a person between 15 and 17 is regarded as a lawful combatant and may commit a crime without being brought to court and punished' (Cassese 1999: 153). Antonio Cassese indicates a potential effect of this gap: 'A commander could therefore recruit minors into his army expressly for the purpose of forming terrorist units whose members would be immune from prosecution' (1999: 153). Although the commanders recruiting child soldiers lack this particular inspiration, the situation is playing out in many conflicts in which child soldiers participate – soldiers under the age of 18 commit grave harms for which they have immunity from accountability under the jurisdiction of the ICC.

The reason for this limited jurisdiction for the ICC is, like most things, a political compromise. In the summaries of the proceedings of the Preparatory Committee there is evidence of a debate. It was widely supported that it would be necessary to include a provision setting an age limit at which an individual could be regarded as not having the requisite mental capacity. The precise age, however, was intensely debated (United Nations 1996: Article 98). Arguments for the minimum age for legal responsibility before the ICC varied between 12 and 18 (Rikhof 2009: 2). 'Eventually, it was decided that the court does not have jurisdiction over any person who was under 18 at the time of the alleged commission of the crime, thereby avoiding setting an age limit for criminal responsibility for minors' (Rikhof 2009: 2).

For persons under the age of 18, however, there should be a juvenile justice system to address criminal contributions to mass atrocity. At what age then should criminal responsibility not apply? Pacifique Manirakiza argues that there ought to be a universal minimum age of criminal responsibility of 15 for international atrocity crimes, below which age children could still be regarded as culpable of criminal activity but only for ordinary crimes under domestic law (Manirakiza 2009). Perpetrators between the ages of 15 and 18 could be prosecuted under the jurisdiction of international criminal law before an international judicial institution, afforded special protection as juvenile defendants. Manirakiza's proposal of the minimum age of 15 seems reasonable given the severity of the stigma attached to a conviction for an international crime (Fisher 2012: 83–102). Manirakiza also suggests that age should not factor into the judgement of guilt or innocence but should be taken into account for sentencing (Manirakiza 2009). The age of 15 is significant because it is the agreed-upon age of minimal legal participation in armed conflict.

It is worthy of note that neither the statute of ICTY nor that of the ICTR preclude prosecuting children for international crimes committed during the temporal jurisdictions of the tribunals. The statutes specify no minimum age for criminal culpability. However, as mentioned above, neither of the tribunals prosecuted any persons under the age of 18.

The tension that community members who must receive home former young combatants feel between regarding demobilized child soldiers as innocent and regarding them as responsible is also reflected on a much larger scale internationally. Despite the argued settling of the prohibition against prosecuting under international criminal law persons who were under the age of 18 at the time the alleged criminal act was committed, there is great inconsistency in the attribution of legal responsibility for young persons who are suspected of committing war crimes. This inconsistency is highly evident with respect to two issues of practical concern: the line between child victim and perpetrator becomes blurry as the child grows up and matures in the armed force, and in the practical experience of geopolitical conflict the line between child victim and perpetrator disappears in some cases depending on who are the victims of the harm and who are the prosecuting agents.

There is a complex relationship under international (and national) law between the non-responsibility of child soldiers and the responsibility that is attributed to former child soldiers who cross an invisible line to become responsible adult agents. The example of two Ugandan LRA members demonstrates this complexity. Both Dominic Ongwen and Thomas Kwoyelo were abducted as children and conscripted into the LRA. Due to their ultimate ranks in the rebel group, they were both indicted by criminal courts. Kwoyelo 'was the first LRA commander to face trial in Uganda's special war crimes court' (BBC 2011). He was subsequently given amnesty according to the provisions of Uganda's Amnesty Act of 2000, but not released and as of the writing of this book, he is in custody in Uganda.[9] Ongwen was indicted by the ICC, is still free, and is considered one of the most wanted suspected criminals in the world.[10]

As mentioned in the introductory chapter, in the aftermath of the Rwandan genocide over a thousand children were imprisoned alongside adult perpetrators in dreadful conditions. The inconsistency of criminal law in dealing with child soldiers, though, is best highlighted with mention of Omar Khadr, a youth who was imprisoned by the US in Guantánamo Bay for seven years, and treated as an adult, prior to his pleading guilty to five charges of war crimes and terrorism before the Guantánamo military commission tribunal (including murder in violation of the law of war and providing material support for terrorism) for the death of American soldier Christopher Speer. Khadr was 15 years old at the time of the fire fight in which Speer was killed (Dore 2008; Friscolanti 2012). The US demonstrates acute contradiction by applying juvenile justice to most perpetrators of crimes under the age of 18 within the US while applying very different standards to persons outside the American borders. Peter Singer quotes Jeb Bush, brother of former US president, George W. Bush, as saying that 'there is a different standard for children. There should be some sensitivity that a 14-year-old is not a little adult'; concurrently, the US was housing underage detainees at Guantánamo Bay, and then-Secretary of Defense Donald Rumsfeld stated that 'these are not children', arguing that they therefore could be treated in the same manner as adult detainees (Singer 2005: 154). Mark Drumbl speaks directly to the problem: 'However embedded, perceptions of the victim status of child soldiers remain somewhat contingent upon the nationality of those persons injured by their conduct. Child soldiers who commit violence – for example, terrorist attacks – against Western targets are seen less like deluded children and more like menacing adults' (Drumbl 2012: 3).

Crane claims that the guilty verdicts of the AFRC leadership by the UN-backed hybrid tribunal mentioned above exist as a clear message about the responsibility of young perpetrators: 'The Trial Chamber sent a clear message to the world that a person who recruits child soldiers into a conflict is a war criminal, but the children recruited and forced to commit unspeakable acts are not' (Crane 2008: 13). It seems, however, that this 'clear message' is actually rather murky. It might depend on the background of the perpetrators, the background of the victims, and the political interests and values that the tribunal and its supporters represent. And, the line between victim and perpetrator is often difficult to draw. However, blanket immunity for those under the age of 18 does not necessarily make the task of accurately and justly dividing the guilty from the blameless easier.

Conclusion

Many conflicts in which child soldiers fight (or contribute to a fighting force) are civil wars that divide communities; and often, child soldiers are compelled to commit brutalities against local civilian communities, often those to which they return after they demobilize. Because frequently, when returning to civilian life, former soldiers must contend with the feelings of those civilians who were also victimized by the violence and who regard the former child soldiers as, at least partly, responsible for the harm that they endured, it is very important to the enterprise of social reconstruction that these feelings are addressed and evaluated for relevance.

The civilian communities to which they return most often recognize that typically young persons who are recruited into or who volunteer to participate in a fighting group that commits human rights violations are 'initiated into violence through a deliberate process of terror' (Honwana 2009: 65). However, there are examples where this reality must be argued and it is likely always to be the case that the general fact of the conditions with which child soldiers contended are known but not felt and not really understood to the full extent. Even when members of the civilian population are made aware of the conditions, there remain the two characterizations of child soldiers that are at odds – the characterization of innocent victimized child and the characterization of agent of harm who prioritized his or her own wellbeing over the wellbeing of others or who revelled in brutality.

It is worth reiterating here that, as mentioned in the introductory chapter, the conception of childhood as a period of innocence is predominantly a Western construct. Nevertheless, even in Western nations the criminal responsibility of minors is a contested subject and responsibility is not denied all persons under the age of 18. Denying that child soldiers (persons under the age of 18) can bear any responsibility for wrongful actions they may have committed is especially at odds with many cultures in which older children and youths are almost adults who assume great responsibility for the welfare of their families and also their communities. To impose a blanket non-responsible quality to all persons under the age of 18 who participated in violent conflict that affected the communities can be incompatible with the conceptions of agency inherent in the culture. The idea that anyone under the age of 18 is to be considered a child and therefore not to be held accountable can be regarded as a newly imported idea to many cultures (Shepler 2005: 205; Aptel and Ladisch 2011: 8–9). The criminal responsibility of minors is a contested subject, both nationally and internationally.

The reality is that many young persons do in fact assume adult roles in their civilian lives. Children in many cultures are expected to be adults long before their age-mates are in Western societies. With these roles come agency, identity, self-esteem, and responsibility. Many child soldiers take on similarly mature roles in the fighting forces, often adopting leadership roles. They also, while at the same time feeling the constraints on their autonomy, exercise and see themselves to exercise limited agency.

The stories told by child soldiers about their own experiences do not reflect across the board the characterization of pure victim who lacks agency. Naturally, former child soldiers highlight the brutality of the conditions of life with the fighting group. They relate their feelings of lack of choices and their fear (Shepler 2005). The conditions under which they began life as a child soldier implicated in severe human rights abuses and the conditions in which they commit these are very harsh. There is no doubt about the terrible circumstances. But, there are also other stories regarding life as a child soldier that point to agency and, just as importantly, perceived agency. There are stories of tactics taken to avoid committing harm, including tales of how soldiers might choose not to harm a civilian and rather let the civilian victim go free, or how they might trick a commander into believing that they had committed the ordered act when in fact they had not.[11] There are stories of decisions to leave or escape. There are stories of actions, and non-actions, taken to protect other soldiers. There are also stories of a sense of belonging and power (Denov 2010: 40), of attempts to win the favour of commanders, sometimes through the infliction of harm on others; stories of young persons in the fighting group brutalizing newer, less highly ranked, less protected members of the group (Beah 2007). And, there are stories of soldiers victimizing civilians because they could and because the civilian population was afraid of them due to their soldier status.

Child soldiers also often report a sense of guilt or responsibility (Akello et al. 2006: 236; Honwana 2006: 108), and although feelings of guilt or responsibility in no way reveal genuine responsibility, such feelings do reflect the sense that many of these causal perpetrators do, in fact, regard themselves as moral agents to whom responsibility should attach. Their stories, along with their feelings of responsibility, suggest that the non-responsible child narrative is difficult for former child soldiers to reconcile with their own assessment of their individual power and agency. Forcing a universalized non-responsible account and feature on former child soldiers could, in fact, leave them feeling disconnected from their own perceptions and identities as capable agents with voice and agency.[12] Finally, former child soldiers who assumed adult responsibilities during their time as child soldiers often do not want to be relegated to the role of child in civilian life (Dickson-Gomez 2003: 344).

There is likely no easy solution to relieving the tension that community members feel, and thereby easing the reintegration process. The non-responsible child narrative, however, seems to cut short discussions about agency and responsibility in a manner that shows disregard for the internal struggles with which community members contend to resolve conflicting perceptions. Taking seriously the emotions and perceptions of civilian victims and child soldiers, even engaging with and unpacking internally inconsistent representations, is important to the enterprise of social reconstruction. Ingrained conceptions of agency, responsibility, and justice must be acknowledged and incorporated into transitional justice practices in a way that shows respect for, and meets the needs of, both demobilized soldiers and civilians. To this end, two important questions must be answered. The first question is whether there is any moral or legal responsibility that can attach to child soldiers. The debate regarding the moral and legal responsibility of child soldiers is thus far still inconclusive and the practices of domestic and international legal bodies offer little help in clarifying matters. The second question concerns how responsibility should be addressed. It asks whether, even if it is to be found that responsibility attaches to child soldiers, there are practical reasons that prosecutions and other means of accountability for child soldiers ought not to be pursued.

3
Moral and Legal Responsibility of Child Soldiers

How closely does the non-responsible child narrative reproduce the reality of the agency and responsibility of child soldiers? Can it ever be said that a child soldier acts intentionally in a manner consistent with attributing to him or her moral responsibility for the actions he or she commits? Jeff McMahan asks the same question from a different angle: 'Do conditions of ignorance and duress in which child soldiers normally act ever make their action morally permissible, even if the war in which they are fighting is unjust and even if they commit war crimes?' (McMahan 2010: 27). How should the factors that affect agency and responsibility influence the narrative regarding child soldiers who participate in mass atrocity?

This chapter argues that despite diminished responsibility based on age and a coercive environment, there is a real sense in which it is possible that child soldiers can be more than causally responsible for their actions, and that in unique cases some persons under the age of 18 can bear significant responsibility for wrongdoing, even to the extent that they might deserve prosecution. This chapter advances the debate regarding the responsibility of child soldiers by building upon the reasoned arguments offered by legal scholars such as Mark Drumbl and Pacifique Manirakiza, philosophers such as Jeff McMahan, and anthropologists such as Alcinda Honwana who dispute the claim that juveniles are not capable of responsibility for atrocity crimes. Child soldiers are victims of bad circumstances, and their moral and legal responsibility is diminished greatly because of their youthfulness and the circumstances in which they act; and yet, some moral responsibility for violent wrongs committed can be attributed to various child soldiers as contributors to atrocity. This chapter also draws attention to the significance of an additional factor in the evaluation of child soldiers' responsibility, as a mitigating as well as aggravating condition: collective action.

The underlying assumption of the doctrine of responsibility is that the responsible agent is free, committing a deed without restraint or compulsion, knowingly, and deliberately. Attributing responsibility for wrongdoing becomes difficult in situations in which actions normally known to be wrong are committed by agents whose freedom to control their actions or whose capacity to make fully informed and reasoned decisions is debatable. Generally, in cases in which serious criminal acts are committed and it can be proven that the act was unintentional or that the agent did not have the mental capability to understand the nature and the consequences of the act, the agent is often rightly exonerated or excused of responsibility on the grounds that he or she lacked the necessary *mens rea* (guilty mind) or intentionality. Intention is a key element in determining the crime, and is the difference between charges of murder or manslaughter, or between a conviction for acting with malice, for negligent homicide, or exoneration for acting out of justified self-defence (Model Penal Code: Sections 210.1–210.4). The difference is in whether the act displays wicked judgement or merely reflects poor or negligent judgement (Carr 1991: 164).

Child soldiers and the contexts in which they usually operate present a challenge to conceptualizing responsibility with a number of factors that can separately each be seen to diminish individual responsibility. Coercion, a feature in the lives of a majority of child soldiers, is a condition that is quite aptly regarded as diminishing or absolving personal responsibility. Imposed extraordinary pressure is often viewed as affecting responsibility for actions if a reasonable person could be understood to see no alternative to committing the criminal act when faced with a serious and credible threat. Youthfulness is also generally seen as a factor that affects legal and moral responsibility. Like the mentally ill, agents under a certain age are considered incapable of the moral judgements and reasoning necessary to commit a criminal act, even if the actions performed are equivalent to a criminal act if they were committed by another agent.[1] Youthful agents who are not completely absolved of all responsibility for their actions because of their age are treated differently according to systems designed to address wrongdoing committed by juveniles and are designed to acknowledge the different nature of juvenile wrongdoing. A normative judgement about the responsibility borne by individual child soldiers must admit consideration of these conditions. Domestic and international criminal law considers both of these factors.

The fact that an act was committed as part of collective wrongdoing rather than against a backdrop of a well-ordered and peaceful environment also affects how acts of atrocity and their perpetrators ought to be judged. Collective action seen as a diminishing factor is not grounded in general domestic criminal law principles – indeed, domestically, the fact that action is committed as part of collective wrongdoing can be considered an aggravating factor, such as in regards to gang participation – but takes on a different meaning when the collective action is widespread and systematically part of the contemporary social order. The mitigating condition of collective action, given too little attention in debates of international criminal law, is particularly significant to a discussion about child soldiers because young people, as a category, are arguably inherently more easily influenced by social norms and pressure.

Given that these three factors exist in combination for many child soldiers, it seems wise to ask whether it makes sense to talk about the personal responsibility of individual young contributors in the context of these atrocities. Many scholars, human rights practitioners, religious groups, and NGOs working in post-conflict contexts argue, in different ways and with different emphasis, that for both moral and practical reasons, young perpetrators should not be seen to bear moral or legal responsibility for the actions they perform as part of an armed group and/or that holding these young perpetrators accountable would not aid in the social healing of the populations in post-atrocity contexts (see: Somasundaram 2002: 1270; Shepler 2005: 200–201; Crane 2008). The issue of social healing will be addressed in Chapter 4 of this book. This chapter critically evaluates the accuracy of the non-responsible child narrative that claims that child perpetrators can bear no moral or legal responsibility and the accuracy of conflicting community views that would attribute responsibility to some child soldiers.

For the purpose of better understanding the tension between community conceptions of responsibility and the non-responsible child narrative, this chapter questions whether any moral or legal responsibility can attach to child soldiers by examining how the responsibility for actions committed can be diminished or absolved based on features of the child soldier experience: duress, youthfulness, and collective action. It explores how these features can function as excuses or justifications for criminal action in some cases; it also explores the limitations of these features as defences for violent crime. By demonstrating that there is nothing about young people *qua* young people that makes them all incapable of responsibility for atrocity crimes, this chapter endorses a reconnection with community conceptions of agency and responsibility that admit the possibility that persons under the age of

18 might be responsible for their acts of atrocity. And, by highlighting the influence of collective action, this chapter argues that transitional justice processes that ignore the importance of social belonging do a disservice to understanding and accurately accounting for a violent past.

Competence and culpability

Are child soldiers simply tools of adult architects of atrocity, morally equivalent to guns or landmines? This question can only be answered by examining what it means to be responsible for an event or circumstance. Significant to the judgement of moral or legal responsibility is human decision-making and the circumstances that surround and affect the capacity to make clear choices. Responsibility arises out of not only acts, but the state of mind accompanying them. Judgement 'presupposes that the agents whose actions are subject to critique qualify as (in some sense) competent or authoritative actors. If competency is lacking, normative critique is meaningless even if agency is present' (Carr 1991: 162).

It is a combination of causal action that produces a particular effect (*actus reus*) and a guilty state of mind (*mens rea*) that influences moral and legal judgement about acts. An individual who pulls the trigger of a gun, the bullet of which strikes another person and kills him or her, is a causal factor of the victim's death. This is true irrespective of any moral arguments that can be made about why he or she might not be morally or legally responsible for the death due to it being an accidental shooting or considering his or her diminished mental capacity. The tricky question is to what extent child soldiers exhibit the mental element necessary for moral and legal responsibility. Freedom is necessary for a judgement of moral and/or legal responsibility. It may not be sufficient that the agent had knowledge of the consequences of his or her actions or that he or she even desired the consequences of the actions, that the outcome was 'both desired and foreseen (i.e. "believed")' (Cushman 2008: 357). The agent's capacity to freely make a choice regarding the actions is also relevant. To be morally or legally responsible means that one is accountable, and is in a position to be called upon to answer for his conduct. He both conducted the action and is to blame for it. A part of the latter is the requirement that 'the judgment "He could have done something else" be valid of the action he has performed' (Held 1970: 472). This choice refers both to the physical and the intellectual ability to do something other than the one harmful option.

In cases of tricky moral puzzles such as deciphering the responsibility that might be ascribed to young participants in atrocity, it is the freedom element that is most complex as responsibility can be obliterated or greatly diminished by either coercion or youthfulness. The fact that child soldiers contribute to collective action is both an aggravating and mitigating factor since the additional influence of collective action affects an agent's decision-making process. There is much to affect the average child soldier's ability to make knowledgeable and free decisions, thereby leading to the assumption that there is some validity to the insistence that the non-responsible child narrative should be adopted by communities with whom it does not initially resonate. The following sections examine these factors and show that this assumption belies the fact that despite diminished capacity, child soldiers can have the facility to exercise autonomous rational choice within the circumstances that shape and constrain their decisions and actions, and that the non-responsible child narrative is too simplistic to apply to all agents under the age of 18 and restricts genuine assessment of individual responsibility.

Coercion

Culpability can be reduced on the basis of imposed extraordinary pressure. As Laurence Steinberg and Elizabeth Scott explain, 'criminal law does not require exceptional fortitude or bravery of citizens' (Steinberg and Scott 2003: 1014), and yet both criminal law and morality demand that pressure to commit wrongdoing be resisted and that individuals comply with the rules that guide society. Criminal attribution of blame rests with the ability to conform to the law. While drawing links to the experiences of child soldiers, this section examines what it means for adult perpetrators to be responsible for acts, side-lining the question of the influence of youthfulness for later.

The defence of coercion, or duress, asserts that the agent who committed the criminal act did not do so of his own free will but committed the criminal act only because he was compelled to do so by another through the use of physical force or threat of immediate serious bodily injury or death. Commission of crime under coercion most often does not reflect bad character or a desire to flout the law. Rather, the criminal action is committed by an agent who recognizes the wrongness of the action but is forced into making an exception because of extenuating circumstance that made it unreasonable to comply with the law. Duress is a recognized but tricky defence that can be employed to absolve agents of legal responsibility or mitigate their punishment for actions performed as a result of pressure from violence or threat or other similar compulsions.

> There are several descriptive factors associated with the duress defense, some or all of which must be present, according to various commentators, in order for legally pertinent duress to exist. These are, in no particular order: 1) The coercion must be real and not just imagined or feared; 2) B's threatened unilateral action must itself be illegal; 3) A has no reasonable third option she could choose under the circumstances; 4) It is not possible (as opposed to risky or dangerous) for A to escape B's clutches or to call the police; and 5) B's threat is credible to A, i.e., A has every reason to believe, and no reason not to believe, that B can and will carry out his threat if A does not do X.
>
> (Carr 1991: 167)

Despite the trickiness in using the defence, its moral foundation is strong: action that is unavoidable has a different moral character.

Some would argue that under certain pressure there is a complete absence of *mens rea*, that the pressure represents compulsion and that the individual was simply an instrument that caused the harm but is in no way responsible for it. In this way, duress can be viewed as a defence against criminal charges as an excuse. An excuse is a claim that although the act was committed and was wrong, the perpetrator is not responsible for his or her actions. Insanity is an excuse, and so, as will be seen later in the chapter, is youthfulness under a certain age. Duress as a justification does not represent an absence of *mens rea*. A justification is a claim that the commission of the act was the right thing to do under the specific circumstances it was done despite the general legal prohibition against the act. Self-defence is an example of a justification.

> Excuses differ from justifications precisely in that with them what a person did was wrong (ought not to be have been done) even though he is excused from blame or punishment, whereas if a person has a justification, what he did was not wrong. Excuses defeat blame or punishment of the particular individual but not the wrongness of his conduct.
>
> (Bayles 1982: 6)

When it is found that the criminal act was committed, a defence against criminal liability can perform in one of two ways: it can be argued that the agent did not qualify as a competent agent at the time of the commission of the offence or that the agent exhibited sound moral judgement in disobeying the law in that situation.

> According to the normative critique of action, we have no recourse but to excuse people for some evil they have (in some sense) brought about if they could not help themselves (absence of agency) or if it is not possible to have expected them to know better (absence of informed competency). The second method demonstrates that the act of disobedience is morally, and hence legally, justified. Disobedience to law in the name of a greater moral good demonstrates good judgment, and where good judgment is exercised one can hardly find criminal wrongdoing according to the principles underlying normative critique of action.
>
> (Carr 1991: 165)

There are two issues here: a question of free will and a question regarding sound moral judgement. If there is no possibility of them exercising free will to decide to commit the action in some capacity, then judging agents morally or legally responsible is akin to 'equating causal responsibility with criminal guilt' (Wall 2006: 741). Are child soldiers capable of exercising free will under the extreme threat of violence prevalent in most fighting groups? If we accept that some agents faced with terrible choices do not lose their capacity to exercise free will, despite their lack of positive choices, then the question becomes one of how much can be expected of the average person. In other words: can certain actions committed under duress be justified while others cannot? When faced with extreme illegal pressure, can a decision to commit certain crimes be seen as sound moral judgement, or at least understandable and reasonable, whereas a decision to commit other crimes be seen as morally reprehensible?

It seems unreasonable to argue that there is no free will in situations of coercion, despite the fact that the constraints on actions are very tight, and the options very limited and disagreeable (Baines 2009: 180–181; McMahan 2010). The agent under pressure is still making a choice within the given constraints and acting according to his or her decision. Under the threat of physical harm, there are at least two options, neither of which is (probably) desirable: one is to commit a crime and the other is to not commit the crime and to risk suffering harm to oneself or a loved one as a consequence. There may be others, but these are the two options that the agent is offered directly, and it is reasonable for the agent to believe that these are the only two options available. While it might seem that the choice between these two options is not really a choice at all, it is more reasonable to view the agent as exercising free will under very severe conditions. The agent retains free will, exercises his or her free judgement, and acts according to a decision, despite the fact that neither of the options available to the agent is satisfying and both lead to bad consequences.

Alcinda Honwana refers to the agency exercised by many child soldiers as 'tactical agency', a process of taking action based on decision-making aimed to maximize the agents' circumstances within a constrained environment (Honwana 2009). Tactical agents aim to make the best of poor situations and try to respond to the demands and pressures of their lives in ways that are most beneficial to themselves (Honwana 2002). In such cases, there can be said to be no absolute loss of free will, despite the fact that the agents' actions are constrained and the agents operate with a limited range of choices, most or all of which are more or less negative. Child soldiers are able to act with a certain amount of discretion. My own research in Uganda (Fisher 2013) finds, as Mark Drumbl explains, that

> Even within the most invidious of circumstances, child soldiers deliberately act in ways to avoid harming others, to reduce suffering, and to protect themselves. They resist orders they find objectionable. Generally, child soldiers actualize their resistance through the means available to them, namely, subterfuge, sabotage, transgression, deception, and by discretely altering their assignments. These means are limited, but discharging them still entails choices, prescience, judgment, foresight, and volition.
>
> (Drumbl 2012: 86)

If there is no absolute loss of free will, can actions committed under duress such as those committed by many child soldiers be considered justified (sound moral judgement) and defensible as such?

Duress has a mixed standing in domestic and international criminal law as a defence against charges of violent crime such as murder, mass murder, war crimes, crimes against humanity, and genocide. In domestic common law jurisdictions, the general policy is that duress is not a viable excuse or justification for the commission of murder. Duress as a defence can be employed against charges of most criminal responsibility, but not acts of taking the life of another. In Canada, the UK, and most states in the US, duress is not available as a defence against the commission of murder (or some other serious crimes), although it sometimes may be proven for the purpose of reducing the charge of first-degree murder to manslaughter (Gardner and Anderson 2011: 166). In civil law jurisdictions, however, duress can be argued as a complete defence for murder. The argument grounding the common law position is that there is no morally compelling, and therefore legally legitimate, reason to privilege one's own life over the life of another. As Carr sums up the moral argument in Anglo-American law,

> the dominant legal view of duress is that the plea should be allowed only where the moral evil associated with the threat prong involves a loss of life or limb and where this evil clearly outweighs the moral evil associated with the action prong. Conversely, the plea should not be allowed where the moral evil associated with the action prong is roughly equal to that of the threat prong (i.e., loss of life or limb on both sides of the choice equation).
>
> (Carr 1991: 172)

The defence of duress is applicable in cases where disobedience to the law can be justified because the agent commits a lesser moral wrong, the illegal action, in order to avoid the occurrence of a clearly greater moral wrong. According to Jeff McMahan, it flies in the face of general moral intuition to believe that it is permissible to kill an innocent bystander as a means of self-preservation. 'The innocent bystander – perhaps as a matter of conceptual necessity – has done nothing to make himself liable to be killed as a means of saving someone else's life' (McMahan 2010: 30). In taking this position, common law jurisdictions regard duress as a possible justification for some wrongdoing, assuming that in some circumstances moral judgement dictates the commission of a crime (but not the killing of another human being) to avoid a greater wrong.

This position is also reflected in some international criminal law, including a particularly significant judgement by the ICTY in the case of Dražen Erdemović, in which the first international application of the defence of duress was attempted.[2] Erdemović, an adult participant in the 1995 Srebrenica massacre, claimed that his life had been threatened and it was for this reason that he committed the acts he did. The majority ruling was that the claim did not absolve him of liability, but that it did act as a mitigating factor and affect his punishment. The judgement in this trial was the result of privileging the common law legal tradition. For the ICTY, there was no customary international rule to guide the choice between the conflicting common law and civil law positions and a decision had to be made. This judgement, subsequently debated, ruled that under international criminal law duress could not be a defence for committing atrocity crimes, but that extreme illegal pressure to commit crime(s) might be considered as a mitigating factor and could affect not guilt, but the severity of punishment. Therefore, coercion would not be viewed, at least according to this majority ruling, as either a justification or an excuse for such crimes. Erdemović's killing of innocent men was neither the right thing to do under the circumstances nor excusable given the conditions under which he acted.

The Erdemović judgement and the prohibition against the use of duress as a defence against charges of serious international crimes has been questioned, and it is interesting to note that, on the face of it, the ICC evaluates the admissibility of the defence of duress differently. Article 31 of the Rome Statute claims that

> in addition to other grounds for excluding criminal responsibility provided for in this Statute, a person shall not be criminally responsible if, at the time of that person's conduct: The conduct which is alleged to constitute a crime within the jurisdiction of the Court has been caused by duress resulting from a threat of imminent death or of continuing or imminent serious bodily harm against that person or another person, and the person acts necessarily and reasonably to avoid this threat, provided that the person does not intend to cause a greater harm than the one sought to be avoided.
>
> (Rome Statute 2002: Article 31.1(d))

This strategy seemingly reflects the civil law tradition, maintaining that the choice presented to individuals under duress is no real choice, suggests a revisiting of debates that stops short of the free will argument, and views duress as an excuse for the commission of criminal action. However, at closer inspection, it would seem that the Rome Statute does not advocate a great departure from the Erdemović judgement.

Arguably, there are practical problems to absolving individuals of their responsibility for harm committed under pressure from others. Carr argues that

> To say that the state should not punish in the event a person disobeys the law because threatened by a bigger, or more immediate hammer, greatly reduces the ability of the state to meet the threat posed by

> terrorists or others who would victimize society by using innocent individuals in order to realize their criminal ends.
>
> (Carr 1991: 186)

Carr's argument, although it brings to light a practical problem, does not speak to the moral issue. If, in fact, it is morally wrong to condemn and punish individuals because of actions that they committed under duress, then the fact that such a prohibition would hamper the work of police is not a sufficient argument to undermine the rights of individuals.

The argument that that there is no morally defensible reason to privilege one's own life over that of another in such situations carries more moral weight. The Rome Statute might reflect this principle more than first reading suggests. Duress has yet to be tested as a defence before the ICC, but it would seem to be applicable to almost no case if the Court admits it according to the strict letter of the Article. The conditions on the use of the defence of duress are firm and restrict its availability to limited cases. Article 31.1(d) of the Rome Statute maintains that criminal responsibility is excluded when a person acts necessarily and responsibly to avoid the threat, provided that the person does not intend to cause a greater harm than the one sought to be avoided.

The defence of duress, according to Article 31, can be successful if the act that the agent performs in his attempt to avoid the threat of serious bodily harm is not intended to cause greater harm than the one sought to be avoided. Arguably most, if not any, acts of interest to the ICC specifically, and ICL more generally, cause serious harm that could be judged objectively as great or greater than many possible threats. Therefore, it would seem that the drafters of the Rome Statute again struggled with the contrasting common law and civil law positions and tried for a more middle ground while staying true to the stance that duress can be a defence if it can be proved that the agent acted with sound moral judgement (of the sort that privileges moral objectivism). Likewise, many of the acts that young members of fighting groups that perpetrate mass human rights abuses are ordered to commit can generally be seen as worse than the threat faced by any one of the youths, despite the fact that the threats they face are appalling. Questions about measuring harm might be left to judges of individual cases.

Even when there is freedom to choose, to exercise free will, there is something in the intention to commit the criminal act that distinguishes an act committed under duress. The agent intends the results of the criminal act but the motivation does not stem from malicious intent. It is reasonably a terrible challenge under some conditions to live up to the moral principle that claims one should not privilege one's own life over the life of another; and for this reason, it seems right to do as the ICTY judges did, to view duress as a mitigating factor, not as an excuse or justification but as a factor that affects the severity of the punishment, and consequently the condemnation expressed by the judicial process. But, child soldiers are not adult moral agents. To what degree should children be expected to act according to such strict moral judgement?

Youthfulness

Young persons are regarded as less culpable, or at least in need of different treatment, based on the assumption that they are both vulnerable (and in need of extra protection) and less-than-fully-developed moral agents. Youthfulness can either affect the existence of responsibility or it can affect the manner in which the perpetrator is treated by the system of law. The minimum age of criminal responsibility refers to a threshold below which a child should not be considered in breach of criminal law. As discussed in the previous chapter, for an agent below the minimum age of criminal responsibility, a lack of *mens rea* is presumed as the agent can be considered not to have the mental capacity to be responsible for the otherwise-criminal actions that he or she commits; he or she is presumed not to understand sufficiently the nature of the crime (Happold 2006: 71; McDiarmid 2006: 86). Between the minimum age of criminal responsibility and the age of majority (at which age the agent is an adult under the law) agents are generally subject to a special penal system for juveniles.

Similar to the disconnect between the international non-responsible child narrative and reasoned conceptions of agency and responsibility is a disconnect between the status of children under international criminal law and under domestic jurisdictions. Under most domestic jurisdictions, children (at least those above a specified minimum age) answer for their commission of the same harmful acts as would an adult, although usually according to the conditions of a juvenile justice system. Youthfulness can influence procedure and outcome, but does not attest to absence of agency or absolve completely responsibility for harmful acts. Like the significant pressure to commit harmful acts that child soldiers face, so should their youthfulness act as a consideration and not an absolute rejection of responsibility. As Drumbl argues,

> Many adults are compulsorily conscripted, as well, yet this does not *ab initio* absolve them from the consequences of their conduct. Many

> adult soldiers are little older than eighteen and live strikingly similar situations to child soldiers. They are thus contemporaries. Can so much differentiation realistically hinge upon a simple matter of chronological age?
>
> (Drumbl 2012: 23)

In America, by 1899 it was recognized that the criminal justice system for adults was not suited for young offenders and a special system was created to address the wrongdoing of young perpetrators (Ludwig 1949). And even though it is argued by some that there seems recently to be a regression in the special treatment afforded young perpetrators in some Western domestic contexts such as the US (Ghetti and Redlich 2001: 34), there is still a general presumption that the culpability of young offenders is different from that of adults and that their age warrants special treatment under criminal legal systems. The two grounds for responsibility reduction – vulnerability and less developed moral agency – are both distinct and interconnected.

Young persons are vulnerable both physically and psychologically. They are more at the peril of adults who may wish to harm them or control them. They are seen as needing protection from dangers in their environment and from the consequences of any poor decisions they might make in their preliminary interactions in the world. Childhood, as envisioned especially from the Western perspective, is a period in which a person is supposed to grow nurtured and safe (Angucia 2009: 79; CRC: Articles 4–6). Generally, it is seen as a period of play and innocent experimentation. Fewer years on this earth represent fewer years to learn how to navigate one's environment and to develop into a full moral agent who can determine right from wrong. Steinberg and Scott argue that 'criminal law implicitly assumes that harmful conduct reflects the actor's bad character and treats evidence that this assumption is inaccurate as mitigating of culpability. For most adolescents, the assumption *is* inaccurate, and thus their crimes are less culpable than those of typical criminals' (Steinberg and Scott 2003: 1014 emphasis original). Arguably, wrongdoing in non-atrocity contexts is often not as much the result of a young offender's strictly malevolent intent as it is a result of pushing boundaries in experimentation, less appreciation for the consequences of actions, and less impulse control – all factors of young brains (Steinberg 2007: 56; Casey et al. 2008).

Young people, particularly adolescents, are presumed to be more sensitive to peer influence, more impressionable and more easily manipulated, to have a tendency to focus more on immediate rather than long-term consequences, and also to be less risk averse and therefore more liable to make risky choices than are adults (Scott et al. 1995: 222; Galvan et al. 2007; Kimmel and Roby 2007: 745; Steinberg 2007). Children and youths who may not grasp the long-term consequences or the potentially serious ramifications of their harmful conduct, therefore, warrant different treatment. Arguably, one of the reasons that children are attractive to atrocity architects is that they are perceived as more fearless and less concerned with long-term consequences of actions.

Despite these assumptions about young perpetrators being more vulnerable, less morally developed, impulsive, and possessing temporal perspectives and risk assessment approaches distinct to their age group, there is a growing sphere of contradictory common intuitions that claim that age does not dissolve responsibility (morally or legally) or automatically warrant less harsh punishment for wrongdoing, especially in cases of violent crimes. In practical terms, saying nothing about the rightfulness or wrongfulness of these conditions, this means that some criminal justice systems try young perpetrators as adults; in the US there was an increase of transference of juvenile offenders to the adult court system (Pagnanelli 2007). In countries such as Australia, England, Switzerland, and the US, the minimum age of criminal responsibility is ten (and as young as seven in the state of Florida). In Canada, Israel, Japan, the Netherlands, and Scotland, the minimum age is 12. In the US and England, depending on the severity of the crime, a young person can be prosecuted under the adult criminal justice system, as was the case for the two young offenders in the UK who in 1993 murdered two-year-old Jamie Bulger when they were each ten years old,[3] and as was almost the case for American Jordan Brown who killed his father's fiancée when he was 11 in 2009. Brown was initially charged as an adult, as is required in homicide cases in Pennsylvania, regardless of the defendant's age, and lengthy deliberation preceded the decision to try him as a juvenile (Fitzgerald 2009).

The fact that most countries have some form of juvenile justice system through which offences committed by persons under the age of 18 are addressed rests on the primary presumption that young perpetrators of wrongdoing ought to be treated in a manner consistent with diminished culpability for their wrongdoing based solely on their age. This presumption may be overridden by factors such as the severity of the crime or the attitude of the young person, but it exists as a base feature of most criminal justice systems that can be reversed under exceptional circumstances. Only the ICC, however, regards all persons under the age of 18 as outside of its jurisdiction of criminal culpability, as was discussed in the previous chapter. Although it has been argued that 'international crimes have such onerous *mens rea* requirements that children will always lack capacity to commit them' (Happold 2006: 71), the limiting of the ICC to adult offenders is not based on any comprehensive understanding of responsibility for the types of actions that are atrocity crimes, but is rather based on political debate and lack of consensus regarding the minimum age of criminal liability discussed in Chapter 2. As Cécile Aptel reasons, 'this exclusion of children from the jurisdiction of international courts does not mean that the age of criminal responsibility is fixed at eighteen; rather it means that children fall outside the scope of the limited personal jurisdiction of the ICC' (Aptel 2010: 105).

While there is considerable inconsistency regarding the legal status of, and response to, young causal perpetrators of wrongdoing, there is little evidence to suggest that typical agents under the age of 18 cannot comprehend their actions or the results of them (Gruber and Yurgelun-Todd 2005; Maroney 2010). In jurisdictions that have juvenile justice systems, such as Canada and the US, the same criminal code applies to young perpetrators and adults. The same acts are prohibited and the same charges can be laid for the commission of the same actions that are in violation of the law. The difference is that persons under the age of 18, but over the minimum age of legal culpability, face different procedures that aim to better protect the young offender from the harshness of the adult criminal justice system. There is also often an aim to focus on rehabilitation and restitution (Pagnanelli 2007; Department of Justice, Canada n.d.). As the Child Rights International Network claims,

> Children are responsible for many actions defined by criminal law as crimes – in so far as they did it. And many are also responsible in the sense that they did know what they were doing was wrong, in one way or another, when they did it. It does not serve our purpose as advocates of children's human rights to deny their immediate responsibility, to belittle their evolving capacities.
>
> (Child Rights International Network 2012)[4]

Despite the image that the general media convey, many child soldiers are not young prepubescent children (Wessells 2006: 7; Schmidt 2007: 54; Drumbl 2012: 50). There are, as documented by the media, very young children in fighting groups that use child soldiers; some are born and grow up in fighting forces and some very young children are admitted or are forcefully recruited. Most child soldiers who commit violent acts are adolescents. And, because conclusions regarding an absolute absence of *mens rea* can be drawn about persons under the age of ten or 12 does not mean that the same conclusions apply to minors who are 16 or 17 years old (Lansdown 2005). Accountability for an offence committed by a person under the age of 18 should not automatically be rejected because of age, at least for a certain range of ages under 18. Within the evaluation of responsibility should be appreciation and reflection of the developing capacities of children, an ascending range of levels of culpability. Many child soldiers are moral agents not very dissimilar from young adults over the age of 18. Responsibility should be determined according to the particular circumstances of individual cases.

Collective action

Collective action is a relevant consideration in evaluating the actions and responsibility of most actors in atrocity contexts, but it is a particularly significant factor when the agents of atrocity are youths who are arguably particularly susceptible to the influence of belonging. Youth susceptibility to collective interpretations of norms and appropriate behaviour is important to the judgement of responsibility, and it is also important that an understanding of responsibility acknowledges and addresses the influence of collective action and the social norms that were prevalent in the fighting group.

The contexts in which child soldiers operate, like so many other atrocity contexts, require the involvement of many people, some with intent, many in fear themselves, caught up in a movement of violence, anxiety, and hatred. The actions of individuals play a significant role in the ability of the collective to meet its violent goals, but the general state of the collective also has a considerable effect on the frame of mind and actions of individuals. This is true whether the individual is a child or a mature adult. This effect of the collective on the individual is not coercion, but it is greatly influential in contexts where the community is wrapped up in its own unique codes of behaviour.

There is the psychological and cultural pressure to conform to the environment of atrocity. This pressure causes persons to act as they likely would not absent the particular environment. Atrocity environments, such as Rwanda in 1994 and Sierra Leone in the 1990s, are chaotic and confusing, and many peace-time norms and values are discarded (Aptel 2010: 98). Agents shaped by the atrocity environment and who act in accordance with it act in ways very different than they do in an environment void of pressure and examples of criminal action. Many discussions of the contexts in which child soldiers operate reveal the very real way in which the rules of social behaviour are unique in these contexts and the environments erode moral codes and exert pressure on agents to conform even in the absence of direct coercion (McKay 2005; Denov and Maclure 2007; Denov 2010: 102–108). Members of fighting groups are typically isolated from civilian life, family, friends, and community members (Human Rights Watch 2003: 48–50; Denov 2010: 104–105). Since membership and good-standing in a group satisfy important emotional needs, the pressure to conform to the social norms of the immediate environment is both visceral and practical.

The collective nature of the atrocity is a feature which encourages, supports, and enhances the harm committed. In Rwanda in the summer of 1994, for example, the radio broadcasts promoted atrocity, the streets were dangerous and exhibited fear and hatred and death, and not acting according to the new rules of behaviour could put persons of the non-targeted Hutu group also at risk. Persons living in, and trying to survive and make sense of, this environment responded to the actions of others around them. Under such conditions, the majority of individuals involved in the atrocity crimes are not so much acting defiantly as they are conforming to their new social environment. Nazi Germany is another great example of collective atrocity that influenced members of the community: 'none of them [German murderers] were likely to commit murder of their own free will' (Arendt 1994: 16). Circumstances in which individuals find themselves evoke in them actions that they would be unlikely to commit removed from that particular environment (Goldhagen 1996). The collective nature of wrongful acts, and its influence, is a significant element of which consideration should be taken in determining ultimate responsibility.

Harmful action committed in contribution to collective wrongdoing, especially mass atrocity, is of a different nature than aberrant criminal activity, though the act may be the same. Because the average actor contributing to atrocity is acting in accordance with the new social norms, his or her actions and motivations are not deviant in the same way. Mass atrocity requires the involvement of people who play a role in establishing the atrocity environment and others who are shaped by it. Being members of a collective arouses ideas, intentions, and actions in individuals who would not otherwise possess or act on them. By far the majority of contributors to atrocity fall into the category of agents shaped by the environment.

Arguably, collective action, despite its influence in shaping behaviour, also creates weightier individual responsibility: contributing to collective action amplifies individual responsibility for specific wrongs committed (Isaacs 2006). Tracy Isaacs argues that focusing too narrowly on individuals risks missing out on the greater harm to which the individual's actions contribute. In line with Isaacs' position, current international criminal law, in that it can charge contributing lesser perpetrators with crimes against humanity or genocide, does indeed reflect the fact that actions contribute to greater harm. There is something to be said for not overlooking how individual acts fit into the broader context of atrocity.

Isaacs rightly argues that 'we fail to capture the extent and nature of the wrong if we do not consider the individual act in the context of the acts of others' (Isaacs 2006: 172). Isaacs' statement is right for her own reason, and also for one completely different from the reason on which she relies. She claims that an act is more morally wrong when it is performed in a larger context of similarly bad behaviour, the consequence of which is worse than simply that one bad act. Her example is running an air conditioner or driving a car. Taken alone these acts are not morally wrong but, combined with similar acts by many others, they contribute to dangerous air conditions and are therefore morally wrong.[5] On the other hand, she seems to ignore the social permission to perform bad acts or the psychological pressure to conform. Acting within this environment and according to social norms results from a different character than the 'bad character' that criminal law is arguably meant to address (Chinapen and Vernon 2006; Sloane 2007; Golash 2010). It is sadly quite possible for the 'reasonable' common person to be led under extreme circumstances to commit terrible acts, including acts of murder or torture according to authoritative directives, state policy, or similar influences. There are, of course, many examples of, and commentaries on, this phenomenon (for examples, see: Milgram 1963; Osiel 2005). For child soldiers as well, brutality can become unexceptional and decisions to commit violence uncomplicated.

Certainly, isolated action inspired and exercised against a relatively peaceful and ordered backdrop, in an environment void of pressure and examples of criminal behaviour, is extremely different from action performed in, and contributing to, an atrocity atmosphere. Understanding acts requires a certain amount of sensitivity to the environment in which they are committed, the background against which the act or inspiration originated. As much as recognizing relative peace and order as the backdrop to many domestic crimes (of murder, theft, assault, etc.)

reveals a particular anti-social nature to the criminal behaviour, recognizing the markedly different environment which functions as the backdrop to atrocity exposes the distinct characters of the acts and actors performing in the atrocity environment. Therefore, taking seriously the context in which individual actions are performed demands the recognition that collective action contributes as a defining element of the perpetrators' intentionality; atrocity contexts should relieve some perpetrators of some responsibility based on the fact that external pressure would likely diminish free and genuine specific intent.[6]

Contribution to collective action is one of the conditions that colours much of the violent wrongdoing that child soldiers commit. 'Perpetrating violence and torture become normal and routine within a culture of violence that pervades every aspect of daily routines and activities' (McKay 2005: 388). And so, without even making any judgements regarding other factors that might lessen individual responsibility, the atrocity context which influences behaviour by changing what it means to accord to one's community's rules and to act as a contributing member of the community might be seen as a reason to claim diminished or lack of responsibility.

And yet, neither the social permission to perform these bad acts nor the psychological pressure to conform is sufficient to excuse or justify serious harms such as those committed in widespread atrocity, even if it might diminish personal culpability. The unique environment in which atrocity crimes are committed demands a recognition of the difference in intention of the average contributor from that of a domestic criminal committing similar crimes and that we judge the acts accordingly, but it does not require that we reject the attribution of responsibility for wrongdoing and the harm particular actions caused. The actions of these agents acting under these conditions may not emanate from the same malevolent intent, but the actions were, in fact, committed knowingly and freely. Collective action might affect the way agents judge certain acts, as agents might assume that if others around them have deemed the activities right then the actions are likely so, or the mere fact of being engulfed by collective action might exert social pressure to conform. However, the pressure is not enough to excuse poor judgement and there is no legal or moral excuse for not exercising one's own judgement, or acting upon it when possible actions seem to contradict one's own judgement of what is right. This is true even for children who can distinguish right from wrong, although collective action might have more significant influence on the very young.

The crimes of contributors to mass atrocity are both worse than ordinary domestic cases of similar wrongdoing because they play a role in the larger scheme and therefore their consequences are more severe, and also less depraved than these domestic cases because they fit the dictates of the current social context in which the individuals find themselves and therefore emanate from different motivations and intentions. Therefore, it is perilous to try to consider the actions of a child soldier as one would judge the actions of another agent of the same age who commits the same acts under conditions of peace. When judging the actions of contributors to mass atrocity, the environment and its influence on individuals ought to be considered as a mitigating factor for individuals affected by the new social norms of the group of which they are members. In assessing the actions of child soldiers, the influence of collective action should receive special consideration. As mentioned above, young people, particularly adolescents, are typically more sensitive to peer influence, more impressionable, and more easily manipulated. Collective action, therefore, while not an excuse for criminal behaviour, should be acknowledged and addressed as a significant factor influencing individual responsibility for atrocity and play a prominent role in procedures of transitional justice.

Conclusion

The tension between the international non-responsible child narrative and the general resentment and conceptions of responsibility and agency held by community members demands this parcelling out and evaluation of the features of responsibility as they pertain to child soldiering. Debates about the responsibility of child soldiers are shaped by questions about whether the power dynamics and conditions under which they committed acts of atrocity make their actions justifiable, whether persons under the age of 18 can understand the acts they commit and the consequences of them, and whether the environment in which they acted obliterated their ability to distinguish right from wrong. Not one of the three factors considered in this chapter – coercion, youthfulness, collective action – should automatically eliminate criminal and moral culpability for grave wrongdoing such as contribution to mass atrocity without an investigation regarding how these factors affected individual agents.

Combined, however, these factors may play an even greater role in the attribution, or lack of attribution, of responsibility. Add youthfulness to social pressure, and it might seem sound to argue that no reasonable young person could see an alternative but to act according to the dictates of the group. If it is true that adolescents are 'less independent in their decision making than adults, and... [are] subject to the influence of both parents and peers' (Scott et al. 1995: 229), then the atrocity environment will have a great influence on the behaviour of young potential perpetrators. We may, therefore, want to claim that their diminished power to judge independently and resist pressure to conform eliminates any criminal or moral responsibility these agents might have. Also, combine youthfulness with duress, and the resulting moral judgement may differ from judgements made about options by adults under duress. 'Because adolescents are less likely than adults to think through the future consequences of their actions, the same level of duress may have a more disruptive impact on juveniles' decision making than on that of adults' (Steinberg and Scott 2003: 1014). Therefore, there must be a clear distinction between children and adults and children used by adults and children who commit crimes of their own determination absent any external influence. Comparisons between juvenile offenders in peaceful countries such as Canada or the US and child soldiers such as those in northern Uganda are useful only to a point, and can be dangerous if the comparisons suggest greater similarity than exists and exclude the aspects of coercion and collective action that greatly affect the responsibility of most participants in mass atrocity.

The claim that young persons generally perceive temporal relations differently, and are more likely to engage in risky behaviour partly for this reason, might suggest that youths faced with very difficult decisions concerning the right actions to pursue in a conflict context might be commonly more likely than adults to pursue actions that have more positive or immediately safer results. Even for adults, the environment that fosters such criminal behaviour is one in which fear for one's own life is a major contributing factor in many of the potential perpetrators' choices to offend or not. Under such conditions, long-term effects or consequences of their actions are unlikely to be forefront in the decision-makers' minds. Since young persons may have a more limited temporal perspective, their thoughts may be even more focused on immediate conditions. On the other hand, the same claim might suggest that youths might take more risks to their own personal safety, possibly in attempts to do the right thing. Sonja Grover argues,

> There is no empirical evidence that the commission of atrocity during hostilities is a function of age of the belligerent; or more specifically,

> that younger children are more likely to commit atrocity than older; or that children are more likely to commit atrocity than are adults under the same circumstances. Indeed, across the centuries most mass atrocity has been committed not by children but by adults whose inhibitory neurological functions are presumed generally to be fully developed.
>
> (Grover 2012: 2)

Youthfulness has an impact on decision-making, but persons under the age of 18 possess moral agency and can act with decision.

Part of what fuels this discussion is the issue regarding what exactly is being judged and condemned in a process of accountability. It is important that judgements do not equate simple causal responsibility with moral or legal responsibility. It is not simply that the harm was a consequence of actions performed by the agents being judged, but that these agents chose these actions and intended the results. Each action must be judged against what another normal person, or 'the reasonable' man or woman, would do and would consider to be the right action. When analysing action, even if the action being judged is not the best possible, most morally correct, or heroic action available to the agent, the question must be whether the action can be judged to be acceptable and reasonable, or whether it should be judged to be morally wrong, despite the poor options available.

It is demonstrated again and again with the first-hand accounts of young persons who participated in atrocity that they knew what they were doing was wrong and in contradiction to local morality, if not also the local laws. Most often report revulsion and regret and shame. And yet, faced with the situation and the external pressure to conform and obey orders, to save their own lives or to progress in the ranks and to secure for themselves certain privileges and comforts, they choose from their limited options. And so, we might say that many of these young perpetrators of serious human rights violations can be seen to be morally responsible for their actions to an extent. Their

> discrete categorization as 'victim' or 'perpetrator' fails to underscore the complexities of shifting roles and experiences such as the seeming paradox of [children] becoming allies with individuals who were responsible for abducting and victimizing them and who continue to... Or, a [child] who has never felt herself to be efficacious might experience the lure that can occur from the power of carrying a gun.
>
> (McKay 2005: 391)

Child soldiers who commit acts of atrocity defy simple characterization as pure victim or pure perpetrator. Many committed crimes for which no moral justification or excuse seems sufficient to obliterate all responsibility, but they fall far from the level of responsibility that would warrant the most serious condemnation of their actions.

Most youths who contribute to serious human rights violation of this type, under these conditions, retain their moral agency. Despite their difficult situation, and the choices that face them, they remain agents who can think and judge and make decisions. They are not mentally defective; they do not lose free will; they do not lack the moral resources to resist the command to fight and slaughter. 'Even if they are cognitively and emotionally immature, and even if they have been brutalized and brainwashed, they are still, it might be argued, sufficiently morally responsible to be able to recognize that indiscriminate killing is wrong' (McMahan 2010: 33). They are not fully excusable because the agent lacked the necessary *mens rea*. And, the decisions that they make to kill and maim and to help perpetuate the atrocity are not always justified as decisions that are morally right under the circumstances.

For the most part, many of these agents occupy a unique position along the responsibility continuum that leaves them not without any moral responsibility for their choices and actions and not fully responsibility for the harm they cause. Each case and each agent is different and each must be considered independently with consideration for age, coercion, and environment. What seems most reasonable is to view child soldiers, as a general category, 'as people who have a diminished capacity for morally responsible agency and who act in conditions that further diminish their personal responsibility for their action in war' (McMahan 2010: 34). There is a sense in which many of these young perpetrators are, in fact, agents who can, although from a position of great weakness, make decisions, evaluate actions and their effects, and choose from a limited number of very difficult options – acting, as Honwana identifies, with tactical agency. Challenges arise when responsibility is interpreted to mean nothing but full responsibility or criminal culpability. This chapter has argued that the category of young perpetrators of atrocity is a unique category of perpetrator, both victim and perpetrator, but not simply fully victim or innocent. The guilty mind element necessary for determining legal and moral responsibility is greatly compromised by conditions and context. The actions of child soldiers, therefore, do not all invite great condemnation; nor do all demand reprieve for their actions.

This chapter has demonstrated that the non-responsible child narrative is a fiction that should not be applied to all agents of atrocity under the age of 18, opening the way for different options to explore the individual responsibility of agents. With child soldier responsibility understood in this way, strides can be made to effectively address the span of responsibility that might be attributable to individual child soldiers in such a way as to reflect the unique factors that affect their responsibility. Particularly, youthfulness and collective action cannot be excuses for illegal actions by all under the age of 18, but both factors should affect how suspected responsible agents should be addressed by policies of post-conflict transitional justice. Additionally and importantly, processes of transitional justice, especially those applied to contexts in which the future society includes former child soldiers who must deal with and move beyond a systemically violent past, should acknowledge, address, and educate about the dangerous influence of collective harmful action, both in order to effectively deal with the past and to promote awareness and caution that can thwart the recurrence of similar mass violence.

4 The Expressive Value of Post-Atrocity Accountability

The claim that justice demands judgement and punishment is a bold statement that does not always hold true. However, even when punishment can be defended as a justified moral response to wrongdoing, the unique role of victim-perpetrator that child soldiers occupy challenges the architects of transitional justice initiatives to devise exceptional means of addressing the harm brought about by most of the child soldiers who are causal agents. Faced with possible prosecutions of child soldiers according to means regularly reserved for adult moral agents (such as the many imprisoned children in Rwanda in the aftermath of the genocide or Uganda's charges of treason against formerly abducted child soldiers[1]), we need to question the goals of retributive justice, and ask what the objectives really demand of transitional justice. In the same vein, blanket amnesties, of the sort that were until recently offered in Uganda to anyone who 'renounces and abandons involvement in the war or armed rebellion' (Amnesty Act 2000: II.4.1(b)),[2] and of the sort granted under the non-responsible child policy, produce reservations in the minds of those who regard some form of accountability for wrongs committed as practically important and morally significant.[3]

Two arguments can be made for accountability. One is that pursuing accountability is the right and just response to wrongs committed. The other is that some form of dealing with the past, accounting for actions, and attributing to individuals appropriate responsibility for wrongdoing is important to the project of social reconstruction. This second argument claims that some measure that directly addresses past harms and considers the contribution of individuals to the atrocity that affected the community is generally perceived as necessary by members of the community who must rebuild in the aftermath. Absent such measures, the transition is hampered by distrust of the community's social institutions and of individual neighbours. There is also a persistent feeling that justice has not been met and that there is unfinished business that hangs over the reconstruction process and over individual lives. This second argument is the focus of Chapter 5 of this book.

This chapter explores the connection between accountability and justice. It questions what it is, beside the natural human inclination to desire that others be identified and punished for their involvement in harms caused, that justifies the use of accountability measures in the post-conflict context. This chapter argues that the same justification that can be used to validate the use of retributive justice mechanisms in post-conflict contexts can also be used to justify a variety of accountability mechanisms, including those appropriate to address the potential individual responsibility of most former child soldiers. It also argues that the theoretical dichotomy between restorative and retributive justice is misplaced and unconstructive.

This chapter first explores possible justifications of post-conflict accountability by examining theories of punishment used to justify retributive justice at the domestic level and assess how the same theories might be applied to the context of mass atrocity and extraordinary international crimes.[4] It advances a retributive-expressive theory to justify international criminal law. It then argues that the same retributive-expressive theory should inform broader transitional justice decision-making and should provide a moral justification for any post-atrocity mechanism of accountability. This chapter provides a normative foundation for the use of post-atrocity instruments of justice in the satisfaction of a particular conceptual goal: the communication and reaffirmation of the community's values and its commitment to them.

It is important to note the dual use of the concept 'retributive' in this discussion. The term 'retribution' can be employed broadly to refer to the whole practice of punishment for wrongs committed, or more specifically as one of a number of justifying theories to explain why punishment ought rightly be imposed on those who commit wrongs. In this chapter, both uses of the word are employed. The distinction between the two understandings of the word will be kept clear by employing the term 'retributive justice' to refer to the broader concept, and the terms 'retribution' or 'retributive theory' to refer to the specific justifying theory.

The broader use, retributive justice, refers to criminal law; it refers to the act of judging and punishing wrongdoers. Our penal systems are based on this conception of justice. Retributive justice can be contrasted with 'restorative justice', which is 'touted as an effective and popular alternative to mainstream justice' (Rossner 2011: 95), a classification of approaches to addressing harm in which the primary focus is not judgement and punishment, approaches that are less adversarial, including mediation and truth and reconciliation commissions.

Since retributive justice, the process of judging and punishing, is the conventional approach to wrongdoing, at least in Western societies, there has been much philosophical debate about the justification of the use of punishment to address wrongdoing. Within this debate, some argue that deterrence is the reason that we punish (Bentham 1962), some include a justification of incapacitation so that wrongdoers are not capable of reoffending, and some argue that it is a moral imperative to punish wrongdoers simply because they deserve it (Kant 1996: 6:331). This justifying theory of desert and paying back the offender for his or her wrongdoing is labelled 'the retributive theory'. The first section of this chapter, *justifying retributive justice*, examines and assesses theories of punishment, including the retributive theory, to justify the use of the broader conception of retributive justice.

Justifying retributive justice

The field of post-conflict transitional justice has by and large uncritically attempted to transpose Western penal practices to international (or internationalized) institutions to address acts of mass atrocity. The current state of justice for mass atrocity, despite those exceptions such as aspects of the Truth and Reconciliation Commission (TRC) in South Africa, embraces holding individuals criminally liable for their actions. And although there is, of course, attention paid to professed restorative measures to foster social healing and return to normalcy and to record events for educational purposes, for the most part, the grand event is a series of court trials by which guilt is established through prosecution, followed by punishment in the form of incarceration. As Robert Sloane points out, 'For better or worse, states have made a decision to devote considerable resources – intellectual, economic, diplomatic, and otherwise – to establishing an international criminal justice system for war crimes and human rights atrocities' (Sloane 2007: 47).

Debates concerning theories of punishment in the context of mass atrocity are still in their infancy (Tallgren 2002; Drumbl 2007; Sloane 2007; Fisher 2012). As discussed in Chapter 3's section on collective action, the nature of wrongdoing is generally different in the context of domestic criminal behaviour and contribution to atrocity, and therefore, it is unreasonable to simply assume that the rationale behind punishing domestic offenders is identical to that which justifies punishment for perpetrators of exceptional crimes.

In some ways, it is right to claim that ICL deals with actions that are unique in spirit; they are not only crimes that the state is unable or unwilling to prosecute, but crimes that illustrate a specific kind of evil (Vernon 2002: 234). The drafters of the Rome Statute captured this view when they wrote that there are 'unimaginable atrocities that deeply shock the conscience of humanity' (Rome Statute: Preamble). Atrocity crimes are crimes that contribute to a wider policy or plan of atrocity and are committed in unique environments that foster and promote particular criminal behaviour. As discussed in the preceding chapter, the average perpetrator in the atrocity context is not asserting his own privilege within his community in the same manner as he would be if he were to commit a similar act under the normal conditions of a lawfully well-ordered society; rather he is acting according to the new standards of his environment (Chinapen and Vernon 2006; Drumbl 2007: 24; Sloane 2007: 41–42, 58–65).

Individual action motivated and exercised in an environment void of the pressures and examples of violent and criminal behaviour is very different from action performed in an atrocity environment. Remember the example, offered in Chapter 3, of Rwanda during the summer of 1994 as an illustration of the type of environment that can be viewed as an atrocity environment. Because of the unique nature of the atrocity context, the acts of judging and punishing perpetrators invite and demand their own justification. In fact, prominent theories that are used and debated in relation to the punishment of agents of 'ordinary' crime are seemingly ill equipped to justify accountability in post-conflict contexts. Theories that justify punishment on the consequentialist bases of deterrence, rehabilitation/reformation, or incapacitation are of very little value in justifying the use of punishment for contribution to atrocity. The deontological basis for punishment expressed as the retributive theory is incomplete in its justification.

Inadequate justifications

Deterrence, either specific or general,[5] is an implausible objective of transitional justice accountability because in almost all variations of the elements – perpetrator, punishment, and intended influenced possible-perpetrator – punishment is unlikely to produce a deterrent effect. Selective prosecution and the sheer numbers of perpetrators may render the possibility of judgement and punishment insufficient as deterrence for minor perpetrator offenders (Drumbl 2007: 169–170;

Mennecke 2007). Child soldiers, except perhaps for an exceptional few, can be the perpetrators who bear the slightest responsibility or are seen to bear the slightest and, therefore, when there are multitudes of perpetrators to address, child soldiers may be the least likely to attract attention. And when the environment which fosters these crimes is one in which fear for one's own life is also a contributing factor in the potential perpetrator's choice to offend or not, as is the case for most child soldiers, the deterrent effect of the possibility of punishment in the aftermath of the violence is likely negligible. For atrocity leaders, including those who illegally recruit child soldiers, it seems probable that the rewards for their criminal endeavours occupy their minds more than the consequences of failure (Pal 1953; Klabbers 2001; Golash 2010).

Similarly, rehabilitation or reformation is not a reasonable aim for punishment for most lesser perpetrators in the context of atrocity. For them, programmes of rehabilitation may be necessary as a means for them to heal from physical or psychological harms they incurred from their experiences, but punishment is not required as a means of repairing a problematically anti-social personality in the same way it is often professed to be needed for criminals acting against the norms of society. Crimes committed against a just and ordered backdrop are generally committed by those who have 'rejected the standards of the larger culture' (Golash 2010: 211), but harm perpetrated in an atrocity context stems from dissimilar motivations, intentions, and attitudes towards society (Waller 2007: 187). Many child soldiers especially can be seen to fall into the category of perpetrators who act in self-defence of their own person and/or are indoctrinated into believing they fight for the side of right. These individuals are not committing crimes against the backdrop of an ordered society against which they are illegitimately asserting their own privilege and therefore, there is not the same anti-social element which punishment, when it is viewed as reformatory, seeks to cure.

Incarceration for the purpose of incapacitation, obstructing the physical capability of perpetrators from committing their crimes again, is similarly impractical and unnecessary as prevention in this context. For those who thought they were doing good for their society or were acting according to the dictates of the environment, a change in surrounding order and attitude will likely dissuade them or prevent them from pursuing malevolent activity. The general stance of the new environment will likely act as dissuasion for those actors predisposed or inclined to commit such crimes, as did the ordered social environment preceding the atrocity. For child soldiers who exhibit aggression and threaten violence, psychological treatment would be better suited to training the children in appropriate means of channelling feelings. Especially for young perpetrators who have their lives before them, incarceration for incapacitation's sake can be nothing but a short-term bandage for a concern that must also be addressed by other means.

And so, the unique environment of mass atrocity and the environment that arises post-atrocity leave little room for the justification of the employment of punishment on consequentialist bases. Punishment, though, can also be justified based on a concept of fair and judicious retribution, following the Kantian deontological school of punishment, in which legal punishment is justified on the sole basis that it is deserved. It is a backward-looking justification, the objective of which is repayment. Retributive punishment

> must embody the idea of something being paid back to the offender (or by the offender, or both) – something akin to what the crime did to the victim(s). The concept of a retributive punishment, therefore, is the concept of a punitive harm, suffering or deprivation, because it is a harm, suffering or deprivation that the acts typically defined as crimes inflict on their victims.
>
> (Bedau 1978: 604)

On this account, it has been argued that punishment is a moral obligation on the part of the ordered community because 'if the law is to remain just, it is important to guarantee that those who disobey it will not gain an unfair advantage over those who do obey it voluntarily' (Murphy 1986: 634). Punishments are '*themselves* consequences of the acts for which they are administered' (Suzman and Cottingham 1987: 27 emphasis original). 'Retribution motivates punishment out of fairness to those who have been wronged and reflects a belief that wrongdoers deserve blame and punishment in direct proportion to the harm inflicted. Otherwise, wrongdoers not only inflict pain but also degrade and diminish victims without a corrective response' (Minow 1998: 12). 'Fit' is a necessary feature of retribution. Retributivism refers to

> any theory of punishment claiming at least (a) that the only acceptable reason for punishing a person is that he has committed a crime, (b) that the only acceptable reason for punishing him with such-and-such severity is that the punishment fits the crime, and (c) that the fit between punishment and crime is independent of the actual or

> probable consequences of the particular punishment or the particular statutory penalty.
>
> (Davis 1983: 737)

The important elements, then, are that punishment is deserved and that the punishment fits the crime.

However, for perpetrators of atrocity crimes, especially those who planned atrocity schemes and motivated and led others to massacre but also for those who contributed as followers and also for those who are victim-perpetrators like child soldiers, achieving proportionality may seem implausible. Drumbl claims that,

> If the retributive value of punishing extraordinary international criminals truly were to be engaged, perhaps punishment would have to exceed anything ordinary. Truly proportionate sentences then might involve torture or reciprocal group eliminationism. That is a terrifying path. In such a scenario, survivors would become as depraved as their tormentors.
>
> (Drumbl 2007: 157)

Of course, a similar argument can be made for retributive justification of punishment for major crimes in the domestic context as well. What is a fair and proportional punishment for rape or murder, or multiple murders? And yet, despite the fact that there are constraints that decent societies impose on themselves, retribution has been employed to justify the punishment of violent domestic criminals. Attempting to 'repay' the perpetrator the harm he caused his victim or society must be done within certain parameters. Within these parameters, suitable punishments are sought. The fit clearly refers, then, to proportionality. More severe penalties are demanded for more serious infractions. Punishment can be distributed on a sliding scale, recognizing that the harm inflicted by the punishing institution will not equal the harm caused by the crime but is deserved as some form of payback. This position, though, raises an important question: why is it just to pay back the harm, especially if there is no other good that will come from it? Retributivists claim that it is the fact simply that it is deserved that justifies punishment, and also that it establishes and confirms a field of fair play (upholding fairness requires making the offender 'pay' for the unfair advantage he or she obtained) (Cottingham 1979: 242–243). For many, while punishing based on desert conforms to common intuitions, this basic justification seems to be lacking a greater telos or goal. As Jan Klabbers points out,

> the one problem with this [basing international criminal law solely on retributive punishment] is that punishment for the sake of punishment rests uncomfortably with our liberal sentiments: we tend to think that punishment must serve a goal higher than punishment itself, and the fact that we have ruled out the possibility of the ultimate form of punishment (i.e. capital punishment) is perhaps an indication that we need to think of something to help us justify punishment.
>
> (Klabbers 2001: 265)

It seems right, then, to see the retributive theory as making sense to a point. It may not necessarily demand (without further rationale) that punishment be inflicted, but it can reveal under which conditions inflicting harm on a person is warranted, and it sets the severity limits: 'just as A's having committed a crime accounts for why A should be punished, A's having committed *this* crime tells us how severely A should be punished' (Klimchuk 2001: 83 emphasis original). It is reasonable to understand the retributive justification as a decent basis for, but not the whole story of, why punishment ought to be inflicted on those judged to have committed atrocity crimes. This explanation requires something more to justify this causing of suffering, in the form of punishment, on any human being.

The retributive-expressive justification

The infliction of punishment on perpetrators, as well as the prosecution and sentencing phases of the judicial event, is most aptly justified according to its expressive value. The expressive theory posits that judgement and punishment are instruments of social communication. The judicial act has a symbolic significance and it aims to communicate to the perpetrator and the broader community a particular message of condemnation for specific behaviour which has been prohibited by that society and promulgated as law. Joel Feinberg writes that punishment is 'a conventional device for the expression of attitudes of resentment and indignation, and of judgements of disapproval and reprobation, either on the part of the punishing authority himself or of those "in whose name" the punishment is inflicted' (Feinberg 1965: 400). Christopher Ciocchetti claims that 'Usually, the hard treatment inflicted on wrongdoers is morally required *because* it censures the wrongdoing' (Ciocchetti 2003: 67 emphasis original). Pablo de Greiff explains that, 'what distinguishes expressionist positions is that they focus on punishment as an expression of condemnation, rather than say, as a deterrent or a tool for incapacitation' (de Greiff 2002: 375). And Drumbl explains how the expressive theory differs from other traditional theories of punishment in the following way: 'The expressivist punishes to strengthen faith in rule of law among the general public, as opposed to punishing simply because the perpetrator deserves it or because potential perpetrators will be deterred by it' (Drumbl 2007: 173).

So, for the expressivist, punishment communicates to the perpetrator and to the community condemnation of a particular action and this communication, as Feinberg suggests, performs 'such symbolic functions as disavowal, non-acquiescence, vindication, and absolution' (Feinberg 1965: 420). By this he means that punishment can communicate that the society renounces and condemns certain behaviour rather than condones it, it reaffirms the authority and strength of particular laws (which would be impotent if not backed by punishment), and also communicates that those who are punished are the guilty parties and absolves any other potential suspects of suspicion. And it aims to persuade individuals of the erroneousness of pursuing certain actions and, moreover, dissuade them from certain behaviour through moral education.

Punishment, according to expressivists, is an educative tool.[6] As de Greiff identifies, 'Since the point of punishment cannot be merely to express a judgment without regard for whether there is any kind of uptake, most expressionist theorists argue that the aim of punishment is to *persuade* offenders and others about the wrongfulness of certain kinds of conduct' (de Greiff 2002: 375 emphasis original). Jean Hampton claims of the expressive theory that

> punishment is not intended as a way of conditioning a human being to do what society wants her to do (in the way that an animal is conditioned by an electrified fence to stay within a pasture); rather, the theory maintains that punishment is intended as a way of teaching the wrongdoer that the action she did (or wants to do) is forbidden because it is morally wrong and should not be done for that reason.
>
> (Hampton 1984: 212)

Domestically, punishment is used as an educative tool the purpose of which is to reconfirm right behaviour necessary for members of society to live peacefully and securely. In the context of atrocity and post-atrocity justice, the aim is similarly to promote such behaviour and to adjust societal norms to support human rights and an ordered and peaceful society. It is also to confirm to a society that has undergone a period of disregard for human rights, law, and order its commitment to these values and to confirm a commitment to going forward with respect for these values. For child soldiers, a process that evaluates and perhaps punishes some perpetrators can reinforce the society's norms and communicate expectations about the limits of behaviour.

The communicative function of punishment can aim to deter by way of re-establishing trust in the rule of law. The expressive justification rests on the view that punishment can express the wrongness, and society's disapproval, of certain behaviour and transmit this message to the broader community; it is not that punishment merely conveys the message that acting in violation of promulgated laws is unbeneficial in a cost–benefit analysis. The goal is to express the community's values and its commitment to them. This is particularly important to a post-conflict society. While one of the benefits (even objectives) of punishment is the reduction of particular anti-social behaviour, expressivists see punishment ultimately as a tool that can be employed to help change attitudes and spread and reinforce particular values. Expressivists are unsurprisingly interested in changing future behaviour, but want to do so by changing norms rather than invoking incentives. Therefore, on this theory the prosecution, conviction, and punishment of offenders act as a communicative (perhaps educative) tool for the promotion of values: the process communicates the values of the community; it reinforces them and emphasizes the community's commitment to these values.

However, the expressive justification of punishment is not sufficient on its own. Elements of the retributive theory must complement and ground the expressive theory. Retributive elements can guide practice and assist in the conveyance of the right message of condemnation and values. The appropriate recipient and means of prosecution and punishment ought to be evaluated according to retributive considerations. That the punishment is deserved and that it must in some way 'fit' the harm – the two primary justificatory features of a retributive theory – is necessary for this right communication of particular values. And this is why determining the right moral and legal responsibility of agents, such as child soldiers, is important. If the judicial body were to convict and punish an innocent or punish too severely, doing so would represent community values that would be very different from those represented by convicting the guilty and punishing him or her in a manner that could be deemed balanced and appropriate within the parameters allowed by the society. The determination of the right accountability mechanism and the calibration of punishment, therefore, are themselves aspects of expressiveness.

Moreover, it is because retributive justice is the right thing to do that punishment is expressively significant. Punishing perpetrators represents evening the balance of justice, repaying harm in a way that demonstrates equality of agents. Unlike negative retribution that assigns restraints, the retributive-expressive theory is grounded in a model of desert, justifies punishment based on the fact that harmful action is intrinsically wrong and that perpetrators deserve punishment, and is expressively significant because it reflects this understanding of punishment.[7]

A possible challenge to this account of a retributive-expressive theory is that the retributive element is unnecessary and redundant, simply implicit in the idea of punishment justified by its expressive nature. A critic might ask why include retribution as an additional justifying feature. A retributive premise is incorporated into this theory for two reasons: as a precaution against using the expressive value of punishment in ways only justifiable according to consequentialist reasoning, and to stipulate that punishment is warranted despite the fact that its communicative value is not preordained and unavoidable. There must be a reasonable expectation of expressive value to a significant share of the audience and the punishment must be deserved. Both responsibility and the positive effects of expressiveness provide a positive reason for punishment, but neither is sufficient by itself (Duff 2001: 19). So, the ability of the judicial response to atrocity to communicate norms and commitment to them is the primary function by which the practice of punishing criminal offenders can be justified, and yet retribution is also an important element in the equation. The practice is validated by its communicative capacity, but the underlying justification for why we ought to punish and why we ought to punish these particular individuals, as well as part of the message itself, derives from a retributive understanding. A foundation in retribution is necessary to determine who to punish and how severely, and punishment inflicted under these conditions also supports and reaffirms the society's commitment to justice, and fair and equal treatment. Therefore, a retributive-expressive theory of punishment provides a solid justification for the enterprise of post-atrocity retributive justice.

Retributive-expressive justification for 'restorative' justice

A retributive-expressive theory also provides a solid justification for the enterprise of post-atrocity 'restorative justice'. Justice can generally be regarded as the promotion of fairness, balance, and equality (Blake 2008; Lamont and Favor 2008),[8] and a genuine respect for people (Oxford

English Dictionary). Post-conflict justice should aim to even the balance that has been tipped by wrongdoing against certain members of the community committed by others and to communicate the equality of persons within the community. It should aim to restore faith in the community's order. One means of attempting to meet these objectives is by employing instruments of retributive justice and punishing offenders. Another is by employing processes of what is categorized as 'restorative justice'. Restorative justice is a concept difficult to define (Ashworth 2002: 578), often described in terms of what it is not, in opposition to retributive justice (Zernova 2007: 1–2), by highlighting the fact that it is concerned less with punishment and desert. The concept is broadly understood as seeking the restoration of peaceful relationships and demanding 'a solution which promote[s] repair, reconciliation, and reassurance' (Zehr 2005: 181). Arguments in support of restorative justice, especially in the context of mass human rights violations, assert that it is more sensitive to the concerns and needs of a community and deals more effectively with the social aspects of grave offenses such as massive assaults on entire communities including crimes against humanity and genocide. Some theorists, such as Priscilla Hayner (2011), claim that restorative justice complements retributive justice and that both ought to be employed for a society to truly recover from the atrocity. Others, such as David Cooper (2001), argue that looking to retributive justice is harmful to the burgeoning new social order and that it is only through restorative justice that the old social order can be held accountable and that the new can be generated.

A useful explanation of restorative justice, one that points to some of the more salient features of the concept, is offered by Howard Zehr: according to restorative justice, crime creates obligations to make things right; justice involves the victim, the offender, and the community in a search for solutions that promotes engagement or participation, that promote the offenders' understanding of the harm caused and the consequences of their behaviour, and seek to repair the harm as much as possible (Zehr 2002: 22–25; Zehr 2005: 181). Another characterization defines it as 'a process of active participation in which the wider community deliberates over past crimes, giving centre stage to both victim and perpetrator in a process which seeks to bestow dignity and empowerment upon victims, with special emphasis placed upon contextual factors' (Hovil and Quinn 2005: 11). What is distinctive conceptually about restorative justice is that it avoids focusing on the offender with intentions to punish and focuses instead on restoring or establishing harmony between the victim and offender and within the community. Distinguishing aspects of restorative justice that define a process as such are its focus on the community, both as participator in the restoration of relationships and as the context in which offences were nurtured and transpired, and its concern for the victim being as great or greater than its interest in the perpetrator. Many proponents of restorative justice talk of healing damage inflicted on human dignity (Minow 2000). Since child soldier experiences often involve multiple parties of victims (including the child soldier and his or her particular victims), a focus on victims and human dignity might seem intuitively appropriate.

The range of restorative mechanisms includes truth and reconciliation commissions of all forms and 'traditional mechanisms' of reconciliation that aim to foster a break from the past, restore relationships, and (when necessary) facilitate reintegration into communities for perpetrators; it includes justice circles, victim-offender reconciliation, and mediation practices. Restorative justice practices are both deep-rooted and novel, historical and innovative. What we now label as restorative justice are practices of restoring relations within communities that have long histories in many societies and are still widely used by aboriginal and traditional African populations (Mantle et al. 2005: 3; Zernova 2007: 7–8). In contemporary Western societies, where penal law has ruled supreme, the use of restorative approaches in lieu of retributive approaches, although slow to get traction, is making great inroads (Zehr 2002: 61–62; Roberts 2003: 116; Zernova 2007: 2).

In post-conflict contexts, the contemporary general design is to promote one or other of these two seemingly distinct approaches to evening the 'unbalance' created by conflict (retributive justice or restorative), or frequently transitional justice initiatives employ, as Hayner advocates, both in tandem in order to aid a society to break from the past, advance justice for previous human rights violations, and move forward. Seemingly, the two approaches have separate goals and grounds for justification. However, at closer reflection, this perceived dichotomy is misguided and, more troubling, possibly detrimental to the transitional justice process. The dissimilarities between retributive justice and some restorative justice processes are not so great and the two concepts should not be held at odds (Pavlich 1996). It would seem right, rather, to regard the options that fall under each categorization as choices to be selected according to how well each, under the particular conditions and in response to particular agents, would satisfy one principal goal: the pursuit of specific targeted communication that aims to restore balance according to retributive-expressive considerations. So-called restorative approaches and retributive approaches can be seen as different manners of satisfying the same post-atrocity objectives.

The retributive-expressive justification for retributive justice approaches (the use of judgement and punishment) is based on the communicative value of the mechanisms employed. And, theories of both retributive justice and restorative justice recognize 'a basic moral intuition that a balance has been thrown off by a wrongdoing' (Zehr 2002: 59). The task is to determine the right exchange that can be expressively significant, communicating the harm and righting the balance. While criminal justice approaches may be the right response to certain wrongdoing, there are cases in which the criminal prosecution and strict corresponding punishment of perpetrators or contributors would convey the wrong message, would in fact express values that the community does not endorse and deny values and norms necessary for peaceful and relatively just co-existence of community members.

To appropriately and effectively meet the basic goals of the transitional justice enterprise, it is unlikely that prosecutions, even if they are communicatively valuable in response to the behaviour of leaders and instigators, would promote the right message and work to even the balance if applied to all participants, especially perpetrators with very complex narratives who generally shoulder minimal individual responsibility for the wrongdoing they committed – like most child soldiers. Sometimes other mechanisms are better able to achieve or promote 'important moral values, values that are far less likely to be attained through prosecution' (Kiss 2000: 69).[9] The right mechanism would need to communicate, among other things, the value and equality of persons under a just regime and concern for widespread victimization and for social healing. Prosecutions could communicate condemnation of the architects of atrocity, those who devise, engineer, instigate, motivate, and compel the atrocity environment, those who hijack political power to the detriment of the community. They can also express disapproval of those leaders and actors who contribute to the brutality, torment, and persecution of members of a targeted group or individuals who get in the way of the organization's plans and policies. They may not, however, be appropriate to express the right attitudes regarding the contributions made by all contributors to the atrocity environment or be useful in expressing condemnation of institutions, policies, or governing structures. And so, mechanisms other than criminal trials are more appropriate to express the society's views about the harm caused by collective entities and also by individuals who bear greatly diminished moral or legal responsibility, like many (formerly abducted) young agents of harm.

Abducted and/or coerced youth contributing to mass human rights violations comprise a unique category of perpetrator for whom the right accountability mechanism must be capable of conveying the right message of condemnation for the wrongdoing while expressing appropriate recognition of diminished capacity for moral responsibility of the wrongdoers. Commission of harm deserves condemnation, to be sure; but in cases of mass atrocity, the many agents of wrongdoing that deserve censure demand different messages for the consistent expression and confirmation of the value of human rights, equality, and balance within the community. Messages must express the right level of condemnation, directed at the right agent, identifying which agents carry the heaviest burden of responsibility and acknowledging conditions that mitigate the responsibility of others. This does not, however, suggest that adult leaders or structures that influence lesser perpetrators are the only ones for which strict condemnation is appropriate.

Often child soldiers fall into a particular category of individuals for whose actions require some accountability and for whom the condemnation that is conveyed by formal prosecutions and punishment is entirely inappropriate. As concluded in Chapter 3, despite the fact that these participants can be responsible as causal agents of serious harm, many of them have, based on their constitution as young and manipulated agents and because of the conditions in which they act, diminished capacity for personal responsibility.[10] This is especially the case where, unlike most contexts of mass atrocity that generate more meaningful distinctions between victims and perpetrators, the youths who are agents of harm are also themselves victims who are forced to commit violence against their own families and communities of origin. For these actors, as discussed earlier, their contribution is such that they acted in a way as to be part of the cause of harm and yet they may not be properly held to be criminally or morally liable, or their personal responsibility is greatly diminished. The message conveyed by criminal prosecutions of these agents would be insensitive to the coercion that these individuals likely faced, would express unreasonable expectations of community members, or communicate lack of compassion or regret for its inability to protect its members. Therefore, the right expression of condemnation, denunciation, forgiveness, or exoneration of actions committed as part of extensive human rights abuses and violent armed conflict by particular actors, and categories of actors, might be best achieved through the employment of mechanisms other than prosecutions.

The same expressive value that justifies criminal judgement and punishment can also be found in other transitional justice mechanisms, and adherence to expression should guide the selection of appropriate post-atrocity mechanisms of justice. Just as different punishments convey the right relative condemnation of certain actions, decided from within a spectrum of punishments acceptable to a liberal society, different mechanisms of accountability can also convey communication regarding values, and the status of perpetrators within the community and the relative status of victims.

Conclusion

Transitional justice initiatives should, at minimum, discover truths, communicate condemnation of the wrongdoing regime or atrocity committed, and convey a clear break from the past. These undertakings act to even the balance, to demonstrate the importance of those individuals who were victimized, restore their human dignity, express equality, and symbolically compensate for harm. Accountability also performs symbolic functions, as Feinberg suggests, that help to differentiate different actions – therefore providing a service that some child soldiers express a desire for, a means of distinguishing their acts from the acts of others so that all members of a fighting group are not uniformly stigmatized (Fisher 2013). To meet these goals, as mentioned, there is an array of options available, options that are generally separated into two categories. The dissimilarities between retributive justice and restorative justice approaches, however, are not so great and highlighting the divergences does a disservice to the pursuit of transitional justice. Positioning these concepts as distinct approaches is not only misleading, but it is also unhelpful as it creates tension and barriers in already challenging contexts. Stressing the differences may mislead and obfuscate important similarities and areas of collaboration.

Both restorative and retributive justice approaches recognize harm inflicted on a human being, 'that a balance has been thrown off by a wrongdoing... the victim deserves something and the offender owes something [and that] there must be a proportional relationship between the act and the response' (Zehr 2002: 59). Although the emphasis might be different, both approaches recognize that harms are offences against both the individual victims and a wider community, and both aim for, as much as possible, the offender to take responsibility for his or her actions and make right the wrongs. Although the term 'accountability' is generally reserved in common parlance to mean legal liability, both retributive and some restorative justice approaches aim to account for harms committed and right the imbalance created by the violation.

Where the two approaches differ may be in the status of the individual victim in the process and on the adversarial nature of criminal prosecutions. Retributive justice focuses on discovering the perpetrators' wrongdoing constrained by formal legal boundaries and rules, whereas most restorative justice approaches aim to engage the individual victims to a much larger degree, 'letting them be heard for their own sake' (May 2005: 4). And yet, retributive justice and restorative justice approaches can be reasonably regarded as alternative measures to reach the same communicative goals.

Attacks against persons, especially attacks of the magnitude committed as part of a widespread scheme of human rights violations, have both elements of individual violation (creating or caused by toxic relationships between persons) and a broader social dimension. Addressing the wrongdoing, then, has to address it both as an offence against an individual and against society. It must communicate society's prohibition and condemnation of harmful behaviour, restore human dignity to victims by reaffirming their value and significance as members of the community, and channel victims' intuitive need for vengeance (May 2005: 4). Also, to adequately address it, the response must be both backward-looking and forward-looking, both dealing with the wrong committed and attempting to restore trust, rebuild human dignity, and influence norms.

The appropriate approach will incorporate some form of individual, and likely institutional, accountability as well as adhere to the tenets of retribution (that it is because one committed wrong and is deserving of blame that he or she should be punished, and that the response must proportionally fit the crime) and possess communicative and norm-altering significance. Possible approaches could include processes of truth-telling (truth commissions), reparation, formal or informal confrontation or mediation between victims and perpetrators, lustration, prosecutions – each of which aims to discover facts about past injustices; ask causal perpetrators to account for their actions, accept responsibility when appropriate, disclose the results of actions taken and accept penalty when suitable; establish a clear break from the past and, in doing so, each process either aims to or is capable of communicating condemnation and values.

The misplaced and unconstructive theoretical dichotomy between restorative and retributive justice is better replaced by a view of the field of transitional justice as pursuing particular expressive goals by engaging a combination of approaches which will best symbolically even the scales, communicate condemnation of wrongful behaviour, reaffirm equality and particular values appreciated as necessary for peaceful co-existence for community members, and reject the privileged status that the wrongdoer seized for himself in committing the wrongdoing. The choice of what scheme to pursue in response to past violations should begin not with the questions of 'What laws have been broken? Who did it? What do they deserve?'[11] nor 'Who has been hurt? What are their needs? Whose obligations are these?'[12] (Zehr 2002: 21), but rather the questions of 'What was the nature of the harm committed? How do we as a community communicate the disapproval and prohibition of the wrongful behaviour and reinforce the value of human dignity of all members of the group?' The answers to these questions should direct the response, perhaps leading to adversarial prosecutions or perhaps leading to mechanisms that allow dialogues between parties or, more likely, leading to a combination of various instruments.

While prosecutions are often considered beneficial and appropriate in addressing past atrocity (Crocker 2000; Roberts 2003), successful prosecutions and adequate punishment of perpetrators are generally regarded as insufficient to make a clear break or heal wounds suffered during the violent period (Minow 1998: 49). Regarding transitional justice initiatives through a lens of viewing post-conflict justice as having multiple tools (drawn from the traditionally categorized retributive and restorative justice camps) will both provide a clearer picture of what processes and mechanisms will best suit any particular context and will also hopefully lessen the degree of separation and theoretical clashing between approaches. The aim here is not to argue, as others such as Hayner have done, that retributive and restorative justice processes are complementary and ought to be employed in tandem for genuine pursuit of transitional justice. Rather, this argument makes no claim about which options are best under which conditions; instead, it promotes a different tactic to thinking about the spectrum of available selections.

It is not always the case that justice demands retributive punishment (Gutmann and Thompson 2000) or that, as Richard Goldstone argues, the ideal scenario for societies which emerge from a period of mass violence is that victims are entitled to full justice, namely trial of the perpetrators and, if found guilty, adequate punishment (Goldstone 1998: ix). He claims that,

> That ideal is not possible in the aftermath of massive violence. There are simply too many victims and too many perpetrators. Even the most sophisticated criminal justice system would be completely overwhelmed. It is for this reason that such societies have to find other solutions.
>
> (Goldstone 1998: ix)

The ideal, rather, is not that simply identified. In the aftermath of mass atrocity, there is an array of needs to be met and an array of perpetrators who contributed to human rights violations with differing actions, motivations, and intentions. There is no single formula for success for all post-conflict contexts. Of course, there are practical limitations and all choices concerning the right options for addressing past harms will be restricted by political, economic, and military considerations. However, the right decision should arise from consideration of possible approaches according to which would best communicate the appropriate concentration of condemnation for actions contributing to the atrocity and confirmation of the values necessary for society's members to live coordinated and peaceful lives.

Viewing the available choices as options to be selected from different and potentially conflicting camps adds tension between advocates of the camps and may make decisions more difficult. Rather than suggesting and arguing that retributive processes are necessary for justice or that truth-telling mechanisms are indispensable to victim healing and restoring relationships, debates should examine the feasibility of all available options and combination of options to best satisfy the principal goal of restoring balance through specific and targeted communication, according to retributive-expressive considerations and reflecting political, social, and economic constraints.

5
Accountability and Social Reconstruction

Every post-conflict society faces the tremendous challenge of rebuilding. This rebuilding must address multiple aspects of the society, including physical, economic, cultural, political, and psychosocial levels (Machel 1996: para 241). Widespread intrastate conflict devastates more than infrastructure, physical features, and individual bodies. It also destroys the capacity for the population to live in peace and tolerance; it destroys the foundational cohesiveness of the community that binds people according to a common identity and interconnectedness; and it destroys the culture and mechanisms that support respect for moral and legal norms of non-violent conflict resolution. Typically, when social cohesion is severely damaged or absent following violent conflict, citizens – combatants and civilians (those who were displaced by the war, victims of the violence, perpetrators) – often find it difficult to locate their places in the post-conflict community (Esuruku 2012: 155). Social aspects of the community especially must be repaired or established if a society is to move beyond a past conflict to a bright and functioning future.

According to the United States Institute of Peace, social reconstruction is a condition in which the population achieves a level of tolerance and peaceful co-existence; gains social cohesion through acceptance of a national identity that transcends individual, sectarian, and communal differences; has the mechanisms and will to resolve disputes non-violently; has community institutions that bind society across divisions; and addresses the legacy of past abuses (United States Institute of Peace n.d.).

Social reconstruction should include the (re-)creation of a culture that recognizes the dignity of each of the society's members and of respect for fundamental human rights (Slye 2000). Social reconstruction is something much more than negative peace or the stability of a political regime. The important question is what elements are necessary to advance the objective of social reconstruction. This is a matter more of practical than moral consequence.

Despite the expressive value of accountability, and the importance of the expression and reconfirmation of social values to the social reconstruction process under most conditions, there is some dispute as to whether accountability comprises an essential element of social reconstruction or whether it can also obstruct or obfuscate the aims of the social reconstruction enterprise and, therefore, should not be assumed vital but only useful within certain contexts. This chapter argues that, because of its ability to confirm the community's commitments to particular values and reaffirm equality and human rights, accountability is a meaningful and critical element of the social rebuilding project. Not only is the pursuit of post-atrocity accountability significant because it is right morally, as argued in the preceding chapter, but also because it produces practical benefits. A society must address past violence and attempt to move forward on a new foot by satisfying both the backward-looking and forward-looking requirements of justice; both are necessary in order to demonstrate respect for the rights of the society's citizens and in order to be capable of moving past the atrocity to cultivate a new healthy culture.

To fulfil the requirements of backward-looking justice, it is accountability that shines brightest. Retribution and punishment primarily are advocated by most Western thinkers. Appeal to criminal legal institutions is, in many respects, the response generally accepted to deal with actions that 'shock the conscience of humanity' (Rome Statute: Preamble). The Preamble to the Rome Statute, the constitution of the ICC, affirms the sentiment by claiming that the most serious crimes 'must not go unpunished and that their effective prosecution must be ensured' (Rome Statute: Preamble).

Accountability can also, arguably, promote forward-looking requirements of justice. Colleen Murphy argues that accountability mechanisms, at least those in the form of international criminal trials, are crucial for the establishment, or re-establishment, of respect for the rule of law, which is 'an important part of the process of repair because relationships structured by law realise three important moral values: agency, reciprocity, and justice' (Murphy 2010: 225). Chapter 4 also argued that prosecutions are not the only means of pursuing accountability. Some so-called restorative measures that ask individuals to account for their actions, take responsibility when appropriate, disclose the results of actions taken, and accept penalty when suitable also satisfy the retributive-expressive aims of transitional justice.

The practical value of accountability is, however, disputed by some academics, NGO workers, and members of religious groups on the grounds that employing forgiveness or non-individualized cultural practices, not retribution, is the right path forward in order to successfully achieve social reconstruction (for discussions, see: Pain 1997; Du Toit 2000; Baines 2005; Hovil and Lomo 2005). According to this position, holding responsible agents to account, especially youthful agents, is detrimental to the social healing of the society. There are two arguments at work. The first is that processes of accountability are too narrow in focus and are ill-suited for addressing widespread violation of human rights; the consequences of employing processes of accountability are that limited resources are wasted and even that these processes can reinforce divisions and animosity between groups and between individuals. Pursuit of accountability can, the argument goes, further stunt the possibility for social harmony.

The second argument questions the universality of individualized accountability. Many of the conflicts in which child soldiers participate are intrastate wars fought on the African continent and some academics and practitioners argue, in reference to attempts to promote post-conflict justice, that Western individualized accountability is not amenable to traditional African understandings of justice. The idea is that retributive justice and the criminal justice system are Western ideals. They are alien conceptions to non-Western cultures. Arguably, 'a penal system anchored in individual guilt and punishment is by nature out of sync with community perceptions of guilt, responsibility and fair outcome' (Komakech 2012: 65). As such, the argument goes, these conventions ought not to be imposed on non-Western cultures. This argument, if true, would be a formidable opponent to a system of accountability that entails criminal prosecution as a fundamental process for dealing with acts of mass atrocity. It would also have profound relevance to any proposal that advocates for individualized accountability of others forms.

This chapter explores these two challenges to post-atrocity accountability. It will show that social reconstruction, the condition of building peaceful and prosperous co-existence after violent conflict, generally demands measures that directly address the past and account for individual wrongdoing, and it defends the (near) universality of this position given the current condition of human relationships and expectations. Naturally, the issue of the value of accountability to social reconstruction is essential to judgements made regarding the moral and practical importance of holding child soldiers accountable for their actions. Child soldiers are not generally architects of atrocity,[1] and so should not be those with whom international criminal law has the most interest, and yet if accountability is a moral imperative and of practical value to social reconstruction, their actions should not be ignored and arguably should not simply be uncritically forgiven but rather recognized and evaluated as acts committed under unique conditions to contribute to extensive human devastation.

Accountability as a critical element of social reconstruction

As a response to mass violations of human rights, individualized accountability that admits the possibility of penalty for harms committed has come under attack from some for not being sympathetic to the concerns and needs of a society dealing with the conditions left behind after the cessation of conflict (for discussions, see: Pain 1997; Du Toit 2000; Hovil and Lomo 2005). Justice in such a context, the argument goes, entails much more than (simply) dealing with those responsible for the widespread harm. The claim is that accountability is limited and does not sufficiently address what is most beneficial to the restoration of the society's infrastructure and harmony. Over recent decades, advocacy for some so-called 'restorative' justice mechanisms, mechanisms that may have some semblance of individual accounting but are not generally themselves designed to lay blame and condemn, has accumulated momentum. Proposals for truth-seeking paired with amnesty, or healing and reconciliation ceremonies paired with amnesty are claimed by some to better meet the needs of the society and to not have the potential to create further rifts that will lead to renewed hostilities. The particular benefits of individualized accountability for wrongdoing, the argument goes, get lost in the vast context of post-atrocity social reconstruction.

The criticism has two components: that accountability is responsively inadequate and that there are better ways to realize justice (perhaps through truth-seeking paired with amnesty); and that because accountability is inadequate, channelling limited resources into accountability mechanisms appropriates from other necessary and more consequentially valuable social reconstruction activities. This criticism has an important point to make, specifically that individualized accountability that asks suspected perpetrators to account for their actions and accept penalty when appropriate is not in and of itself sufficient to meet the requirements of justice. Individualized accountability is typically limited by practical considerations in the number of perpetrators it can address, it may not be the best source for a coherent and encompassing picture of the atrocity environment and criminal activity,[2] and the focus is not on relationships or the needs of victims but on the perpetrators and the harm committed. Individualized accountability as a critical component of social reconstruction, however, can be validated on practical grounds that complement the moral grounds established in the previous chapter because some measure that directly addresses past harms and considers the contribution of individuals to the atrocity that affected the community is generally perceived as necessary by members of the community who must rebuild in the transition (Gutmann and Thompson 2000: 26; Key Principles for Children and Transitional Justice 2010; Hayner 2011: 3). Absent such measures, the transition is hampered by distrust of the community's social institutions and of individual neighbours. There is also a persistent feeling that justice has not been met and that there is unfinished business that hangs over the reconstruction process and over individual lives. Given the significance of individualized accountability to the project of social reconstruction, resources allocated to accountability, provided they are well used, are well assigned.

One of the arguments in opposition to individualized accountability is that 'If past abuses have been numerous, no criminal process will be equipped to bring most of the guilty to justice' (Greenawalt 2000: 189). Individualized accountability is limited in scope and therefore typically leaves much of the atrocity unaddressed. Therefore, complements to individualized accountability should include processes that aim to get broader community involvement, and that are, as a result of their nature, less consuming of time and resources per capita for each individual participant and therefore able to address a broader scope of the harm. A truth commission, for example, might be more capable of effectively revealing the details and scope of the atrocity environment than can ordinary legal procedures (Greenawalt 2000: 189).

However, justice is not simply a numbers game. Despite the seeming reasonableness of the argument, there is something inherently wrong with one that claims that if a particular process can bring to light more offenders and their actions than another, and the latter will allow many, and likely some of the most responsible, offenders to slip through the cracks, the process that deals with the greater scope of wrongdoing can bring satisfaction to a greater number of victims and is the better choice. Victims often resent such arguments that see their perpetrators receive amnesty for their recognized wrongdoing (Maepa 2005: 69–70; Hayner 2011: 30–31). It is not simply that the details of past abuses should come to light, but also that individual perpetrators are made to answer for their actions that is important to the restoration of social harmony. Social harmony develops from a sense of common purpose and existence, and such feelings derive from the opinion that one is a respected member within the community. Therefore, victims must feel satisfied that attempts to restore their dignity were made, that they are treated as esteemed members. They must feel that the government and their community's members (and, in some contexts, the international community) have acknowledged the wrongs committed against them and have addressed the wrongs appropriately. In this vein, victim perception and satisfaction is important.

Resentments must be addressed if reconciliation is to be achieved (Komakech 2012: 66). Taking seriously the feelings of resentment that victims have includes communicating and supporting the satisfaction of their legitimate desire for reprisal when warranted. Their negative attitudes towards perpetrators should be acknowledged 'as legitimate and worthy of respect' (Brudholm 2006: 23). That their emotions are acknowledged as legitimate is important to the wellbeing of individual victims and to the broader society (Stauffer and Hamber 1996).

Even the most limited satisfaction that comes from acknowledgement may be lost for some victims when wrongdoing is completely overlooked because of the limitations of the process, especially when choices were made to pursue one option at the expense of another that had broader implications. However, it is important to note, as Greenawalt reminds us, that amnesty is not the same as failure to prosecute or failure to convict. If accountability practices express a particular regard for the victims, for equality before the law, and human rights, then amnesty can express a lack of such regard. Greenawalt claims that offering amnesty is treating offenders 'better than they deserve from the standpoint of justice... That the offenders are identified and may feel remorse hardly cancels this injustice' (Greenwalt 2000: 200). Therefore, victims may feel short-changed when the wrongdoing from which they suffered is neglected for any number of reasons, but the feeling of neglect might be better than the impression that the community has deliberately closed its eyes in order to excuse the wrongdoers for political reasons.

The satisfaction and possible recuperation of a sense of dignity that comes from victim involvement in transitional justice mechanisms can also be sacrificed to the pursuit of individualized accountability when particular suspected perpetrators are not brought to account. The lack of victim involvement is even a weakness of some forms of individualized accountability, especially criminal trials. Victim involvement is said to affect victim satisfaction and processes that more generally focus on the victims as well as the offenders are argued to better satisfy the emotional needs of the victims (Latimer 2005). Most proponents of alternative non-retributive justice talk of healing damage inflicted on human dignity. Martha Minow claims that trials miss this important goal and, she asserts, it is a dangerous oversight. 'Failure to address damage to individual dignity and to the very idea that members of targeted groups are persons with dignity ensures that the consequences of mass violence will persist and may give rise to new rounds of revenge' (Minow 2000: 236). If part of the practical grounding of accountability is its capacity to bring about a certain amount of victim satisfaction, promote peaceful co-existence, and restore personal dignity through institutional processes, efforts must be made to maximize victim involvement.

Since processes that allow victims greater and more autonomous involvement in the process are seemingly more sympathetic to the feelings of victims, as much as possible, accountability mechanisms should attempt to involve victims to the highest degree feasible without compromising the appropriate expression of condemnation or the basic human rights of the suspected offender. There are reasons that, at least in response to the most senior leadership of atrocity schemes, limited individual victim participation and influence is appropriate. The first is that while the individual victims are naturally of concern to the process and their satisfaction with the process desired, justice is equally concerned with the broader community as itself a victim of the atrocity. Offences that are of interest to systems of criminal law, and transitional justice more generally, are offences against the community and its rules as well as particular individuals and for which community condemnation accompanies sanction (Hart 1958). Accountability expresses commitment to values to the whole community, therefore benefiting and satisfying a great number. It also fosters social reconstruction by eliciting a feeling of a common public. The second reason is that, although victims should not feel removed from the process or feel that they are peripheral or superfluous, such feelings, when they develop, generally do so as a response to safeguards that need to be in place for the just pursuit of officially pursued accountability that most victims actually want (Wilson 2001; Longman et al. 2004; Brudholm 2006). The need for accountability, in its purist form, must be balanced with precautions for those accused.

Non-accountability responses, such as mechanisms paired with amnesties, can in fact offer at least a minimal degree of satisfaction for victims in that they can identify individuals, groups, and policies responsible, but they rarely satisfy the natural human aspiration that wrongdoers are truly brought to answer for their actions. Even if they do not necessarily invite or demand responsible agents to account for their actions or accept traditional punishment, some non-accountability restorative mechanisms can bring to light wrongdoers by the naming of names, which can occur through the testimony of victims, witnesses, or other perpetrators. Such a process can create a record of what harms were committed and by whom, therefore attributing responsibility to individual and other agents. 'This record will give *some* satisfaction to those who have suffered, and constitutes a kind of official acknowledgement and minimal accountability' (Greenawalt 2000: 190 emphasis original). This very minimal accountability, despite offering nominal satisfaction in its acknowledgement, is not however generally considered sufficient or legitimate accountability by victims who bore the effects of mass atrocity (Gibson 2002; Hayner 2011: 1–3).

Amnesty generally leaves victims, despite any ability to be heard and to confront their offenders, often feeling short-changed, deeming justice not really to have been done, as the example of South Africa's TRC can demonstrate. 'If a government openly failed, for no cogent reason, to prosecute a murderer, torturer, or rapist against whom it had overwhelming evidence, few would doubt that an injustice was done' (Greenawalt 2000: 194). Priscilla Hayner, in her book about truth commissions, points out that 'Despite the efforts of the Truth and Reconciliation Commission, many South Africans still demand strict justice and punishment for their perpetrators' (Hayner 2011: 3). Likewise, survivors of the Rwandan genocide supported accountability and penalty for wrongdoing. According to research conducted in post-genocide Rwanda in 2002,

> respondents strongly supported using trials to punish the guilty (92.3 per cent agreed or strongly agreed) and to reveal the truth about what happened in 1994 (94.0 per cent agreed or strongly agreed), but they also supported using trials to separate the innocent from the guilty (89.4 per cent), rebuild trust in the community (87.1 per cent), and recognize the suffering of survivors (83.2 per cent).
>
> (Longman et al. 2004: 212)

Victims generally regard punishment as the appropriate response to wrongdoing. Retributive justice has a long history. In almost all cultures across time a society's means of responding to anti-social actions or those that violate the prescribed behaviour of the group was a process of judging and punishing. This universality is addressed later in this chapter.

Sometimes amnesties are necessary for political and practical reasons, but they must be justified on the basis that the injustice of not pursuing a process of accountability is trumped by the political and practical needs that necessarily conflict with retributive processes. Accountability, in its many forms, can accompany non-accountability 'restorative' justice practices as a means for a fuller sense of justice to be met and for justice to be seen to be met. Lack of accountability and denunciation can only be excused if there is a greater threat to the society that is avoided by circumventing accountability. As such, lack of prosecution or individual accountability might be excused, despite the injustice, if there were reason to believe that further harm would befall innocent civilians if amnesty were not granted. For an example, we might look to the case of South Africa and the argument that to truly bring an end to the systemic abuses and bring to light the harm caused so that further harms were not committed, truth-telling and amnesty was the best approach. And yet, as Hayner suggests, despite the arguments and despite the good work that the TRC did, many South Africans still believed that strict justice and punishment should befall their perpetrators. Retributive justice is coveted likely as a means to satisfy a desire for revenge, but also because the acts of judging and punishing perpetrators themselves speak volumes about the relative value of the victims and perpetrators in their society and to the audience of the transitional justice process. Therefore, in post-atrocity contexts, we might want to claim, as Hayner does (2011: 91–109), that a wide range of accountability and non-accountability processes ought to be used, but that a lack of accountability hinders a society from truly recovering from atrocity.

Finally, mechanisms that focus on individualized accountability are criticized also for their lack of attention to relationships within the community. Arguably, they do nothing to promote or support the re-establishment of relationships, at least such an aim is absent from the objectives of retributive processes like criminal trials. In addition to their not promoting or supporting the re-establishment of relationships, processes of individualized accountability might be seen to exacerbate rifts. As a time-consuming process, post-atrocity accountability may continue to reinforce divisions that absent the ongoing process of accountability would begin to heal with time (Bachmann 2013). If the goal is to lay 'the groundwork for more harmonious relations between former adversaries, continuing criminal trials may exacerbate old wounds and impede efforts to move beyond past wrongs' (Greenawalt 2000: 191). Conversely, although accountability does not promote the mending of relationships, such an interest is a very lofty goal not likely realized by any post-atrocity mechanism. Amnesties, though, may permit broader feelings of anger and blame to fester since the official response did not curb retributive inclinations, and a policy of amnesty might allow rifts to grow and lead to renewed hostilities. Post-atrocity justice is meant to bring an end to the cycle of animosity and settling of scores. Transitional justice mechanisms should necessarily aim to heal divisions and restore dignity and equality to groups within the community. While accountability mechanisms do not aspire to repair relationships, they do seek to restore balance within the community, therefore rebuilding a just social foundation from which healthy relationships can develop.

Reconciliation programmes absent any means of addressing and accounting for past wrongs are likely to be most often ineffectual. Accountability programmes should precede (or co-exist with) attempts at reconciliation. 'Reconciliation programs seek to promote tolerance and mutual respect, reduce anger and prejudice from the conflict, foster intergroup understanding, strengthen nonviolent conflict resolution mechanisms, and heal the wounds of conflict' (United States Institute of Peace n.d.). Criminal trials, at least for those considered most responsible for the human rights abuses, are generally seen as an essential element for transitional justice as they support victims in their pursuit of regaining their dignity, part of which demands that they are shown due respect and concern (Wilson 2001). In extreme cases, the benefits of criminal trials must be weighed against other political and practical considerations, but the worth of retributive justice, both moral and practical, is such that all attempts must be made to pursue retributive justice for those who deserve it. In fact, there are legal and moral obligations for holding those most responsible for mass atrocity accountable in criminal proceedings (Convention on the Prevention and Punishment of the Crime of Genocide: Article 1; Rome Statute). And, a history of unaddressed massive abuses is likely to be socially divisive, generating mistrust between groups and individuals (ICTJ n.d.). To properly address abuses, accountability that asks perpetrators to answer for their wrongdoing is the most expressively salient. Accountability in its many forms is crucial for a society to demonstrate respect for human rights, equality, and the value of its victims.

Given our current world, with its particular history, mechanisms of accountability have a very specific function and circumventing accountability speaks volumes in a tone that lacks sufficient respect for victims who have come to know accountability as the measure of international, national, and local concern. However, different approaches and outcomes of accountability, as will be argued in Chapter 7 of this book, are appropriate for different manners and degrees of responsibility. Accountability mechanisms of a form different from formal criminal trials are included in the options to satisfy the need for accountability. For example, local neo-traditional trials that deviate from the structural procedures of criminal trials can be seen to satisfy the need for accountability. Despite their being beset with problems, it was found in the same Rwandan study mentioned above that domestic and gacaca trials (local neo-traditional trials in Rwanda) were overwhelmingly seen as contributing to reconciliation in Rwanda (Longman et al. 2004: 219). Other processes are also viable solutions to meeting the need for accountability.

This chapter concerns practical implications. What are the benefits to the transitional society of accountability practices? And, do they outweigh the potential disadvantages mentioned above, such as the potential disappointment of victims when criminal trials or other mechanisms of individualized accountability might only be able to deal with or penalize some perpetrators and not others, when they, the victims, are not central to the process and are sidelined as the process focuses on perpetrators, and when resources that are channelled to fund trials or other individualized mechanisms are not available to also fund other needs of the victims of atrocity? The answer is that the victims' need for retribution, in its expressively significant form, is so strong that the lack of such a response to serious wrongdoing communicates something else. It seemingly expresses a lack of appropriate regard for the victims commensurate to the regard victims feel they deserve. It might express that the victims' bitterness towards the causal perpetrators is illegitimate and that the harm inflicted on the victims was deserved, excusable, or forgivable. It is an added insult to suggest that victims' resentment cannot be retained on genuinely moral grounds (Brudholm 2006). Since individualized accountability has this expressive significance, perhaps it is true, as Geenawalt claims, that 'A government owes prosecution to victims and their relatives and perhaps to the law-abiding public at large' (Greenawalt 2000: 194).

Universally meaningful justice

Central to the above arguments is the position that individualized accountability is meaningful to the population of the transitioning society. Individualized accountability, however, has come under attack for being a foreign imposition and not able to convey the right message to some populations due to different histories in dealing with conflict and offences against society. The idea advanced by some is that the criminal justice system and other attempts at attaching personal responsibility and punishment are Western ideals. As such, the argument goes, these conventions should not be imposed on non-Western cultures, especially if they take the form of international instruments, because such imposition is hollow and offensively paternalistic to the transitioning society. If this argument is true, it would mean that individualized accountability would be at best inconsequential, rather than of great significance, and at worst detrimental to the social reconstruction enterprise.

This debate was central to questions of justice in South Africa at the end of apartheid and was being played out especially in discourse concerning the ICC's involvement in Uganda. Dullah Omar, the South African Minister of Justice, claims that gross violations of human rights could be 'addressed on the basis that there is a need for understanding but not for vengeance, a need for reparation but not retaliation, a need for ubuntu but not for victimisation' (Omar n.d.). Archbishop Desmond Tutu regards non-retributive justice as 'the characteristic of traditional African jurisprudence', the central concern of which is 'not retribution or punishment but, in the spirit of ubuntu, the healing of breaches, the redressing of imbalances, the restoration of broken relationships' (Tutu 1999: 54). As suggested earlier, part of the reasoning behind the establishment of the TRC and the accompanying amnesties was practical: there was concern that the truth about the structure and policies of apartheid and what happened to individual victims would never come to light if perpetrators did not come forward and tell their stories and that this would only happen if amnesty was granted. Another part of the reasoning was the thinking that African conceptions of justice do not focus on fixing blame and punishing. The African conception of justice, the argument goes, favours the re-establishment of harmony in the relationships between people or parties in conflict through forgiveness. Already in the last section it has been suggested that South Africans did not comprehensively whole-heartedly support the amnesties. This 'African conception of justice' deserves more inquiry. This criticism of accountability, particularly in regards to the 'African' conception of justice, is noteworthy and worrisome in that although the use of child soldiers is a global problem, many of the conflicts in which child soldiers participate are intrastate wars fought on the African continent.

When the ICC announced in January of 2004 its intention, in response to President Museveni's referral of his state's situation, to investigate the atrocities committed during the course of the conflict in northern Uganda and to arrest and prosecute those individuals most responsible, the announcement was met with little enthusiasm from Ugandan civil society (Perrot 2010: 194). Two reasons were expressed for this discontent: it was feared that prosecution would undermine the offers of amnesty that accompanied attempts at peace talks, and 'it was argued that international approaches to justice were inappropriate to the current context, and possibly undermined traditional approaches to justice' (Baines 2005: 1). As Tim Allen explains, assertions were made that 'the ICC reflected flawed and compromised systems of justice, and that it could not comprehend the meaning of real justice known to the Acholi [northern Ugandan tribal group], grounded in what are asserted to be traditional... values' (Allen 2006: 86).

Part of the claim is that African societies in general, and Ugandan communities specifically, are more community-centred than Western societies and that individualized retributive justice is not appropriate in the African context. In fact, in terms of cultural values, African societies (especially tribal societies) do seem to regard the community in a different way than do Western cultures.[3] Western ideology tends to veer to prioritizing the individual, while African cultures tend to promote the community. And because they do, in response to criminal activity, some tribes accept the guilt of the offender and compensation offered to the victim is usually expected to be contributed to by the entire tribe of the offender (International Center for Transitional Justice 2005: 51). The community owns the wrong.

While these arguments can be seen as problematic for accountability grounded in criminal justice, with its aim to judge and punish individuals according to promulgated laws, these arguments also cast a shadow on the wider range of instruments of individual accountability. If it is true that African conceptions of justice are generally more focused on community and restoring bonds and run counter to Western individualism, then there might be a lack of justification for any punishment or other means of individualized accountability in African post-conflict contexts. This section challenges this argument and, by employing field research that explores the prevalence of individualized judgement and punishment in historic mechanisms of justice in Uganda specifically, reveals important similarities between traditional 'restorative' justice and retributive justice approaches to reconciling conflict and further emphasizes the argument of Chapter 4 that the dichotomy between restorative and retributive justice ought to be abandoned.

This section dismantles attempts to characterize African traditional mechanisms as lacking retributive elements by challenging the notion that Ugandan local traditional mechanisms of justice reject retribution for a focus on community and restoring relationships. Ugandan traditional mechanisms of justice championed by the restorative justice literature have, overwhelmingly, aspects of judgement and punishment. The lines dividing traditional mechanisms, espoused by restorative advocates, and Western-style retributive justice, as could be administered by the ICC or local or national criminal justice systems, are blurred. This position reveals important similarities between some so-called restorative justice and retributive justice approaches to reconciling conflict, again demonstrating that the distinction between restorative and retributive justice is misleading, and challenges the argument that traditional societies, such as communities in northern Uganda, would be unsatisfied with Western-style prosecution because their sense of justice is based on attempts to restore relationships rather than punish offending parties.

It is important to show that individualized accountability is historically valid and therefore credible as an option that does not run counter to the intuitions and conceptions of justice of those for whom the process is intended to be expressively significant. Making this argument will show why blanket amnesties are unfavourable, and suggests why in post-conflict contexts it is important that individuals are held personally responsible for their wrongdoing in order for the transitional justice mechanism to communicate the right condemnation of harm.

There are dozens of recognized ethnic groups in Uganda.[4] The Acholi tribe on which much has been written, speculated, and debated, and whose traditional mechanisms have been most ardently promoted, is the group most affected by the recent conflict in northern Uganda. It is the children and young adults of this tribal culture who have been abducted, tormented, killed, and used as soldiers and sex slaves; it is the men and women of this tribal community who have been murdered, abducted, disfigured, tortured, displaced, and raped. What will first become obvious in this discussion is that traditional mechanisms heralded as the optimal means of dealing with returnees from the conflict in Uganda, such as Mato Oput of the Acholi people, most definitely traditionally have individualized responsibility attaching to perpetrators. These perpetrators ask forgiveness of their victims, provide compensation, and participate in a reconciliation ceremony. Even those who herald 'restorative' approaches as more authentically African do not suggest that these traditional mechanisms have no acknowledgement of individual wrongdoing (Komakech 2012). The troublesome claim, though, is that acknowledgement of wrong and a request for forgiveness is generally adequate to satisfy the dictates of justice. These reconciliation ceremonies, with their element of restitution, are argued suitable for those who have committed egregious human rights violations. It is also argued that personal punishment of individual offenders is not amenable to African conceptions of justice that aim to promote community harmony rather than focus on the perpetrator's desert (Komakech 2012: 65).

And so, if it is the case that African communities are, in fact, not interested in attributing individualized responsibility that results in punishing offenders, then it might stand to reason that the offences of all atrocity perpetrators, but especially those of individuals whose responsibility is greatly diminished, ought to be ignored in the interest of community harmony. If the most serious of harms committed by competent adults, against the backdrop of order and peace are traditionally dealt with only through a reconciliation process where the perpetrator asks for forgiveness and he and his relations offer compensation, then there does appear to be a significant distinction between African justice and Western focus on retributive accountability.

Mato Oput is a highly publicized traditional Acholi reconciliation ceremony performed after a killing, but 'was traditionally not applied for killings that happened in war, but rather to those occurring between clans that had up to that point maintained friendly relationships with each other' (Harlacher et al. 2006: 79). This ceremony is one of clan- and family-centred reconciliation which incorporates the guilty acknowledging a wrong committed and asking for forgiveness, and then offering compensation. Ultimately, both sides of the dispute share a bitter drink, the bitter herb of the Oput tree, to symbolize the swallowing of the psychological bitterness that prevailed in the minds of the parties to the conflict (Baines 2007: 95).

This ceremony, interestingly, is not truly specific to the Acholi; the name and the particulars may change but the process for reconciliation is relatively the same across the country.[5] For example, in the Langi practice of Kayo Cuk, 'a perpetrator [is] expected to take responsibility, ask for forgiveness from the victim's family and pay compensation which was standard in nature, i.e. seven (7) cows payable to the victim's family and an eighth one which is slaughtered and eaten by the elders mediating between the families' (Lamony 2007: 3). Nor is Mato Oput the only reconciliation mechanism available to the Acholi. Tumu kir is a ritual ceremony that reduces or resolves smaller-scale local conflicts in Acholi society. It heals *kir*;

> behaviors that constitute *kir* across clans are those that might kindle or accompany already-existing conflicts, ... quarreling over land, at the water source or for firewood, burning somebody's hut, uttering curses, sexual activities in the bush or with relatives and various forms of violence (including fighting between husband and wife or father and son, and even throwing food at another person).
>
> (Harlacher et al. 2006: 75)

The process for this ceremony includes sacrificing either a goat or a sheep (depending on the offence), in which the offender holds 'the head of the animal to show acceptance and repentance for the crime that has brought uncleanness [dirt] into the family' and the offended holds the legs (Harlacher et al. 2006: 77). The animal is cut open and the intestines are removed and put on the feet and the chest of the victim and some are sprinkled on the house to clear the home of the offence.

The main objective of Mato Oput and similar reconciliation ceremonies is to restore relationships between the perpetrators and the victims of the crime and reintegrate the perpetrators into their communities. The 'restorative', or non-retributive, nature of this particular ceremony has been widely explored and publicized and it has led to a widespread understanding of Ugandan traditional justice as categorically non-retributive in nature. However, this understanding of the local mechanisms for conflict resolution and reaction to wrongs committed against the community is mindful only of the final stages of the historic process, ignoring significant steps that must occur before reconciliation can ensue, including judgement and punishment. The importance of judgement and punishment in the historic iterations of these traditional mechanisms of justice in Uganda goes a long way to dispelling the idea that a unique African conception of justice avoids retributive individual accountability.

Even in traditional societies, to which some legal theorists and practitioners are looking as proponents of alternatives to retributive justice, in most cases there is punishment meted out to the perpetrators. In fact, traditional mechanisms of justice in Uganda have more in common with 'Western-style' retributive justice institutions than much of the current literature on these mechanisms suggests. Even the debate central to philosophy of law, that of the primary purpose of punishment, is alive and well among those who practice or remember the practice of traditional ceremonies performed in the villages to restore relationships after conflict. They cite retribution and satisfaction for victims,[6] deterrence,[7] and rehabilitation.[8] Another similarity that seems to emerge in many discussions on the topic is the function of contrition. Admitting one's guilt, saying 'sorry', and asking forgiveness play important roles in traditional mechanisms and can go a long way to mitigating punishment.

Common understanding of some of the tribal communities' cultures (found in a Ugandan textbook) demonstrates a strong retributive element which includes punishment for wrongs committed (Nzita and Niwampa 1993). Conflict resolution practices have 'strong consistencies across tribes and ethnic groups' (Oola 2012: 58). For example, for the Lugbara of north-western Uganda, an intra-clan murderer was fined a bull or a cow and an inter-clan adultery case was serious enough to require capital punishment (Nzita and Niwampa 1993: 141); for the Bafumbira from the south-west of the country, punishment ran the gamut from verbal discipline (for a woman at fault for divorce) to a drink of poison (for poisoning another to death) to death by spearing or beating (for thievery) (Nzita and Niwampa 1993: 66). The currently used Ker Kwaro Acholi *Law to Declare the Acholi Customary Law* lists offences and their corresponding fines (Ker Kwaro Acholi n.d.). All tribal communities in Uganda examined express their own codes of conduct which detail what is considered a criminal or anti-social act and offer a strict range of appropriate responses that can be taken for each offense.

As mentioned, I extensively argued in a previous work that tribal communities have their own ways of determining the guilt of suspected offenders and calculating appropriate sentences relative to offences (Fisher 2012: 144–167). This is evident in each of the studied tribes, primarily the Acholi, Langi, Iteso, Baganda, and Banyankole. Punishment varies from tribe to tribe, as does the level of individual responsibility and accountability.[9] An element of punishment is present in the traditional processes of justice for each of the examined cultural groups. Punishment must not be confused with compensation which, while essential to Ugandan judicial culture, aims to satisfy another objective. The responsibility and burden to befall the perpetrator does not begin and end with compensation.

For the Langi, offences against society generally, 'something that doesn't affect an individual but hurts the pride of the community',[10] could be punishable by death (Driberg 1923: 209), or community service (such as hard labour). Offenses against individual persons, such as homicide or assault or theft, were reportedly responded to with demands of compensation and fines,[11] and perhaps physical punishment (caning). For an inter-clan crime, the entire clan would contribute to the compensation, but would deliver punishment to the perpetrator itself.

The Iteso never employed capital punishment, but an inter-clan murder was punishable by revenge killing, as is the case with most tribes, if justice was not seen to be met by the cultural judicial process. This process would administer punishment such as beating (caning) for theft, compensation and fines for accidental murder. For intentional murder, a perpetrator would be sentenced to pay much heavier fines; he might be banished from the community, and it was common practice that he would be confined to a secured home with guards while the negotiations determining the punishment (fines) were occurring.[12] These negotiations would take a couple of months. As some Iteso elders explain it, this confinement, without visitors, was a severe punishment and shame.[13] The perpetrator would have his head shaved, ceremoniously, by a clan elder, before being admitted to confinement.

The Banyankole might have also often side-stepped the more formal processes in favour of mob justice to exact immediate revenge for a murder. For an inter-clan murder, once a perpetrator, or a family to which the perpetrator belongs, was identified, a killing would need to occur to revenge the murder.[14] The entire clan of the victim was involved in this revenge, and it may not have mattered if the victim's clan killed the perpetrator or another member of his clan, or even a visitor.[15] On this account, there is little evidence of individual accountability for inter-clan murders in mob-justice of the Banyankole tradition. Usually, however, the clan elders would be called to the body to investigate the occurrence, suspects would be determined, a culprit would be identified, and punishment would be established; if it was an inter-clan murder, the punishment would be banishment to avoid inter-clan clashes.[16] For accidental killings, the punishment would resemble that for theft: public caning, compensation and fine of double the value of the stolen item, and perhaps a much larger penalty for lack of contrition. Community service, such as cleaning the well or other public ground, was also appropriate. Now, however, elders of the Banyankole culture accept that their tradition of revenge killing is no longer appropriate.

They refer cases of murder to the formal national legal system, expecting it to exact retribution for them.[17]

Punishment and individual responsibility are also evident in the Acholi tradition, although as in the other Ugandan traditional systems they are not as apparent as in Western-style judicial systems. For the Acholi, responsibility and punishment are and were as much communal as they are individual. Punishment, like responsibility for the crime, was assumed by the perpetrator's clan.[18] Usually it consisted of repayment, or symbolic compensation, including a monetary or material fine. Compensation and fines would be suitable punishment for most crimes, including theft and murder, and help lead to reconciliation between the perpetrator and his clan and the victim and her clan. The perpetrator's entire clan was expected to contribute to this compensation and fine. There are different accounts of what percentage of the fine the perpetrator himself was required to pay. On most accounts, he was to pay a large percentage (perhaps 50 per cent), because he 'must feel the pain'.[19] If the perpetrator did not admit his guilt and refuted the accusations against him, he would be fined double the value of the stolen item once he was found guilty of the theft; however, if it was a case of murder, most explanations of the process claim that the compensation and fine would remain the same whether he admitted his guilt or not. Repeat offenders, though, would be treated to more serious punishment including public caning or banishment.[20]

In each of the Ugandan traditions examined, a combination of compensation and fine is among the punishments available for the perpetrator; it was also the most commonly employed. Even if the perpetrator was not able to or was not expected to impart the entire value of the demanded compensation and fine, it was his burden. The penalty was given to him and it was he who had to seek assistance. It was meant to be his shame.[21] All this to demonstrate that the historic traditional mechanisms of justice to which proponents of 'restorative' justice point are ones in which there is personal accountability, judgement, and punishment to a much greater effect than anything evident in the reconciliation ceremonies. The reconciliation ceremony is a last step. And the steps of individual accountability, judgement, and punishment are necessary before any reconciliation ceremony can occur.

Conclusion

Social reconstruction, the condition of peaceful and prosperous co-existence after violent conflict, generally demands that accountability transpires, that measures are employed which directly address the past and ask individuals to account for their actions, take responsibility when appropriate, disclose the results of actions taken, and accept penalty when suitable. Accountability need not take the form of a criminal justice system, or it may take (and likely should take) multiple forms within a post-atrocity transitional context. Criminal trials are one option, prone to be the best option to address the wrongdoing of the architects of atrocity. Other options such as neo-traditional mechanisms of justice can also satisfy the need for accountability. Some measure that directly addresses past harms and considers the contribution of individuals to the atrocity that affected the community is generally perceived as necessary by members of the community who must rebuild in the transition. Absent such measures, the transition is hampered by distrust of the community's social institutions and of individual neighbours. Without any accountability it is likely that there will exist a persistent feeling that justice has not been met and that there is unfinished business that hangs over the reconstruction process and over individual lives. This is true for most of the globe's communities.

Finally, the peace-versus-justice debate that has dominated much of the transitional justice literature and practice has only in these pages been briefly mentioned. On one side of the debate is the position that justice must sometimes be circumvented for the goal of securing negative peace. In this chapter, the argument has been made that accountability should only be evaded in extreme cases when it is essential to do so for the sake of protecting the lives and physical security of community members. There is also good reason to believe that international obligations, at least under customary law, require or are moving towards requiring accountability (Schabas 2011).

However, it has been argued that granting amnesties and refraining from punishment could avoid creating deep and lasting political cleavages (Bachmann 2013) and avoid prolonged conflict, anarchy, and perhaps the eventual toppling of governments (Levitt 2012: 4). When the ICC announced in response to Ugandan President Yoweri Museveni's request that it would investigate the atrocities committed during the course of the conflict in northern Uganda and would arrest and prosecute those individuals most responsible, Ugandan civil society retorted that pursuing justice by holding individuals criminally responsible for their wrongdoing could hinder attempts to bring lasting peace to the region and obstruct aims of social reconstruction (Branch 2007: 184). At that point, northern Uganda was not a post-conflict situation. Arguably, attempts to pursue accountability before the cessation of the violence are not helpful to negotiating peace. At the time, there were hopes that the LRA rebels would negotiate and sign a peace treaty with the government of Uganda. The ICC indictments, it was argued, would impair this process. In regards to such situations, the peace-versus-justice debate is animated. Uganda is a great case study.

Identifying the potential benefits or disadvantages of initiating pursuit of justice during ongoing conflict is a difficult task. Some have argued that the ICC indictments have, in fact, assisted in the peace process by motivating LRA leader Joseph Kony to negotiate, if even only to attempt to bargain prosecution off the table or because the practical impact of the warrants left him with few options but to negotiate (Akhavan 2005: 404). It is, however, hard to prove such advantages of initiating mid-conflict accountability.

Despite some claims that lack of retribution often comes with a reward (Bachmann 2013), there is a more overwhelming concern that lack of accountability generally only masks and strains tensions. Jeremy Levitt argues that in the vast majority of cases (at least in Africa) blanket amnesties and schemes of power-sharing have neither ended violent conflict nor produced sustained peace (Levitt 2012: 4). Louise Mallinder, on the other hand, points out that although many amnesty laws have failed to break cycles of violence, in some contexts such as Spain, South Africa, Tajikistan, and Mozambique the countries experienced profound improvements in democracy, rule of law, and human rights following the enactment of amnesty laws (Mallinder 2009).

Amnesty comes in a multitude of forms. Amnesty laws can require amnesty beneficiaries to perform tasks ranging from surrendering, disarming, and participating in DDR programmes to engaging with non-retributive transitional justice processes such as some forms of truth commissions (Mallinder 2009: 14). Some forms can offer limited satisfaction, as suggested above. However, it seems important given the significance of accountability to the social reconstruction project that peace be secured but that accountability not be overlooked or sacrificed to the prospect of immediate peace. It is also vital to distinguish between positive peace and cessation of violence, where positive peace is more than the absence of violence, 'in which peace is a long-term condition that must be facilitated for the future, through building trust and encouraging greater interaction between previously antagonistic parties' (Clark 2011: 36). Accountability is both morally and practically relevant and beneficial to post-atrocity reconstruction. There is, therefore, good reason to continue the trajectory of international criminal law that is moving towards obligating all states to hold responsible agents accountable.

Northern Uganda is now, for all intents and purposes, post-conflict. The fighting has ended; civilians have moved home and are trying to rebuild their lives and their communities. Questions of accountability are perhaps more relevant now than ever before; Uganda has just recently allowed the 12-year-old Amnesty Act to expire in order to open the possibility of domestic prosecutions of atrocity perpetrators.

The international community has made great strides forward in establishing particular parameters of warfare and interstate interaction. It is arguably working towards a prohibition on amnesty in its fight against impunity. If such a prohibition is realized, amnesty will over time simply cease to be a considered option. As Stephen Oola argues, however, there is a need to combine prosecutorial justice processes with traditional justice principles to facilitate meaningful justice (Oola 2012: 62).

6
Trauma, Truth-Telling, and Post-Atrocity Justice

Armed conflict affects children (and adults) psychologically and emotionally, with long-term consequences at both the individual and community levels. The effects of trauma are a particular hazard of conflict that can affect victims, witnesses, and perpetrators. Chapter 5 argued that effective accountability is critical for successful social reconstruction. It explored a pair of political and cultural criticisms voiced against the pursuit of accountability in post-atrocity contexts and found neither of them to be sufficiently robust to be reasons for which accountability should not be pursued. This chapter addresses another factor on which social reconstruction is reliant – the psychological wellbeing of the society's citizens. It particularly addresses the intersection of trauma and accountability by taking up another manner of challenge. It explores the major objections raised against accountability based on the notion that the psychological wellbeing of individuals and the community can be further threatened in the aftermath of mass atrocity by engaging in truth-telling and reviving past traumatic experiences. This chapter argues, however, that remembering and truth-telling, rather than causing re-traumatization, should be viewed as significant components of projects of individual and social healing.

During widespread atrocity, the society, its individual victims and witnesses and often even the perpetrators endure acute psychological trauma. Trauma is defined as a physical or psychological threat or assault to one's physical integrity, sense of self, safety or survival or to the physical safety of another person significant to the individual, and it is in itself shocking and can lead to post traumatic stress (PTS) that affects the sufferer after the traumatic episode has subsided and affects the sufferer's capacity to function (Moroz 2005: 2). A society of individuals who collectively find difficulty in functioning at high levels due to the challenges that accompany PTS will have a very difficult job of rebuilding. Therefore, fundamental to successful recovery and reconstruction in post-conflict contexts is particular concern for and pursuit of the psychological wellbeing of the society and its individual members (Machel 1996; Wessells and Monteiro 2001).

The American Psychiatric Association defines Post Traumatic Stress Disorder (PTSD) in its *Diagnostic and Statistical Manual of Mental Disorders* (DSM-IV-TR/DSM 5) as exposure to a traumatic event that results in particular symptoms. A traumatic event is one in which the person experienced, witnessed, or was confronted with actual or threatened death or serious injury, or a threat to the physical integrity of oneself or others.[1] Symptoms include persistent intrusive re-experiencing of the event through distressing recollections such as thoughts or images, flashback episodes, or distressing dreams. In children, there may be frightening dreams without recognizable content (American Psychiatric Association 2000/2013: code 309.81).

There are debates concerning the best tactics to heal individuals who have suffered trauma, but the standard assumption, at least from the Western perspective, is that talking about the traumatic experience, discovery, and exploration of emotions lead to healing (Cohen et al. 2004; Getz 2012). Some of the post-conflict social reconstruction literature, however, disputes the Western approaches to psychosocial healing, including confidence in truth-telling and accountability and the healing effects they deliver (Machel 1996; Zarowsky and Pedersen 2000; Summerfield 2004; Shaw 2005). And, even for those who believe in the benefits of this healing approach, questions exist about the benefits and dangers of asking individuals to recount traumatic experiences not for healing purposes but for the pursuit of accountability (Mendeloff 2009). This chapter engages with this lack of confidence in truth-telling and accountability and considers whether there can be justice in the suppressing or forgetting of the past. Of interest are particular psychosocial considerations, such as whether, due to the social and traditional contexts of some post-conflict societies, truth-telling is at best ineffective and at worst harmful to the pursuit of individual (both child and adult) and societal healing.

Different individuals and societies have different reactions and understanding of traumatic events and they deal with the manifestations and challenges that arise from the trauma in different ways. Each of the cases for sacrificing truth-telling and accountability for suppression has different bearing on particular individuals or particular societies, depending on the history of trauma and the history of understanding trauma.

These cases offer as reasons for foregoing truth-telling and accountability evidence of negative consequences of pushing individuals or societies to acknowledge and recount past trauma and explore their emotional and intellectual responses to it. The first criticism that this chapter addresses is similar to, and yet different from, the argument against individualized accountability in the African context examined in Chapter 5. It argues that Western psychological approaches are inimical and do not apply to societies that possess very different ontologies and social and cultural patterns. The argument is that by recalling past events, the society can be hindered in its ability to move past the pain; in some ways, the argument claims that dwelling can re-traumatize the community. The second criticism argues that processes of truth-telling effectively re-traumatize victims who are already vulnerable and fragile persons, therefore unjustly prioritizing the seemingly immediate needs of the society to address past harms over the wellbeing of individual weak members and consequently the overall long-term wellbeing of the society.

In their aim of recovery and reconstruction, a high priority for transitional justice processes is the physical and psychological wellbeing of the society's members, especially the children as their vulnerability demands special attention and they comprise the future of the society. As Kathleen Moroz writes, 'young trauma victims often come to believe there is something inherently wrong with them, that they are at fault, unlovable, hateful, helpless and unworthy of protection and love' (Moroz 2005: 4). The long-term effects of trauma, on individual adults or children, will challenge a society – especially one that is weak and vulnerable in the aftermath of violent conflict where the infrastructure does not function effectively and there is a large segment of the population that is either dead or dealing with severe physical disabilities. Long-term effects of exposure to acute or chronic trauma can include aggression against oneself and others, mood swings, problems with social attachments (resulting in either excessive dependence or isolation), the inability to modulate sexual impulses, emotional irritability, anxiety, depression, dissociation, problems with attention and concentration, impulsivity, loss of trust and hope and personal agency, and the lack of will to prepare for the future (Van der Kolk et al. 1996; Moroz 2005: 4). The result of exposure to trauma is that individuals may be unable to serve as contributing members of their community (Maynard 1997: 205). And so, a main concern for a post-conflict community in transition is ensuring the minimization of the effects of PTS and avoiding unnecessarily reintroducing trauma to individuals (victims, witnesses, victim-perpetrators, and even perpetrators) or the society. However, this concern must be tempered with other considerations of justice and the potential long-term effects of suppressing trauma and supporting impunity.

What is trauma?

Trauma and PTS are prevalent in conflict and post-conflict environments, and in cases of widespread or particularly horrific traumatic events, the broader society as well as individuals feel the effects. Therefore, in post-conflict contexts, particular attention to trauma and the effects of trauma is important for reasons of individual rights and also the health and wellbeing of the broader society. Individuals who have experienced traumatic events, whether they were involved as victims, perpetrators, or witnesses, ought to have access to mental health care. It is simply the right thing morally. Practically, for the good of the transitioning society, the mental health of citizens is important. In war-torn societies, healthy social patterns can be replaced by distrust, apprehension, and outrage that can impair community cohesion, interdependence, cooperation, and mutual protection (Maynard 1997: 207).

Moreover, particular attention to the psychological and emotional needs of former child soldiers is essential for both moral and practical reasons. In post-atrocity contexts where there are child soldier perpetrators of atrocity, special attention should be directed towards them given that theirs are unique experiences and that from these experiences there is a great potential for children to suffer from PTS. The experiences that these young actors endure can have serious effects on the psychological and emotional make-up of these individuals and their experiences can negatively shape their own self-created identities. These young persons have suffered from their experiences and deserve attention, as every victim deserves attention. And, given that children are less-fully developed individuals and are in special need of protection, their psychological and emotional needs should be high priority. They are also part of the future of the transitioning society, and therefore their health is of paramount importance for the future health and prosperity of the society. This section explores trauma, how it affects individuals and society more broadly, and how it can be addressed.

Psychological trauma affects a person's response to future events in his or her life. Exposure to traumatic events can result in a range of conditions, including severe dysfunction, distress, or even no lasting effect (wellness) if the victim is particularly resilient (Silverman et al. 2008).

Resilience is determined by a number of internal and external factors, including the intelligence and natural optimism of the victim as well as circumstances such as community and family support (Masten and Powell 2003). Different individuals will respond to experiences differently. As mentioned, long-term effects of exposure to acute or chronic trauma can include a long list of psychological and social ailments. Such afflictions can seriously affect an individual's ability to live a decent life (Silverman et al. 2008).

Careful assessment of individuals who have experienced traumatic events and the availability of mental health care should be a main concern. Those who appear well may, in fact, not be. Accountability of perpetrators may have little impact on the social healing of a society when its individual members suffer from the effects of PTS. It is also important to recognize that conditions after exposure to trauma are rarely stable, and for this reason, the availability of mental health care should be a long-term endeavour (World Health Organization 2003). Future events or the experience of particular developmental stages (like getting married, having a child, or experiencing the death of a parent or other loved one) can call forth memories and trigger negative reactions (Rice 2004). The effects of trauma can have long-lasting consequences for victims, seeping into every aspect of their lives and the lives of loved ones and those with whom the victims interact. One of the principle concerns of a society in which individuals suffer from PTS must be the alleviation of these symptoms so that they can regain control over their lives and themselves, regain their dignity, and function well in society.

The enduring negative effects on a community can include the distress inflicted on the social cohesiveness of a community as individuals trust less and react more readily with anger. They can include lower productivity in the community as a result of many members suffering from trauma. They can include the encumbrance of traumatized individuals on the health of the society. In a community plagued by physical and social chaos, the psychologically traumatized are of little help to the rebuilding of the society, may require extensive care, can be a drain on limited resources, and 'quickly become marginalized and a burden to society' (Maynard 1997: 206). These negative effects that traumatized individuals have on the rebuilding process impact the future prospects of the society. The traumatic experiences of some, if not appropriately dealt with, can have far-reaching effects in the social reconstruction process that affect society more adversely than simply draining resources. 'The paranoia and distrust common among the mentally disturbed may influence the community mindset at a time of intense vulnerability, decreasing the odds for reintegration' (Maynard 1997: 207). For these reasons, addressing trauma and minimizing the disturbing effects of processes of justice are essential to the wellbeing of the post-conflict society.

There are a number of approaches to healing trauma; cognitive behavioural therapy (CBT) with a focus on trauma, with seemingly the best evidence, aims to help the individual process and evaluate thoughts and feelings about the traumatic episode and its lasting effects (Cohen et al. 2004). It is also considered to be the first choice of treatment of PTSD in children and adolescents (Kar 2011). CBT is arguably 'proven to be a safe and effective treatment for posttraumatic stress disorder (PTSD)' (Harvey et al. 2003: 501). The idea behind this and similar treatments that promote relating experiences is that the best way to deal with traumatic past events is to talk about them (Bryant et al. 1999: 1784; Harvey et al. 2003: 502). Although there is some debate as to why exposure is beneficial, Allison Harvey and her co-authors suggest that possible reasons include: promoting habituation and therefore reducing anxiety, promoting correction of the belief that anxiety remains unless avoidance occurs, impeding negative reinforcement associated with fear reduction, promoting the incorporation of corrective information into trauma memory, establishing the trauma as a discrete event that is not indicative of the world being globally threatening, and enhancing self-mastery through management of the exposure exercise (Harvey et al. 2003: 503).

Suppressing or ignoring thoughts about past trauma can be unhelpful by possibly intensifying or prolonging the negative effects of the traumatic experience. 'Thought stopping', a possible anxiety management skill, has been challenged because there is evidence that attempting to stop or suppress thoughts relating to a trauma may actually fuel these thoughts (Wenzlaff and Wegner 2000; Harvey et al. 2003: 503). The benefits of CBT and similar approaches, however, depend on certain factors, such as a safe environment in which to talk and the use of learned strategies to manage stress as it arises during the exploration of the past events and emotions.

In general, the best way to prevent the development of chronic PTSD is early intervention (Bryant et al. 1999: 1780). However, early intervention is not usually possible for victims of ongoing conflict, including former child soldiers. In the case of child soldiers, abuse is often long-term and constant, many times persisting over months or years and the first possible access to psychological health care is available once the former soldier returns to civilian society. Although not all individuals who experience post-traumatic stress reactions develop persistent PTSD, the risk is present for all who experience traumatic events. Although almost everyone in the transitioning society is at risk of PTSD when the home community is the battlefield, priorities must be determined in societies that have finite resources and widespread need. A priority for psychological treatment should be, along with civilian child victims, former child soldiers.

Ontologies and individualization

Although the dynamics of trauma and trauma-induced distress transcend culture, there is a sense in which culture and cultural sensitivity play a big part in the effectiveness of approaches to healing. Part of addressing trauma effectively means acknowledging and working within the cultural parameters of the post-conflict society. Part of what accounts for the differences in effects and treatment of trauma is the social environment in which afflicted persons exist. An individual's psychological wellbeing is often tied to his or her interactions with the immediate environment and much of what shapes interactions and perceptions of how interactions should be are histories and cultural norms that the community and its individual members have internalized. In her report on the impact of armed conflict on children, Graça Machel calls attention to the dissimilarities in different cultures in understanding and coping with the symptoms of traumatic stress:

> The ways in which individuals and communities cope with, react to and understand stressful events can differ markedly from one culture to another. Although many symptoms of distress have universal characteristics, the ways in which people express, embody and give meaning to their distress are largely dependent on social, cultural, political and economic contexts. Likewise, the manner in which different cultures deal with manifestations of emotional distress is based on different belief systems.
>
> (Machel 1996: para 174)

Accordingly, Western-inspired designs for post-atrocity individual healing, that endorse recollection and talking about the traumatic event, come under attack for not representing the ontologies and conceptions of justice held by some local populations for whom the processes of transitional justice and healing (both individual and social) are supposed to be most valuable. According to some arguments, Western psychological approaches to post-atrocity healing are inimical to the African context and do not apply to societies that possess very different ideas about the nature of persons and communities and that possess very different social and cultural patterns (Honwana 1997; Akello et al. 2012: 55). Machel claims that 'Western diagnostic approaches can be ill-suited to a context in which people are more likely to turn for assistance to family, friends and traditional healers than to seek medical help for their problems' (Machel 1996: para 174). Likewise, recounting past bad events to the community is sometimes seen as counter-productive to the community's attempts to move beyond traumatic events.

The argument goes as follows: Western debate about trauma has focused on the psychological effects of what is seen as extreme violation of individual integrity and identity and this is

> in line with the western view of the individual as the basic – and autonomous – unit of society, and that our psychological nature is closer to our essence than our social or religious ones. But non-western peoples have different notions of the self in relation to other and the maintenance of harmonious relations within a family and community is generally given more significance than an individual's own thoughts, emotions and aspirations.
>
> (Summerfield 1996: 6)

As mentioned above, Western approaches to trauma and healing generally fall under the category of cognitive behavioural therapy, the aim of which is to help the individual process and evaluate thoughts and feelings about the traumatic episode and its lasting effects by talking about it. According to Moroz, an important stage of healing is that of remembrance and mourning, which 'is usually understood to include the telling of the story of the frightening and harmful events that have derailed the individual and the experiencing of sensitive, empathetic and attuned responses from a person who can offer' a sense of safety and security, and which brings about 'a transformative experience that enables them to experience themselves differently' (Moroz 2005: 21). The approach, this argument claims, is either ineffective or harmful to individuals and communities who live according to other basic conceptions of what it means to be a person and a community member.

In contradiction to the prevailing Western view that champions the benefits of delving into the past through memory and dialogue, some cultures believe the best way to move beyond the pain is to put the former episodes in the past and not to think or talk about what happened. Individuals, as is the custom in their societies, manage their own trauma and the possible anxiety of the members of their communities by quietly trying to relegate the past to distant memory and not broaching the subject. Some former child soldiers who said they deliberately avoided thinking about their bad war experiences actually seemed to fare quite well (Wessells 2006: 139). To them, the best way to deal with traumatic memories – for their own sake and seemingly for the community at large – is avoidance.

Even in situations in which those with past trauma might have been helped by talking about their experiences, in some societies healing ceremonies act as a cut-off point, after which time it is unsuitable to revisit the past. Studies in Mozambique reveal that in 'many cases, those involved want to start fresh after ritual procedures, which do not emphasize recalling the traumas suffered, as western-style counseling would' (Fegley 2008: 45). After the healing ceremony, the past is in the past. 'Soldiers who have completed a purification ritual are typically told not to "look back," that is, to avoid talking about their war experiences or the ritual, lest the bad spirits return' (Wessells 2006: 202). Cleansing rituals, which take different forms, generally aim to symbolically shut the door to the past, as they purge the individual of the contamination of war and death and sin and guilt and offer protection from the spirits of anyone the recipient of the ritual killed (Honwana 2006: 104, 110).

Unlike Western conceptions of psychological trauma and healing, some societies regard the negative effects of past bad experiences that are regarded by Western medicine as psychological effects of trauma – such as nightmares, difficulty concentrating, panic attacks, unfounded or amplified anger, and poor impulse control – as caused by spirits. These communities believe that the spirits of the dead can torment their killers, causing them illness and possibly even death (Baines 2005: 10, 12–13; Honwana 2006: 108). Alcinda Honwana reports that soldiers as well as any civilians who witnessed a murder are said to be particularly susceptible to insanity that is caused by the spirits of the dead (Honwana 2006: 108). According to these communities, the way to bring to an end these negative effects is not to explore the memories and help the afflicted to come to terms with them, but to appease the spirits. Once this appeasement is done, there is no reason to mentally revisit the past experiences. Talking about past events and the lingering memories is not only uncomfortable for the former fighter, but the act is regarded as ineffective as a means of dispelling the negative emotional or physical by-products of the conflict.

Those who return from war are seen by these communities as polluted and potential contaminators of society (Honwana 2006: 105; Baines 2007: 92–93). In societies where views of the world and social interaction are filtered through traditional conceptions of the influence of the spirit world, traumatic experiences such as witnessing or causing death can be seen to result in a harmful relationship between spirits and living persons. Randall Fegley, in discussing Mozambique, claims that 'local society emphasizes the importance of ancestral spirits and other supernatural forces in the causation and healing of mental health problems. Therefore, the reintegration of child soldiers must begin with community rituals' (Fegley 2008: 45). 'In Mozambique, community-based healing and reconciliation mechanisms dominated the rural areas in the absence of state-led strategies' (Honwana 2009: 66). Similar traditional cleansing rituals are used in Angola, Sierra Leone, and Uganda. In rural Angola, dreams are viewed as channels for communicating with spirits (Wessells 2006: 150). Individuals, then, often interpret their dreams not as bad memories with which the person must come to terms, but as angry spirits haunting the dreamer. A similar conception of dreams exists in northern Uganda where persons can be followed by the *cen*, the spirit, of someone deceased (Akello et al. 2012: 47). Cleansing the person of the spirit is necessary for him to live a blissful life. In traditional communities, healing and cleansing ceremonies can effectively indicate the birth of the former combatant as a new person. The aim of these rituals is 'to purge and purify the children of the contamination of war, death, and the sense of guilt and sin that can surround them and of the avenging spirits of those who may have been killed by the children' (Singer 2005: 203).

The cleansing rituals are as much for the benefit of the community as they are for the benefit of the individual former soldier. Once cleansed, the former soldier is in a condition to be regarded as a potential contributing member of the community. In this way, these rituals are reflective of the interconnection that community members feel with the spirit world and also the more community-based nature of the society and how an individual is viewed in relation to the relationships he or she has with others. 'The angry spirits of those killed during the war pose a threat to those who were directly involved in combat and, through them, to the families and communities they rejoin after demobilization' (Honwana 2006: 106). Therefore, in some societies, cleansing ceremonies alleviate concern in the community regarding the harm that can accompany the former combatant because of his or her former acts, and such ceremonies can also go a long way to instilling in the former soldiers the sense of security and trust that Western modes of healing aim to achieve. Honwana argues that these rituals 'present a holistic approach to health, addressing the physical, psychological, and social dimensions of the affliction in order to treat the whole person' and that healing all aspects is important because social imbalances also manifest themselves physically (Honwana 2006: 108).

Therefore, the unease with Western healing processes such as CBT and transitional justice processes that promote recollection and truth-telling is that they seemingly reflect more individualized conceptions of harm and responsibility and overlook the more community-centric concerns of some societies. Community-centric approaches to healing and to harms caused, it is argued, focus on restoring good connections between community members and between the community members and the spirit world. Western approaches to healing that ask individuals to relive and recount the pain that they endured in a healing session, or processes that aim to promote individual and social healing through accountability that asks individuals to relive and recount pain as a witness or perpetrator in a criminal trial or other means of accountability, run counter to approaches to healing that aim at putting the past aside to simply move forward (while working to minimize risk by ensuring that those who could be potential contaminators are stripped of their possible harmfulness). For these reasons, Western approaches to healing (individual psychological healing and also social healing through accountability) may not foster the desired results because they arguably do not address the real concerns or requirements of those who need the healing and they can be seen in the light of bothersome external imposition or even dangerous imposition that hampers the social healing of the community.

The problem with this argument against Western approaches is twofold. It is essential that the designers of transitional justice (including healing) processes are sensitive to these concerns and needs, but avoiding addressing past harms risks endangering the wellbeing of individuals and the broader society. First, arguably, the psychological and physical effects of trauma are universally realized and although the benefits of social acceptance can go a long way to relieving PTSD, there are aspects of the effects of trauma that require more specific attention and ongoing treatment. Careful assessment of psychological health is important. It may be the case that particular individuals who experienced trauma are able to arrive on the other side relatively unscathed,[2] or that healing ceremonies might be sufficiently meaningful to some individuals to counteract the symptoms of PTS. Other individuals, however, likely require additional intervention. There is also the risk that continued suffering of symptoms of PTS will be hidden by individuals who have undergone cleansing ceremonies for fear of the consequences of demonstrating that the ceremony did not work and bad spirits remain a danger. Attempts at suppression, as mentioned earlier, can encourage thoughts and symptoms. While cultural sensitivity should be heeded, especially since ignoring the customs and belief systems of a particular culture can be additionally upsetting and dangerous to the psyche of victims and the broader society, it should be heeded in the context of trying to truly understand the consequences of trauma on individual members of the society and offer healing rather than challenging individuals to suppress and forget, which might ultimately be more dangerous to individuals and to the broader society.

Second, accountability is generally seen as important to the dignity, self-respect, and satisfaction of victims. Whether it is a result of the interconnectedness of communities globally that allows the Western need of accountability to seep into other cultures, or whether traditional practices that are wholly non-retributive were never really sufficient to satisfy the needs of victims of violence, individual victims of atrocity do, in fact, need to feel that their victimizers are not coddled and that their harms are not disregarded and/or excused. This is true of victims in contemporary African communities and in Western contexts. These potential contaminators of society, as threatening as they and their danger may be, are also the real perpetrators of brutal harms that have already affected the society. And, as examined in the previous chapter, traditional African conceptions of justice did, in fact, apply individual judgement and responsibility, and identified individual and group victims as recipients of reparations. Like so many complex problems, dealing with the perpetrators of atrocity whose actions caused individual and communal harm from which individuals and the society must recover demands a sensitive and considered approach – one that represents the local understandings and customs and concerns as well as addresses the real pain of individual victims and that communicates respect for the law and for international human rights norms.

Honwana points out that often cleansing rituals are not used in isolation in contemporary times, even in rural settings where they are used often (Honwana 2006: 110). She argues that people from these traditions explore different options, including Western medicine, to find that which is most effective for healing particular ills. It is also true that people from such societies also have very strong views of personal harm and conviction that he or she who committed wrong against them might be forgiven but that it should not be demanded of the victim that he or she forgive and forget. Admittance and contrition precede forgiveness. Therefore, a similar exploration of different options and combinations of processes will likely be the most effective as a tool of justice and communication. Internationalized processes that respect a commitment to accountability must also find a way to respect local practices.

The experiences of children and youths in combat have profound consequences both for the individual young person and for the wider society to which he or she belongs. The violent acts to which the young person in some way contributed affects the victim, the society, and the perpetrator. So too will the effects of trauma that the perpetrator feels not only affect him or her but also influence the wider process of social rebuilding. Trauma, therefore, is not individual-centric. But, addressing individual symptoms and individual responsibility is important for the wellbeing of the society at large. And, the consideration of trauma must be meaningful both to the individuals affected and the broader circle of affected persons and post-conflict social development.

The risk of re-traumatization

As a result of their involvement and participation in fighting groups, many child soldiers were witnesses and/or perpetrators of intense physical violence that included murder, torture, rape, mutilation, bombings, forced displacement, and summary executions. Participation in, or witnessing of, such brutality can leave individuals, adult or child, with severe crises of identity and other psychological problems that demand, as argued, treatment so that these individuals can pursue happy and productive lives. There is a tricky balance that must be performed between pursuing justice for victims (including victim-perpetrators) and aiding in the healing (or minimally, not adding to the trauma) of community members. As discussed in previous chapters, the benefits of knowledge, acknowledgement, and accountability are considerable in a post-atrocity context. But, it is important that the pursuit of knowledge, acknowledgement, and accountability does not endanger individuals, including victims, witnesses, or victim-perpetrators. This section argues that the risk of re-traumatization, if appropriate care for the psychological wellbeing of individuals is taken, is not as significant as the risks of avoiding truth-telling and accountability.

The Western world, for the most part, has confidence in the ability of recounting past events, discussing emotions, generally sharing knowledge about what happened, why it happened, and how it affected different people to advance individual and social healing. Positive effects can result from story-telling in therapy, as discussed above, but also, arguably, the act of recounting past traumatic events (for a truth-commission or trial, for example) can itself be cathartic, and 'bringing one's voice to the public sphere is also a healing exercise' (Aptel and Ladisch 2011: 13). While such remembrance and story-telling can be very beneficial and therapeutic to many individuals, such acts can also have very negative effects on some. There is the risk that truth-telling, either as a means of investigation and accountability or as a tool for healing, can lead to the re-traumatization of individual participants – including former child soldiers and their victims.

The need for truth-telling exists for investigations and during any accountability process. And usually the act of truth-telling can be engaged in voluntarily. Victims or witnesses may be encouraged, or even pressured, to share their experiences through truth-telling, but it is rarely the case that they are compelled to do so. In regards to the perpetrator, however, participation in accountability processes is not usually entirely voluntary. Perpetrators may not be forced to recount stories, but their participation in the process and therefore their attendance during the examination of events of which they were a part is the minimal re-exposure that they can likely expect. Therefore, pursuit of accountability for harms committed by victim-perpetrator child soldiers seems to necessitate forcing victims who are also perpetrators to engage in truth-telling or at least a process of investigation and evaluation. The risk, then, is to further harm individuals who deserve special care.

Re-traumatization is a risk that results from the involvement in accountability mechanisms and from processes aimed at healing that do not provide sufficient support. Machel argues that 'in-depth clinical interviews intended to awaken the memories and feelings associated with a child's worst moments risk leaving the child in more severe pain and agitation than before, especially if the interviews are conducted without ongoing support for follow-up' (Machel 1996: 175). As mentioned, some studies have shown that sometimes it is the youths who deliberately avoid thinking about what happened during the conflict who show the fewest negative psychological impacts, and that this is true of individuals from Western societies as well as those from more communal societies (Jones 2002; Wessells 2006: 139). It is reasonable that the practice of exposing and reliving past traumatic experiences may be beneficial for some victims, but not for all, despite what was once believed about the near-universal benefits of truth-telling (Brounéus 2010). For some victims, the process of recounting these past episodes, especially for accountability purposes, can be disempowering and cause emotional shock, the risk of which designers of transitional justice processes must be aware and endeavour to avoid.

Avoidance of such re-traumatization that former victim-perpetrator child soldiers might be put in jeopardy of is desirable and necessary out of concern both for the individual former child soldiers, who are protected by human rights concerns and also rights exclusive to children, and also for the broader community. Children have the right to proper concern and support for their physical and psychological wellbeing. Some child soldiers experience severe mistreatment during the conflict and are able to rejoin civilian life relatively unscathed (Cortes and Buchanan 2007; Blattman 2009: 231; Klasen et al. 2010). One coping mechanism for some child soldiers is to disassociate oneself from the self that is the violent soldier. Demobilizing, as well as participating in a cleansing ritual, may be all that is needed for the former soldier to leave that old self behind and move forward. Dredging up the past and examining those acts as acts committed by the same self could be very traumatic in itself. Asking a former soldier who had disassociated in this way to revisit past experiences, especially when he or she is now in a different and safer environment, could possibly cause more psychological harm than did the original experiences.

Inflicting psychological harm on a victim-perpetrator before he or she is even deemed guilty of misconduct with no corresponding long-term benefit to the victim-perpetrator, his or her victims, or society, seems equivalent to a cruel and unwarranted punishment. And yet, arguably, the benefits of such accountability and truth-telling to victims and society are great. As argued in previous chapters, accountability is an important element of post-conflict social reconstruction and a means by which the broader community can communicate its respect for human rights and its concern for the victims of the conflict. Especially given our global history of punishment as a communicating act, accountability that admits the possibility of punishment is a significant statement that the harms inflicted are taken seriously by the society (Wilson 2001: 536). And so, the question becomes twofold: how do we avoid inflicting traumatization in a consequentialist 'the end justifies the means' manner and how do we accomplish a balancing act that aims to minimize re-traumatization and maximize the beneficial effects of accountability?

Significant to this evaluation and balancing act is the weighty point that not only is retelling of stories potentially re-traumatizing but so too is suppression. There can be great danger in attempts to push to the background, to ignore and suppress experiences and memories, and to avoid thinking of those experiences. In fact, attempts to suppress thoughts of past trauma generally fail to contain memories, emotions and other effects of PTS, are often counter-productive, often assuring the very state of mind the individual was trying to avoid, and have themselves been implicated in sustaining in persons who experienced the trauma depression, generalized anxiety disorder, specific phobia, and PTSD (Purdon 1999; Wenzlaff and Wegner 2000; Aikin et al. 2009).

And, just as individuals often suffer from recurrences of symptoms of PTS, so too societies struggle with the suppression of past injustices and victims who feel that their interests were not met by the society. Not appropriately addressing a legacy of past human rights abuses can risk a society's relapse into violence, disorder, and abuse. This points again to the great value of pursuing backward-looking elements of justice. The advantages of an accountability process, especially one that also seeks to promulgate broader truths about the conflict, to advancing social reconstruction and successful reintegration of those agents into communities, benefit former child soldiers as well as other members of the society, as long as risk of harm is carefully managed and there is adequate attention to the psychological welfare of participants and opportunities for counselling and healing.

Therefore, it is likely that successful social healing will develop from a process that acknowledges harms committed and explores the facts related to the harms, but that also incorporates or takes advantage of tools that address the psychological health care needs of victims and victim-perpetrator child soldiers who participate in the process (Allan 2000). Single-minded concentration on accountability or on trauma-healing will not make available the tools necessary for individuals and the society to address and get past events of the atrocity context. As Phil Clark stresses, suspected perpetrators and civilian survivors are justified in anticipating a painful process but the accountability process is necessary for long-term peace and can be a training ground for non-violent conflict resolution (Clark 2011: 232). The transitional justice process, though, must encompass a number of complementary instruments that aim to address different needs, including psychological, physical, and economic needs.

The psychology of the non-responsible child narrative

Judith Lewis Herman, in her study of trauma and recovery, explores the desire to suppress and forget. The desire to forget the past is strong with victims and the society who want to move beyond the past and its pain and ugliness; it is also strong with perpetrators who have very self-serving motivations to disregard the past and move forward into the future. 'In order to escape accountability for his crimes, the perpetrator does everything in his power to promote forgetting. Secrecy and silence are the perpetrator's first line of defense' (Herman 1997: 8). A victim narrative that can also include a perpetrator narrative, then, is enthusiastically suppressed to be overshadowed by the non-responsible narrative that denies any admittance of a responsible perpetrator narrative and distracts by allowing 'for the problem of responsibility in the war to be shifted onto the task of recovery itself' (Coundouriotis 2010: 192). Grace Akello also points out that ex-combatants, who were being treated and supported to regain a 'normal life' after the extreme events 'they were forced (or willingly) committed, found the paradigm palatable' because a redefinition of their sometimes ruthless acts of violence as 'acts performed under duress by traumatized innocent children' was a gateway to being accepted by family and kinship (Akello 2012).

This conception of non-responsible child soldiers seems so useful to the former child soldier that some adopt it at favourable times. It has been argued that former child soldiers, in their attempts to navigate the complex terrain of post-conflict civilian society, adopt a variety of personas. Of former young soldiers in Sierra Leone, Shepler explains:

> Among their friends and fellow soldiers, they try to maintain the status that being part of the fighting gives them. They wear combat clothes and sunglasses and brag about firing rocket propelled grenade launchers. With NGOs they adopt the persona of the traumatized innocent, usually requesting aid in furthering their education. With community members and in school they act like normal kids, never mentioning the past.
>
> (Shepler 2005: 198)

If the account that Shepler recounts is true, the multiple personas that accurately attach to former child soldiers add to the complication of social reintegration and social reconstruction, and the non-responsible child narrative can be notably useful as a tool for extracting basic necessities from the foreign aid agencies.

The non-responsible child narrative, however, unlike other blanket amnesty schemes, suggests a lack of genuine agency; it is a narrative that can help relegate the former child soldier to the voiceless periphery. A result of the narrative is that former child soldiers can be expected to 'become mute and return to their place at the bottom of the social hierarchy' (Shepler 2005: 205). Ignoring the past and asking former child soldiers to humble themselves without a voice does nothing to acknowledge the capacity of former child soldiers to act with agency, make choices, and impose their decisions on the world, or to demonstrate respect for the rights of the former child soldiers or the other victims of the violence. Therefore, by accepting this conception of childhood that denies children real agency, former child soldiers benefit in one respect but suffer a loss in another; there may be an added simplicity to their reintegration process, but they lose real agency and public esteem as morally relevant agents. And so, what may seem a conception of the former child soldier that is advantageous to the returnee and the society may, in fact, be less supportive of real social healing.

A concern of abandoning the non-responsible child narrative for one of responsible agency and the pursuit of accountability for those for whom it is appropriate is that 'an approach which locates responsibility purely at the local individual level will freeze identities' (Karekezi et al. 2004: 75), with those to whom responsibility for wrongdoing is attached firmly indentified as killer and criminal. The idea is that by categorizing all former child soldiers as non-responsible entities, the community avoids the possibility that groups of individuals will be stigmatized with a negative label, or that if such a label already exists that it will be reinforced and become entrenched. However, the non-responsible narrative paints all former child soldiers with the same brush, thereby stigmatizing them all equally in whatever way that child soldiers are stigmatized by the community. One possibility is that former child soldiers are all recognized equally as innocent of any wrongdoing by community members with whom they must interact. Alternatively, and as suggested in Chapter 2 the evidence supports this interpretation, they may also be all equally considered at fault. This narrative does not admit any means of distinguishing those who are truly innocent of wrongdoing from those who have something for which to answer.

Another fear of abandoning the non-responsible child narrative is the worry that some might interpret the possibility that some child soldiers bear responsibility for some of their acts to mean that they bear full responsibility, therefore attributing too much blame to child soldiers and absolving others of any responsibility. An additional fear is also that placing responsibility on the shoulders of child soldiers can result in the unacceptably harsh treatment of juveniles. Sometimes the response to appalling harm is treatment that does not accord to human rights standards, such as the treatment of suspected perpetrators of genocide in Rwanda after the summer of 1994 or the treatment of terrorist suspects held in Guantánamo Bay by the US. There is good reason to want to protect children from such treatment. On analysis, it seems that the solution, however, should not be invoking the non-responsible child narrative, but rather working to compel the enforcement of human rights standards and protection of juveniles when accountability is warranted.

Conclusion

A high priority in social recovery and reconstruction is the psychological wellbeing of the society's members. A society of individuals who collectively find difficulty in functioning at high levels due to challenges that accompany PTS will have a very difficult job of rebuilding and of existing as a peaceful, ordered, and flourishing society. Since they comprise the future of the society, it is especially important that the social recovery process concentrates on children and youths. In post-atrocity contexts, the aim is to bring individuals, social groups, and institutions to a place where they together

> develop a shared vision and sense of collective future (community); establish mutual ties and obligations across lines of social demarcation (interdependence); accept and actively promote individual rights, rule of law, tolerance of social diversity, and equality of opportunity (social justice); and adopt non-violent alternatives to conflict management (non-violence).
>
> (Longman et al. 2004: 207)

Part of doing this, as the argument developed in the past chapters claims, is acknowledging wrongs committed and taking seriously the bitterness of victims towards those who were the cause of their suffering. In the case of severe wrongdoing committed by child soldiers, the needs of all categories of victims (civilian victim, child soldier victim-perpetrator, and the broader community victimized by the conflict) must be balanced with the potential for additional harm caused by any post-atrocity accountability initiative and the harm that could result from suppression of the truth and avoidance of accountability. In the aftermath of disaster such as widespread violence, the priority is to foster resilience of communities and individuals and to avoid the likelihood of causing additional stress on individuals or on the enterprise of social reconstruction. Avoidance and suppression are not the solution.

Much of the effectiveness of both the traditional approaches and the Western approaches to psychological healing possibly comes from the social acceptance received and internalized by the former fighter and the assurance that he receives that he and those around him can move beyond past events. Derek Summerfield argues that a society's attitude about particular events, harms, and trauma shapes what individual victims feel has been done to them, the vocabulary they use to describe what happened and how it affects them, whether they seek help, and their expectations of recovery (Summerfield 2004). Part of the healing effect of cleansing ceremonies is that they are also 'a process of socialization in which the [individual] is incorporated and reconciled with the community' (Finnström 2008: 161). Children who have been traumatized tend to view the world as a frightening and dangerous place and they can act accordingly, with fear, helplessness, and misplaced anger. Improved community acceptance is associated with positive psychosocial adjustment (Sendabo 2004: 67; Betancourt et al. 2010). Part of healing from trauma is experiencing security, feeling sheltered and confident in the rules that dictate social interaction and behaviour.

In a study conducted in post-genocide Rwanda mentioned in the previous chapter, 63 per cent of respondents who were asked if it were better to try to forget what happened and move on answered that it was. However, of the same group, 96.8 per cent claimed that it was important that those who committed crimes during the war be prosecuted (Longman et al. 2004: 219). Interviewees in my own qualitative research conducted in post-conflict northern Uganda also voiced internal inconsistency in their statements regarding punishment and amnesty; amnesty for child soldier returnees was a good thing, but it was also felt that those who committed atrocities in the bush should be punished for their harmful acts (Fisher 2013). Conflicting attitudes and desires abound. Participants in the Rwanda study demonstrated the need for accountability to serve a number of purposes such as revealing the truth about what happened, exonerating the innocent and punishing the guilty, helping to rebuild the community, and recognizing the suffering of victims (Longman et al. 2004: 219). Accountability is a significant step in the social reconstruction project. Giving all members of society a voice to express their emotional and intellectual responses to their own experiences and ensuring that some accept responsibility when appropriate is essential to rebuilding a foundation on which respect for human rights, and moral and legal norms of non-violent conflict resolution can flourish. Bringing facts and emotions to light aids in the social and psychological healing of communities in the aftermath of widespread atrocity.

Accompanying post-atrocity accountability must be psychological health care. Support must be available for the long-term, it must be readily accessible, and a special effort to reach children who participated in accountability mechanisms, as victims, witnesses, or victim-perpetrators is critical. And, designers of transitional justice processes should endeavour to appreciate and apply local understandings of trauma and healing. As Machel argues, special consideration given to meaningful cultural practices will facilitate better healing of individuals and the community. 'Integrating modern knowledge of child development and child rights with traditional concepts and practices may take time, but it will result in more effective and sustainable ways to meet children's needs' (Machel 1996: para 179). It is also the most effective means of meeting the community's needs.

Practices of blanket impunity and non-individualized attention would, in most cases, be out of sync with the communicative aims and obligations of the post-conflict social reconstructive project. Suppression of facts, emotions, and discussions regarding agency and responsibility is not the answer. 'Equally as powerful as the desire to deny atrocities is the conviction that denial does not work... Remembering and telling the truth about terrible events are prerequisites both for the restoration of the social order and for the healing of individual victims' (Herman 1997: 1). What is important is that attempts at healing members of the community, especially civilian children and child soldiers, exist, and that past harmful actions should be addressed in such ways that produce understanding and appropriate accountability and foster the acceptance of perpetrators back into civilian society as clean and having repaid any debts that they might have incurred.

7
Accountability for Child Soldiers

Given the distinct category of perpetrator that is child soldiers and the expressive significance of the choice of accountability mechanisms employed, there are important questions about how closely mechanisms of accountability for persons under the age of 18 ought to resemble those used to address adult suspects. For the majority of child soldiers, motivations restricted to tactical considerations, and diminished capacity for high-level deliberation and full-picture appreciation for the consequences of their actions (due to conditions and the age of the participants) demand that their actions be addressed by mechanisms reflective of these conditions, likely mechanisms other than criminal trials. For the most part, even those who bear personal legal or moral responsibility do so to an extent greatly diminished by context. Mechanisms employed to address the acts of child soldiers must be sensitive to the fact that despite their causal responsibility many child soldiers can be excused their actions or that their personal responsibility is diminutive, and must be sensitive to the unique needs of youths who face processes of accountability.

This chapter argues that since the choice of accountability mechanism is expressively significant, special care to reflect the severity of the crimes of which individuals are suspected and the special characteristics of suspects, such as age, must be taken into consideration in the design. It demonstrates that the same communicative value and the same communication of values can be found in a range of mechanisms. Criminal prosecution that respects the rights of the child may be appropriate for some child soldiers, but not for most. As argued, the use of mechanisms of accountability other than criminal trials can be defended according to the same theoretical underpinning used to defend the use of criminal prosecution of atrocity crimes. Whereas criminal trials would inappropriately communicate harsher condemnation than would effectively be needed to communicate the right qualified understanding, disapproval, and/or blame regarding the majority of child soldiers, a process of modified mediation might be an alternative mechanism able to properly satisfy post-conflict needs for accountability and communicate the right sensitivities.

Defending accountability according to its expressive function means that accountability mechanisms must be evaluated according to their ability to suitably communicate the right values of the community. Different means of holding individuals to account and different means of penalty convey very different messages. Evaluating the right means of holding former child soldiers to account for the acts that they committed rests on the determination of what values and messages are to be communicated and to what extent these values and messages can be conveyed through accountability. The accountability mechanism must be both appropriately retributive and expressively significant. Transitional accountability is significant to the transitional process and the form that transitional accountability takes sets a foundation for the subsequent social order; the form and substance of transitional accountability makes a strong imprint on the emerging post-transition society. Therefore, understanding the expressive significance inherent in employing one accountability mechanism over another is as critical as acknowledging the importance of post-atrocity accountability.

The category of child soldier is not uniform. One subcategory would be those who genuinely can be said to bear no moral responsibility for any wrongdoing either because their participation in the fighting group was not significant enough to be considered material support or because they have defences that absolve them of responsibility beyond simple causal responsibility. Another subcategory includes those who are both causally responsible and can be judged as bearing some diminished moral and legal responsibility for harms that they inflicted on others. Operating within very harsh and restricted conditions, they exhibited tactical agency, made decisions, and acted on them to the severe detriment of others and to some extent their own personal benefit to safeguard their own wellbeing or standing in the fighting group. Another subcategory would include those child soldiers who delight in the tasks of killing and terrorizing, who went beyond what they were forced to do, and/or who took up leadership roles. A transitional society's choice of accountability mechanisms, and the system that binds them, must reflect these different categories and degrees of responsibility.

In the case of accountability for atrocity in which child soldiers participated, a balance must be struck between three necessary components: recognition of harms committed and the possibility that persons under the age of 18 bear responsibility for these harms, consideration of coercive conditions under which the average child soldier operates and acknowledgement that age affects the critical faculties of agents, and appreciation of the need for knowledge and justice for social reconstruction. This balance can likely be found in a combination of mechanisms that acknowledge different degrees of responsibility in the post-atrocity context. For those who fall within the last subcategory (agents who delight, who pursue death and terror of their own initiative, who take leadership roles), and whose age was above a reasonable minimum age for criminal responsibility at the time that the crimes were committed, a model of criminal trial may be suitable. For others, their participation in other mechanisms is more appropriate. For all categories, any mechanisms employed must be child-sensitive and work to promote the wellbeing of children (Aptel and Ladisch 2011).

The harsh condemnation expressed by criminal accountability

Criminal trials alone, themselves communicative, should not be used to address the majority of wrongdoing in contexts in which child soldiers were agents of atrocity, especially when they were forced to commit terrible acts as a part of collective wrongdoing. Before judgement, sentencing, or punishment, criminal trials express a particular level of concern regarding the act(s) committed and condemnation for the responsible agents of that harm. Criminal trials express the existence of promulgated laws and a formal system that operates to uphold them. Each criminal trial expresses the reasonable suspicion that the individual on trial has violated the laws of the society (despite the presumption that he or she is innocent until the completion of the judgement portion of the trial). The job of criminal law is to decide what should be punished by the state, and not merely what the state may disapprove of (Wall 2006: 736). The particular expressive significance of criminal trials is severe condemnation of anti-social behaviour that violates law. Criminal trials establish that a criminal act has been committed by proving that the accused committed the prohibited act and that the accused had the necessary *mens rea*. An indictment and commencement of a criminal trial assumes sufficient evidence to support reasonable suspicion that both the accused commission of the crime and *mens rea* exist.

For child soldiers for whom such assumptions can be made, accountability can be processed through an international(ized) juvenile criminal justice system for atrocity crimes or a war crimes unit of the national youth criminal justice system already in place. There are some examples of such processes, including one found in Sierra Leone's approach to post-conflict justice. In Sierra Leone there was a special youth system created to address the crimes of child soldiers.

> The strategy recently adopted in Sierra Leone toward child soldier perpetrators seems the one best suited both to serve the interests of the victims and promote long-term stability and societal recovery. While the statute of the special court does allow for the prosecution of those between the ages of fifteen and eighteen, the prosecutor has not taken such action yet, instead focusing his efforts on the adult leaders. Children implicated in particularly heinous crimes are given hearings in special closed juvenile chambers (to keep their identity secret) as well as psychological counseling and other forms of assistance. They are not sentenced to prison with adult perpetrators, but placed in special custody, rehabilitation/demobilization programs, and foster care. This response seems to best recognize the unique war crime that is child soldiering, where the perpetrators are also the victims.
>
> (Singer 2005: 155)

Some child soldiers do in fact, despite their age and situation, commit serious crimes that could qualify as genocide, war crimes, and crimes against humanity (Manirakiza 2009: 722). As examined in Chapter 2, international law does not prohibit the prosecution of persons under the age of 18. International agreements on the protection of children express as much (Paris Principles: Articles 3.6–3.7, 3.9 and 8.7–8.11), and statutes of international and hybrid criminal tribunals also provide for the possibility of prosecuting juveniles, such as the Special Court for Sierra Leone (SCSL) which does so expressly and the ICTY and ICTR which are silent regarding the age of perpetrators. In cases in which an adolescent child soldier was in control of his actions, was a leader, and was not forced to commit the atrocities, not holding the child accountable would arguably deny justice to victims and could be communicatively detrimental to the community and to the particular individual suspected of wrongdoing. Chapters 2 and 5 explored the desires of victims of atrocity for prosecutions of perpetrators, even those who had not reached the age of 18. In some cases, as Amnesty

International argues, 'child soldiers must be held accountable for their actions' (Amnesty International 2000: 2).

Naturally, a system of juvenile criminal justice for atrocity crimes would need to be established consistent with international standards of fair trials, offering the same rights as anyone charged with the commission of a war crime, crime against humanity, or genocide. It must also offer special protection for juvenile suspects. Any accountability mechanism that aims to address the acts of child soldiers must uphold human rights standards and accord with the rights of the child as established through international agreements and principles (CRC; Paris Principles). Since situations in which child soldiers contribute to human rights abuses are often ones in which child soldiers are forcibly recruited to participate, the process of accountability employed should also reflect this fact, allowing for the defence of duress. Those who were threatened should be able to argue that they acted under duress, either as a defence (if the situation warrants it) or in mitigation of penalty (Amnesty International 2000: 2).

International criminal law is the result of effort on the part of the international community 'to eliminate the persistent climate of impunity which has so often sheltered those who commit serious international crimes' (Robinson 2003: 482). International criminal law generally and particularly international tribunals, such as the ICC, specifically claim jurisdiction over the most serious crimes of concern to the international community as a whole that must not go unpunished (Rome Statute: Preamble), with the practical effect of the court being that it investigates and prosecutes those individuals most responsible for mass atrocity. Criminal prosecutions should not be reserved only for the architects of atrocity, but there should exist within international and national criminal justice systems a significant distinction between the prosecutions of architects and lesser perpetrators of atrocity.[1] For young perpetrators of atrocity, especially those who were likely subjected to forceful recruitment, harsh treatment, and tactics of terror, a further distinction must be made and must be reflected from the outset by the nature of the process of accountability. International criminal tribunals or domestic trials of atrocity crimes themselves express the gravity of the criminal act(s) that are investigated and the severity of the condemnation that will follow a judgement of guilty.

In some cases it is desirable for the enterprise of post-atrocity social reconstruction that juveniles are brought to account before criminal proceedings. Special care for the protection of young defendants must be taken, but the need for such care does not seem an obstacle to establishing a special justice system to address atrocity crimes committed by juveniles. However, the majority of child soldier perpetrators of atrocity do not warrant criminal prosecution and, therefore, other options for the pursuit of post-atrocity accountability must be available. For child perpetrators, there is an inherent presumption that the *mens rea* element is affected by their age, and children's rights demand that persons under the age of 18 be protected from the full weight of judicial condemnation (Paris Principles: Article 3.6–3.7). Children may not always lack the capacity to commit atrocity crimes, but the commission of criminal acts by the average child soldier would generally require a form of accountability that expresses reduced condemnation. Youths who do, in fact, intentionally commit or order grave violations of international criminal law with malice, fully understanding the consequences of their actions, may be dealt with by a criminal justice system, but should be afforded appropriate protections for youthful defendants.

Despite the fact that acts of atrocity committed by some child soldiers warrant such trials, according to juvenile justice standards, the motivations and capacity of many of the young perpetrators demand that their responsibility for harms be assessed and addressed through different means. It would seem a severe and unwarranted condemnation of many of the child soldier perpetrators if the accountability mechanism used to address their actions suggested that they were in violation of the highest breaches of the community's moral and legal codes. The conditions of their cases demand a more sensitive and nuanced approach. The severe methods of criminal justice are restricted and leave little means of justly dealing with responsibility other than by judging actions justified or excused or by harshly penalizing them as criminal. The unique conditions of child soldiers as perpetrators of harm and the context and goals of post-atrocity reconstruction mean that accountability must promote justice by addressing wrongs committed and precisely isolate responsibility, and yet not re-victimize those who have already been hurt by the conflict. It must not too harshly condemn and penalize those who have diminished culpability and ought not worsen the stigmatization of the group of former child soldiers to the detriment of their ability to reintegrate. A wider and more nuanced range of approaches to assessment and means for perpetrators to accept and make amends for responsibility beyond criminal trials ought to be available to properly reflect the right balance of competing priorities and values. While the focus and the priority of post-atrocity accountability should be on addressing the crimes of the architects of atrocity, and in regards to child soldiering on those who recruit children to participate in armed conflict, combating impunity and respecting the rights of victims should mean that the specific brutal human rights violations committed by young persons must not be overlooked. Given the age and features regarding their recruitment, most child soldiers and their acts should be addressed in a distinct manner that itself helps to facilitate understanding of the difference between atrocity leaders, adult perpetrators, and dissimilar youths who commit atrocity crimes.

Mediation as accountability

There are alternative accountability mechanisms available within the fields of transitional justice and domestic criminal justice that are becoming normalized and could help meet accountability and social reconstruction needs in post-conflict contexts. Decisions about the right mechanisms for particular contexts should come from consultation with children as well as adults. Children should be actively involved in designing, as well as participating in, transitional justice policies and mechanisms. Creativity is needed for devising context-specific solutions. For most potentially responsible juveniles a unique mechanism of accountability is likely necessary. It must be capable of expressive significance, able to communicate the right level of blame, and address the complexity of the victim-perpetrator status. It must allow responsible agents the opportunity to account for their actions, communicate the right relevant values, and help with healing and social reconstruction.

Dialogue is a good basis from which to satisfy these aims and a community-based system of modified mediation could be the right answer, satisfying the needs for accountability and information and reflecting the complex nature of actors and responsibility in this post-conflict context. Mediation is an act of social exchange (Shnabel and Nadler 2008). In a context where there is no easy dichotomy of victims and perpetrators, mediation can emphasize the potential victimization of multiple parties participating in the process and the need for understanding by the different parties.

Mediation, usually identified as a process of restorative justice, can play a significant role in retributive criminal and civil justice systems. Victim-offender mediation has been used to respond to criminal and civil matters in North America since the 1970s (Umbreit et al. 2004). It promotes offender accountability as well as a meaningful role for victims. 'Specifically, victim offender dialogues were designed to hold offenders accountable to the person they harmed and to give victims a voice and an opportunity to have their needs met' (Amstutz

2009: 7). This process is particularly relevant to the child soldier context because of the unique position of victim-perpetrator held by most child soldiers. A system of modified mediation could itself take many forms including one similar to neo-traditional mechanisms of justice, such as those advocated by some in northern Uganda to deal with all members of the LRA. This particular form will be explored later in this section. Modified to incorporate procedural fairness and compliance with reasonable retributive justice outcomes, neo-traditional mechanisms of justice could satisfy post-atrocity accountability needs in regards to certain perpetrators. To apply to child soldiers, precautions must be taken to ensure that this process also conforms to juvenile justice standards and the rights of the child.

Mediation is a process of conflict resolution and accountability. Together the participants of the mediation process investigate what happened, explore the circumstances that caused the offender to commit the harmful act, examine how people have been affected by the actions, and investigate what can be done to help repair or pay back the harm that was suffered. Mediation of this form (victim-offender mediation) has for the most part, 'been applied to lesser offenses within the criminal justice system, however, successful work has been done with cases of a more serious, violent nature, such as rape, armed robbery, car-jacking and even families of homicide victims' (Stauffer and Hamber 1996). In providing a safe place in which the dialogue can be constructive by offering a third-party who helps by guiding, interpreting, and channelling the intensity of emotions and the sensitivity of the information, mediation allows victims and perpetrators to engage in dialogue so that parties to the harm can understand the damage and move beyond the past.

Mediation emphasizes the importance of holding offenders directly accountable to the people they violate; it can lead to a greater sense of community safety through community building and through victims interacting with offenders to ascertain that the actions were not representative of a bad character (Umbreit 2001: 1). Victims and perpetrators together, through dialogue, settle on an account of events and on what is needed and fair to right the wrong as far as possible. As the child soldiers are generally victims as well as possible perpetrators, with reasonable grievances against the society and the particular group that recruited them, useful is a dialogue that aims to air all concerns, complaints, and points of view to bring about emotional release, feelings of being heard and respected, redress, and conciliation (Baines 2009: 186–187). Those who study victimization have identified as a basic need of victims to know what happened and why (Achilles and Zehr 2001: 89) and to know that what happened to them was 'wrong' and that their emotions are legitimate (Stauffer and Hamber 1996; Brudholm 2006). A community-instituted system that facilitates dialogue between child soldiers and victims allows both groups to explore the wrongs they suffered and the responsibility borne.

As mentioned earlier in this book, traditional justice has been pushed to the forefront of debate, discourse, and policy in many societies, especially African societies, transitioning from conflict to peace. A process of mediation, especially one that incorporates or gives space for traditional healing and reintegration ceremonies, can easily combine traditional and Western formal accountability and documentation elements. Another way to look at the suggestions of this chapter could be to view this mediation process as a neo-traditional form of cultural processes of justice and reconciliation, adapted to incorporate and satisfy accountability and documentation. Some traditional mechanisms do in fact feature aspects similar to mediation, and the Ugandan Acholi tradition of Mato Oput is one. Indeed, the Mato Oput Project of Gulu University in northern Uganda speaks of the traditional process of Mato Oput as a mediated process (Mato Oput Project 2009). Traditional ceremonies must be evaluated for their reconciliatory effect. Popular cleansing rituals, despite having their role to play once the process of accountability is finalized, 'are unlikely to provide survivors with a meaningful experience because they tend to emphasize individual cleansing rather than a two-way process of reconciliation, justice, or relationship-building' (Mato Oput Project 2009: 6). Mato Oput, as described in Chapter 5, is a traditional reconciliation process that holds individuals responsible, asks them to account for their actions to their victims, and provide compensation before participating in a reconciliation ritual to put the animosity between the parties behind them.

Mato Oput, like other mediation processes, consists of negotiation between parties to a conflict, although at a distance. In Mato Oput, unlike other mediation processes, the parties do not generally communicate directly with each other. Rather, they communicate through a third-party neutral and do not at all engage in face-to-face dialogue until the price of compensation is settled. In Mato Oput, as with most other mediation processes, participation is voluntary. And so is the acceptance of the outcome. The outcome of the mediation, or Mato Oput, is in the hands of the parties to the conflict and while the mediation might help to guide the parties to a resolution acceptable to both sides, the parties must in the end own the process and the outcome. Nevertheless, under the structured guidance of the right mediators and procedures, a modified mediation/neo-traditional mechanism of justice can appropriately explore and express the right level of personal responsibility for harms committed and help parties settle on appropriate means of restitution and/or retribution.

There is a useful balance that can, and should, be struck between local traditions and imposed judicial procedures. Traditional practices often have an important relevance to transitioning societies, thereby increasing the likelihood of the meaningfulness of processes (Carlson and Mazurana 2010: 288). On the other hand, as David Kaulemu argues, sometimes talking about traditions 'creates a blind spot about the usefulness of what is being conserved' (Kaulemu 2012: 83). By critically examining the aspirations of transitional justice and the ability of traditional mechanisms to meet these aspirations, choices can be made about what elements of traditions should be retained and which should be revised so as not 'to miss real opportunities and useful cultural and traditional tools that could help transform or solve' conflicts (Kaulemu 2012: 87). In some cases, traditional elements are no longer relevant or possible in modern or unique circumstances (Baines 2007: 93; Komakech 2012: 68). A modified mediation/ neo-traditional form of accountability and reconciliation should ensure dialogue, a formal method of recording an agreed-upon narrative of the facts, and some means of deliberating on penalty and restitution. It must also ensure that there are formal protections for participants similar to those offered participants in legal cases.

Mato Oput is a good example of many traditional practices that bear some similarity to Western practices and can offer familiarity to local populations, quiet concerns of Western imperialism, and tender important elements of accountability. An interesting element of Mato Oput is the negotiation that takes place to reach 'a common understanding or account of the history' (Mato Oput Project 2009: 14). In this way, informal reporting exists in this traditional practice. Formal documentation of this account can be made, but often these records remain only with the clan chief who presides over the ceremony.[2] The ceremony of Mato Oput can vary between clans, but the essential elements of negotiation, compensation, and reconciliation are always present (Baines 2005). Some adaptation that retains at least two of these features – negotiation, compensation/restitution/retribution– and at least tries for the latter, seems like an appropriate approach to post-atrocity accountability for those who do not bear sufficient guilt for their actions to necessitate criminal prosecution, but who do in fact likely bear some responsibility for which victims and society are owed some accountability.

A modified mediation process must be clear about its goals and limitations; there can be no requirement that the process result in reconciliation or that victims must forgive. A lack of cool hearts was cited by the Mato Oput Project as a major challenge to the use of Mato Oput.

> This was with respect to the victim and the perpetrator; the victim's clan must be willing to forgive, and the perpetrator must admit to their offenses in order for mato oput to occur. Many participants felt that victim's clans might not be ready to participate in mato oput in light of the freshness of atrocities, even if the perpetrator was willing to confess.
>
> (Mato Oput Project 2009: 18)

A modified mediation process, or neo-traditional process, might be more effective as a mechanism of accountability, and one step in the social reconstruction venture, if the victim were not required to be ready to forgive at the onset of the process. It may be unjust to demand that they must (Brudholm 2006).

A modified mediation process might even be able to overcome some of the challenges that attempts to employ traditional reconciliation processes would face. Arguments that support the use of traditional mechanisms as a means to draw from meaningful traditions of a people and to avoid impositions of Western cultures often oversimplify the universality of culture in post-conflict contexts. Particular traditional mechanisms often lack universal appeal and relevance within a single post-conflict context when the violence was widespread. The specific traditional means by which to pursue accountability can differ between groups, and the particularities some culture or tribe is familiar with may not resonate with another. In fact, this is the case in Uganda where local traditional conflict resolution can be used in the villages, but Western-style systems of criminal justice are employed in the cities in which members of disparate ethnic backgrounds and diverse practices converge. As Kristopher Carlson and Dyan Mazurana explain it in regards to the population of northern Uganda, 'The Lango, Madi and Iteso all also have their own systems of accountability. It is unclear to what extent, if any, these groups would be willing to accept Acholi rituals to achieve accountability and reconciliation' (Carlson and Mazurana 2010: 257). A modified mediation or neo-traditional process could theoretically solve problems of relevance by incorporating similarities between different systems, including Western formalism, but not force any groups to adopt the mechanisms of another cultural group.

A modified mediation process of this sort, to be as meaningful as possible, should be developed through a collaborative effort between local actors (including children) and international advisors. It should incorporate some of the significant elements of the traditional reconciliation processes, ensuring that accountability and documentation are adhered to, and feature modifications that mitigate some of the challenges of inclusion, need for forgiveness, and need for material compensation of the traditional processes. Restitution of some sort, including community service or service to particular victims, could be the outcome of the mediation process when it finds particular individuals warrant it, with the understanding that restitution does not make up for the loss the victim sustained but rather is symbolic.

A drawback to this proposal, of course, would include any resistance to the idea of changing or updating traditional rituals or replacing them with something similar but not the same. One argument is that doing so 'would be considered an insult to...culture and ancestral custom' (Carlson and Mazurana 2010: 259). Another challenge to the modified mediation proposal is the reluctance of individuals to admit their harmful acts and engage voluntarily in mediation with victims or representatives of victims. There is the associated challenge of acts of harm being known without knowledge of victims, or known acts without known perpetrators. There are victims for whom establishing the identity of the individual(s) who harmed them could be impossible. 'Less commonly, there are also scenarios in which a perpetrator comes forward and confesses to his crimes, but does not know who the victim(s) of his offenses are' (Mato Oput Project 2009: 19). It can be hoped that investigation and the use of documentation produced by projects like that of the Justice and Reconciliation Project in northern Uganda and from previous mediation processes could alleviate some of these tensions. However, investigation will likely not be able to answer all questions. In some cases, stand-in representatives for victims might be needed to accomplish the task. Victims whose perpetrators cannot be identified might be paired with perpetrators whose victims are unknown so that, in a sense, there is a resolution and an opportunity for important dialogue, including acknowledgement of the awful circumstances under which terrible acts were committed.

Modified mediation should be able to address both harms perpetrated by child soldiers and grievances that child soldiers have against those who perpetrated against them and the community that failed to protect them. By not maintaining the strict adversarial nature of criminal prosecutions, there is more room for modified mediation processes to explore multiple aspects of harm committed and suffered. In the aftermath of mass atrocity, modified mediation should also be able to examine the social pressure to conform to the atrocity environment and the process should be able to reinforce the values of the ordered and peaceful community.

Another important balance to ensure is that the local needs and local ownership of the process are balanced with objectivity, consistency (beyond any particular small village), and a sense of a broader systemic arrangement. Any system adopted by a post-conflict environment to deal with child soldiers should involve the whole country for consistency and ensure that the system is a representation of the community by the state or state-representing adjudicator. There could be an accountability process in every village or neighbourhood, at least all that have been affected by the conflict, with locally elected judges or third-party neutrals and mandatory participation by the local population and demobilized child soldiers suspected of having participated in violations.

Such an accountability process has two outcomes; it can act as a form of truth-telling that brings to light information about what happened, and it can act as a tool of social healing that brings individuals in conflict together to discuss the experiences and emotions of each and that out of respect for both the victim and perpetrator explores responsibility with the aim that relationships will improve with understanding and penalization when appropriate. Naturally, truth-telling is not a positive experience for all participants. It may not be immediately beneficial to some former child soldiers or to civilian victims who participate, but the process and the improved understanding that results from the process is valuable for broader social reconstruction and long-term healing of victims, victim-perpetrators, and the society. Ideally, 'transitional justice processes should promote accountability while fostering learning, self-respect and dignity' (Machel 2010: xii). Creativity can ensure that appropriate and feasible outcomes are reached. Out of the individual mediation sessions that bring together individual perpetrators and victims in dialogue will likely arise the need for more comprehensive investigation or reporting of the community's wrongdoing and/or inability to protect its most vulnerable citizens.

Truth commissions

Truth commissions also allow victims and perpetrators to voice their stories and feelings; they collect for the community these stories in a report and offer recommendations about what policies can be used to move forward, to address past harms, and to ensure that similar atrocities do not happen again (du Toit 2000; Rotberg 2000). Truth commissions have become a standard option used by transitional societies as a means to address a legacy of mass violations of human rights (Hayner 2011). For example, the Sierra Leone Truth and Reconciliation Commission was mandated to 'create an impartial historical record of violations and abuses of human rights and international humanitarian law ...; to address impunity, to respond to the needs of the victims, to promote healing and reconciliation and to prevent a repetition of the violations and abuses suffered' (Truth and Reconciliation Commission Act 2000: section 6(1)).

Truth commissions can circumvent genuine accountability when they are paired with general amnesties, and can threaten the aims of transitional justice (Smith 2010: 52–53); or they can help meet goals of accountability when they admit the possibility of individual penalty when appropriate. Even when they are paired with amnesty and can thwart significant individual accountability, it is possible for truth commissions to be effective in the pursuit of collective accountability by examining, judging, condemning, and/or censuring groups or institutions. Recommendations could include a proposal for memorialization, lustration policies, and the use of accountability mechanisms if they have not already been employed. A truth commission offers the opportunity for a community to explore crimes committed by members of the fighting force and also the responsibility that the community had to children to protect them from being recruited into combat.

A truth commission is capable of examining, evaluating, and (when necessary) condemning group behaviour, institutions, policies, and governing structures, as was argued was necessary in Chapter 4. Besides holding individuals responsible for their personal acts, it is important to the enterprise of transitional justice and social reconstruction that institutions, policies, and governing structures are evaluated and overhauled when necessary. While individuals contribute to the wrongdoing, there is a sense in which collective action is distinct from and can be worse than the actions of individual contributors and such structures must be addressed. The appeal of truth commissions is their 'ability to offer a broader historical perspective' (Teitel 2003: 79). Attributing responsibility to a collective may not be reducible to attributing blame to individual members of that group. There are characteristics of the structure of collectives that make them capable of actions that would be unavailable to individuals. Collectives ought to be held responsible for the outcome of policies and actions exercised by the group because their own internal structures lead individual members to act as they would not have absent their membership or roles in the collective (Harbour 2003: 78). A collective is something distinct from a simple aggregate of its members. As May explains them, collectives are 'social groups' as 'individuals *in relationships*' (May 1987: 9 emphasis original). He argues that although collectives are nothing more than their parts, 'those parts are not merely people but the structures and relationships among those people as well' (May 1987: 14). And, through the prosecution of individuals, it is unlikely that the right examination and expression of judgement of structures and policies can be appropriately engaged. A truth commission can examine the roles of entire sectors of a society in enabling and failing to prevent mass violence (Minow 2000: 239). Transitional justice that examines responsibility beyond individuals can explore interconnecting levels of responsibility which led to the victimization of children and their victims (Baines 2009: 183).

For armies comprised overwhelmingly of young perpetrators who were either abducted or coerced into wrongdoing, some without the maturity to engage in advanced decision-making such as the high-level moral evaluation of the options available to them, the structures are self-perpetuating and sustain the violence. These groups are good examples of collectives that act as a unitary group although the decisions do not reflect the desires or intentions of all individual members detached from their roles within the group. The group itself grows or maintains itself by forceful recruitment (or by accepting volunteers whose voluntariness is questionable), and sustains membership and dependability through a policy of fear; members act in ways they would not absent their membership in the group (because of identification with the group or because of fear), committing violent acts against the perceived enemy of the group and against other members of the group to ensure their membership, constancy, and effectiveness in meeting the group's goals. Young perpetrators recruited into the armed forces or militia group are generally, in addition to committing violent acts against the enemy, forced to commit against other recruits violent acts to compel obedience and loyalty to the group (Honwana 2006: 50). Some are forced to aggressively recruit others and to inflict corporal punishment to penalize betrayal of the group (Wessells and Kostelny 2009: 113). Some examination and condemnation of the group's activities in total is required.

Overlooking the group and its membership entirely for the prosecution of the highest level of leadership disregards the fact that without the involvement of the recruits much of the brutality would not occur. It also discounts the fact that many of these soldiers adapt and conform to their new environment, accept and excel at their functions within the group, often becoming over time fervent participants (Wessells 2006: 57–58, 65). It problematically insinuates that youth forces are odd entities to which no responsibility can or should attach beyond that ascribed to the few top commanders.

We need, then, mechanisms of justice that can examine, evaluate, and (when necessary) condemn group behaviour, institutions, policies, and governing structures. The right mechanism would communicate condemnation of harmful collective activity, group structures, and the foundation from which such a group was able to spring. And, as declared above, it would communicate the right values of equality of persons under a just regime, human rights, and reasonable expectations of members of the community towards their neighbours. Violations of human rights committed by way of group policy require a response that addresses multiple agents, the collective and its policies and governing structures. Truth commissions can be useful as a means of publically examining group policy and expressing condemnation of institutions, policies, or governing structures; they can be the impetus for necessary changes or mark stark divisions in social norms.

Children have participated in the work of truth commissions in Sierra Leone and Liberia. As with other transitional justice mechanisms, the involvement of children in truth commissions must be carefully monitored for the protection of the children. There should be agents available to young participants to ensure that they understand the procedures and to guarantee that the rights of the child and the best interests of the child are adhered to. As Saudamini Siegrist shows by examining the decisions taken by the Truth and Reconciliation Commission(s) (TRCs) in South Africa and Sierra Leone, assessments of the best interests of the child can lead to different outcomes (Siegrist 2010: 17–19). With the South African TRC, the decision was made in 1996 to exclude children from the process to protect them from exposure to public and political glare. The conventional wisdom of five years later, however, led to the conclusion that the involvement of children in the Sierra Leonean TRC was essential. Specific safeguards should be established to protect children and to comply with human rights, children's rights, and juvenile justice standards. Meeting recognized standards, however, does not deny all children particular roles in transitional justice accountability and non-accountability mechanisms.

In the case of a policy of amnesty

Some communities in conflict offer blanket amnesties in order to facilitate an end to the violence, and some post-conflict communities do so with an aim that the peace is stable and will not be sacrificed to a return to violence by those who had put down their weapons. When there is a policy of amnesty, there is no significant accountability process for the atrocity leaders or other responsible adult perpetrators, including those who recruited and abused child soldiers. Under such conditions it would seem problematic to recommend that a subcategory of lesser perpetrators, child soldiers, undertake a process of accountability for their actions and take responsibility when appropriate. Would it be unfair to ask former child soldiers to account for their actions when no significant prosecution of those most responsible is possible?

Under policies of blanket amnesty, there is no means for formal accountability that leads to punishment by the state. In many cases, there is no accountability for any participation in the conflict – neither adults nor child soldiers are required to provide accounts of their actions, accept responsibility when appropriate, report the results of their actions, or accept penalty when appropriate. This is true of northern Uganda. Although there are ICC indictments for the top four LRA leaders (after Raska Lukwiya was declared deceased in 2006), there is no robust system (despite the existence of the ineffectual International Crimes Division (ICD) of Uganda's High Court) to hold atrocity leaders or other perpetrators of war crimes or crimes against humanity criminally accountable at a national level in Uganda. And, although civil society has called for a truth commission, there is no political will to support such an endeavour (Makumbi and Eriku 2011).

In 2000, Uganda enacted an Amnesty Act that provided blanket amnesty for any Ugandan 'involved in acts of a war-like nature' (Amnesty Act 2000), including LRA members who might otherwise be charged with war crimes, crimes against humanity, and/or gross violations of human rights. Uganda's Amnesty Act was written very broadly. It applied to just about any fighter – captured, surrendered, or 'rescued' – who 'renounces and abandons involvement in the war or armed rebellion' (Amnesty Act 2000). Much of Ugandan civil society supported the Amnesty Act as a means to entice fighters back home

(Baines 2003: 7; Branch 2007: 184). With hope to end the conflict, the Act was renewed between 2000 and May 2012, when it was quietly allowed to expire (Schenkel 2012). There is, however, continued debate as to whether it is still relevant. Even now, as there are seemingly no immediate security concerns, the Amnesty Act is still regarded as a peaceful means of bringing out of the bush those who are still fighting in neighbouring regions. However, as one civil society member described the situation, it is 'like forgiveness motivated by intimidation'.[3] Even now there is some fear that, if provoked, the LRA can make a revival and return.

Uganda, with this Amnesty Act, has seemingly tied it own hands in the options it has in terms of dealing with the perpetrators of atrocity. This is apparent from its dealings with Thomas Kwoyelo and Caesar Achellam, both considered within the top five of the leadership of the LRA at the time that each was taken into custody by the Ugandan Army (UPDF), in 2009 and 2012, respectively.

When the Amnesty Act was in force, there was a provision, an amendment to the Amnesty Act added in 2006, that allowed Uganda's Minister of Internal Affairs to prohibit certain individuals from being granted amnesty. Verbatim, it reads, 'a person shall not be eligible for grant of amnesty if he or she is declared not eligible by the Minister by statutory instrument made with the approval of Parliament' (Amnesty Act 2000: Section 2A). Until the date the Amnesty Act was allowed to expire, this provision had not been employed. Written into the Act were no further guidelines as to how, why, or on what timeline, amnesty could be denied. Since the Act has expired, there is serious debate about what this means for accountability in Uganda. Whether Kwoyelo or Achellam face criminal justice in Uganda is significant, but does not erase the amnesty granted many other commander perpetrators of atrocity. It is important to note here that both Kwoyelo and Achellam, along with Dominic Ongwen who is one of the leaders indicted by the ICC, are reported to have been originally recruited into the LRA as abducted child soldiers.

In 2009, Thomas Kwoyelo was captured by the UPDF. He applied for amnesty under the Act, his application was denied, and he was put on trial by the Ugandan government. Kwoyelo 'was the first LRA commander to face trial in Uganda's special war crimes court' (BBC 2011). He was subsequently given amnesty according to the provisions of Uganda's Amnesty Act, but not released and he remains, at the time of writing, in custody in Uganda. In May 2012, the UPDF announced that it had in custody Caesar Achellam, and questions began to sprout as to what fate awaits this LRA commander allegedly responsible for some of the most egregious abuses against children and civilians. Should he be prosecuted in a court of law or granted amnesty and allowed to rejoin civilian life?

Neither of these two alleged top LRA commanders was among the list of LRA leaders indicted by the ICC. It would seem that given the enactment of the Amnesty Act, Uganda has limited options in terms of how it can address the alleged crimes of Achellam. Achellam, it would seem, should be granted amnesty. Despite its near-blanket qualities, the Amnesty Act does allow for some individuals to possibly be held accountable under domestic jurisdiction. For instance, under the Amnesty Act, amnesty is a one-time deal. Achellam would not be eligible for amnesty if he had already been granted amnesty but then returned to fighting – there is no indication that this is the case. There is also the aforementioned provision that allows Uganda's Minister of Internal Affairs to prohibit certain individuals from being granted amnesty. Despite the fact that Achellam might seem to warrant investigation and possible prosecution as one of the leaders of the LRA, it seems unreasonable given Uganda's history of amnesty that he be put on trial. This is true especially since it was ruled in 2011 that Thomas Kwoyelo was eligible to be granted amnesty (Kisige 2012).

This makes an interesting situation for a proposal that child soldiers ought to participate in some accountability process. How does it make sense to hold child soldiers accountable when the highest ranking commanders of the force that abducted them and compelled them to commit their brutal acts avoid criminal trials? The answer naturally is that child soldiers should not be expected to accord to stricter policies of justice than adults. If amnesty is granted so that adult perpetrators avoid mechanisms of criminal justice, then so too should persons under the age of 18. Amnesty, however, does not preclude all forms of accountability. As Uganda's Amnesty Act states, amnesty 'means a pardon, forgiveness, exemption or discharge from criminal prosecution or other form of punishment by the State' (Amnesty Act 2000: I (2)). It does not preclude facilitated dialogue. It might not even preclude negotiated penalties; in communities in northern Uganda, individuals who were granted amnesty can participate in Mato Oput and provide restitution to victims of their acts. In cases in which amnesty is granted, mediation that reflects neo-traditional practices of justice might reasonably be employed to address the acts of all suspected perpetrators. So, too, would participation in truth commissions be possible under policies that grant amnesty from punishment by the state.

Conclusion

The adoption of a variety of individual and collective accountability mechanisms – including prosecutions, post-conflict mediation when appropriate, and even some forms of truth commissions (allowing for penalty when appropriate) – is an important step to acknowledging and addressing the diversity of agents of atrocity. Employing a unique mechanism, such as a modified mediation process, is itself a great signifier of the unique status of child soldiers who bear limited moral responsibility for severe harm inflicted on innocent victims of society according to judgements made amid very difficult and choice-limiting environments. Accountability, in its different forms, signifies recognition of the needs of victims for the offences against them to be acknowledged and not simply brushed aside. Child soldiers can and should be held accountable for the responsibility they bear and the instruments of accountability used should reflect the unique conditions that surround perpetrators who were under the age of 18 at the time that their acts were committed. In an environment that pursues post-atrocity criminal justice, all agents under the age of 18 should neither be treated as adult perpetrators of the worst crimes nor avoid all accountability simply based on a stark division between 17 and 18. Some might deserve criminal prosecution that takes account of their age and offers juvenile protections. For the bulk of child soldiers, there are options more appropriate than criminal trials to evaluate and address their actions. For most, a unique process might be warranted, perhaps a mediated dialogue.

Mark Drumbl, unlike the argument of this chapter, does not view criminal law as an appropriate response in post-conflict contexts, for adults or child soldiers. Although he challenges the non-responsible child narrative, what he calls the faultless passive victim image, and argues that understanding the nuances of the variety of experiences and agency of child soldiers could lead to better solutions than those currently employed, he argues that responsible agency should not be taken as grounds to prosecute (Drumbl 2012). Despite the fact that some child soldiers bear responsibility for their actions, Drumbl argues, the general policies that exclude persons under the age of 18 from criminal prosecutions for acts committed as part of mass atrocity are right to do so. 'Although excluding child soldiers from international and national criminal trials may well be appropriate as a policy *result*, the current *rationales* for so doing, and the forces that propel those rationales, have come to overshoot their mark' (Drumbl 2012: 22 emphasis original). His position in regards to criminal prosecutions for child soldiers is consistent with his position that for all perpetrators of atrocity current international sentencing schemes do not fit well with the considered aims of international criminal law generally (Drumbl 2007: 149–180), and likely by extension transitional justice.

Arguably, however, Drumbl fails to accept the significance of prosecutions as a means of upholding and expressing commitment to human rights and equality under the legal system of the society. Such confirmation, as discussed earlier in Chapters 4 and 5, is critical to social reconstruction. Rather, Drumbl argues that 'one way to redress this blind spot [of coming to terms with the participation of child soldiers] is to trim the emphasis on criminal law binaries of guilt or innocence, corruption or purity, victim or perpetrator, and adult or child' (Drumbl 2012: 24). Nevertheless, the binaries that Drumbl cites are not as stark as he sees them nor as inapplicable as he suggests. A judgement of guilt is influenced by conditions; although the criminal justice system does usually promote a dichotomy of victim and perpetrator, there is room for a blurring of the two that still recognizes the wrongness of particular actions by and against an individual. Criminal legal systems have their role to play, as do other accountability mechanisms.

Children's participation in transitional justice mechanisms is important for the wellbeing of the post-conflict society, but there are significant considerations to consider to ensure the valuable and safe participation of children in accountability mechanisms. For one, all processes should be adapted to suit children's particular needs and vulnerabilities. Second, a minimum age of responsibility must apply to all practices – not only to criminal prosecutions. Children who are too young to be judged by systems of juvenile justice may also be too young to participate as perpetrators in other accountability processes such as mediation. This is not to claim that very young children should be denied participation in non-accountability processes, like truth commissions for which the goal is a record of events and not the judgement and punishment of individuals or processes of memorializing or apology, or participation as victims in accountability processes if they wish.

Accountability mechanisms, both criminal trials and alternatives, should aim at two outcomes: communication to victims and communication to perpetrators. An accountability process should communicate to victims that those who are suspected of committing acts of harm against them warrant investigation and possibly condemnation by the community and its official authorities because their acts and the consequences of them are serious enough to merit such attention. An accountability process should offer victims information about what happened, how and by whom, and compel those who committed acts of harm to contribute to some semblance of balance by respectfully providing to victims, the families of victims, and the community information about harms as fully as they can. An accountability process should also communicate to the perpetrators the nature of their acts as determined by the community in relation to its promulgated values, aim to help perpetrators come to realize their responsibility for their actions and come to terms with these actions, and allow them to accept penalty when appropriate.

Therefore, a process of post-conflict accountability has to strike a difficult balance of expressive significance. Both the process and the result of evaluation convey a substantial message about the suspected criminal action and its agent. The choice of accountability mechanism is itself expressively significant. It may not be seen to accomplish its primary expressive goals if the mechanism chosen is too harsh, is conceptually associated with acts generally deemed far more serious or agents considered far more malevolent, or is in some other way inappropriate. The accountability process must also be capable of drawing distinctions between different perpetrators and distinguishing between different levels of responsibility. And importantly, any accountability mechanism employed to address the wrongdoing of child soldiers must be sensitive to the rights and peculiarities of dealing with children.

8
Distinctly Girl Soldiers

This book has challenged the accuracy and usefulness of stereotypes that try to relegate all child soldiers to a homogeneous class. The common image of a child soldier is one of a young boy holding a gun that is far too large for his small frame. He is dark skinned since most recent conflicts in which child soldiers have participated are on the African continent. He was kidnapped and brutalized. He exudes innocence. Dispelling the generality of these stereotypes, this book has argued that many child soldiers are not young boys but youths, that there are many different forms of recruitment and participation in fighting groups, and that child soldiers who commit violent acts do so according to different temperaments, different levels of identification with the cause, and different aims and goals.

Another problem with the image of the young boy with the big gun representing the average child soldier is that it belies the large number of female child soldiers. Girls play a much larger role in these fighting groups than many of the media images and some of the studies suggest. In fact, by some accounts girls make up from 25 per cent to nearly half of the child soldiers in some fighting forces (Brett 2004: 31; McKay 2005; Pillai 2008: 26; Eichstaedt 2009: 3; Krishnan 2011). They assume many roles, including active fighters, cooks, caregivers, gatherers, laundresses, and nurses. In many of the fighting groups, females typically also have the role of forced 'wives', sexual slaves of male commanders or soldiers to whom the privilege of being given a 'wife' is granted. When girl soldiers are acknowledged, it is often this latter role that is used to represent their experiences, with little appreciation of the multiple supportive and combative roles that females play (McKay 2004: 23; Honwana 2006: 75–82). Often, there is a general perception that females are not soldiers. Boys can be soldiers; girl child soldiers, if acknowledged at all, are often characterized with the non-responsible child characterization to an even greater degree than are boys. Despite this characterization, however, they are generally met with more negative reception upon returning to civilian life. They are intensely stigmatized for their victimization, especially if they return with children who were born while the female soldiers were associated with the fighting group (Kamya 2012; Tonheim 2012).

Girls 'are often a very vulnerable and marginalized group even among children who are already excluded and rejected by society' (War Child n.d.). Special attention to female members of society must be afforded in transitioning communities for the ultimate goals of positive peace and a just society to issue from the transitional justice processes. Too often, post-conflict justice and reconstruction studies focus on only one gender, male, while relegating females to the sidelines (Kamya 2012: 68). When transitional justice and social reconstruction does attempt to exhibit gendered considerations, the result is generally one-dimensional, highlighting sexual violence (Machel 2010: xiii). Because both the experiences that female child soldiers face within the fighting groups and the experiences they face as they attempt to reintegrate into civilian life often have a gendered component, female demobilized child soldiers require special attention.

For a just society to emerge on the other side of the transitional phase, gender equality and respect for women's rights must be a priority of transitional justice processes. For this reason, gender-based violence within the fighting groups must be acknowledged and justice for gender-based violence must be pursued. Also, the agency of female community members and female ex-child soldiers must be acknowledged. There is more to be said about female child soldiers than simply that they can be generalized as being sexually exploited passive victims.

Many countries in which transitional justice is needed have histories of disregard for women's rights, and social, familial, and political relationships and roles are defined according to gender inequalities (Sierra Leone Truth and Reconciliation Commission 2004: Vol. Three B, 92; Manea 2013). Women are often great advocates for change and workers for establishing peace, but when it comes time to establish transitional justice processes and new social and political structures, the needs and agency of women are often overlooked (Scanlon and Muddell 2009). For example, women in northern Uganda are particularly active in civil society, but the fact that women are relegated to peripheral roles in traditional mechanisms of justice such as Mato Oput is rarely central to the debates about whether such traditional mechanisms of justice are appropriate (Justice and Reconciliation Project 2007; Mato Oput Project

2009). Although there is increased attention to gender-based violence in armed conflict elsewhere, in Uganda there is also little or no attempt to address gender-based violence that was committed during the conflict, and no attempt to consider the agency and moral responsibility of female members of the LRA.

After exploring the unique experiences and perspectives of female child soldiers, this chapter addresses two gender-specific needs that must be addressed by transitional justice. The first is the need to somehow incorporate a means of investigating and addressing sexual violence committed against female child soldiers in the fighting group without further stigmatizing and harming the victims. The second is the need to address the possibility of responsibility borne by female returnees, recognizing that female child soldiers are capable of committing brutal harms for which they are responsible. Lastly, this chapter justifies the need to pay particular attention to gender-based issues in transitional societies, highlighting the fact that addressing gender-based discrimination and violence is vital to entrenching post-conflict peace and justice.

Distinctly female experiences

The experiences of female child soldiers are similar to and distinct from those of male child soldiers. This is true of their experiences with the armed force or armed group, as well as their experiences demobilizing and returning to civilian life. Female child soldiers face many of the same conditions and occupy many of the same roles within the group. They are targets of violent recruitment, training, fear, hunger, discomfort, and abuse. They act as porters, gatherers, disciplinarians, and fighters. Female child soldiers also face distinctly different treatment and gender-based violence as part of the fighting force: the principle responsibility of cooking usually falls to them and they are also expected to be available for sex and to care for any small children who are present (Kamya 2012: 71). Female child soldiers also face particular gendered challenges as they attempt to reintegrate into civilian life at the same time as many face the same challenges as male child soldiers: they can be stigmatized as fighters, violent and unpredictable (and unfeminine); they can lack education and possess fewer skills than their non-child soldier age-mates that could aid in procuring employment to support themselves.

The distinctly different reception they face is usually a result of the gender-based violence they suffered at the hands of other members of the fighting group. In cases in which girls were used for sexual gratification by the male members of the fighting group, upon returning home these 'girls appear to have experienced unique forms of rejection and stigma' (Denov 2010: 166). In many cultures to which child soldiers return, there is a premium on virginity at marriage. These female child soldiers are stigmatized for their victimization by sexual violence. This stigmatization also falls to the children born of members of the fighting group, often labelled 'rebel children' (Mazurana et al. 2002: 115; Baines 2005: 35; Kamya 2012: 76).

It is important to note that although some lines can be drawn according to gender divisions, the experiences of females in different conflicts are themselves dissimilar and based on the characteristics of the communities from which they come, the nature of the conflicts, and the roles of women according to the social norms of the societies. Their entrances into the fighting forces, like that of the boys, come in different forms. 'Depending upon the context, girls enter fighting forces through recruitment, joining, abduction, being born of mothers who are in a force, or because they leave home to escape abuse' (McKay 2004: 22). Despite the fact that sometimes young females (like males) join fighting forces out of ideological leanings or pursuit of a job, often they join fighting forces against their will or out of desperation. 'In Africa, the predominant – although not exclusive – pattern has been for girls to be abducted or coerced into forces, either being taken from their homes and communities, or being forcibly recruited in a school setting' (McKay 2004: 22).

So too are their roles in different conflicts different. In many cases 'the bodies of abducted girls, and their domestic and sexual labor, are commodities to be traded. For example, in Columbia, Sierra Leone, and Uganda, male commanders are rewarded with abducted girls forced to become their 'wives' and sexual and domestic slaves' (Mazurana et al. 2002: 111). In Uganda and Sierra Leone sexual violence was rampant in the camps. In Angola girls were forced 'to live with and sexually serve the chief and other men on demand. They were also forced to dance and entertain the men in preparation for battle' (Keairns 2002: 3). Although it is the case that in many fighting forces girls are often subjected to sexual violence (rape by one or many men) and dangerous pregnancies and labour experiences, this is not the case of all groups. 'In some forces where girls serve primarily as combatants, sex is consensual or forbidden, and severe punishment directed to sexual perpetrators was reported in Colombia, the Philippines, and Sri Lanka' (McKay 2005: 389). In Sri Lanka, the general rule was that sex was prohibited (Human Rights

Watch 2004: 6). In the Philippines, the stated policy was that males and females were not permitted to be alone together and they were to be treated equally and were to have respect for one another (Keairns 2002: 3). For the most part, the existence and nature of sexual exploitation depends on the disposition of the fighting group, but even within groups different females have different experiences and experience the same events in different ways.

The issue of children born of sexual encounters between fighters is also treated differently by different groups. In some groups, a pregnancy means for the female release, a dangerous abortion, or death since she will hold up the group and there is no need or desire for newborns (Mazurana et al. 2002: 114–115; Wessells 2006: 100). In other groups, pregnancies, while dangerous for the mother, are greeted warmly. The primary role for females is providing sex and being a wife who gives birth 'to children who are raised within a rebel force to be fighters' (McKay 2005: 389). In Uganda, approximately half of the 'forced wives' have given birth to children fathered by the men or boys to whom they were given (Carlson and Mazurana 2010: 237).

Life as a female child soldier, like life as a male child soldier, is harsh – and frequently short. They are subjected to brutal treatment, go hungry, are made to walk long distances, and risk their lives by participating in fighting. To be chosen as a 'wife' is often a positive thing in this harsh environment of the fighting force. A 'wife' can be spared sexual abuse by multiple partners. A 'wife' also often has access to better resources and security; there are particular privileges to being the 'wife' of a commander (Michels 2006: 137; Cortes and Buchanan 2007: 49; Kamya 2012: 72–73). This is seemingly the case both in fighting groups in which girls are forcefully taken as wives and in fighting groups that have strict policies forbidding sexual relationships without the consent of the female. In most groups 'there were power differentials between the men and the young girls and many of the girls agreed to a sexually intimate relationship when they recognized it brought with it benefits such as more food, better living conditions, opportunities to ride rather than walk long distances and other privileges' (Keairns 2003: 3).

As members of the group, females might find ways to reduce their own hardships but they are generally victims of serious harm due simply to their gender. Girls return with similar health concerns as do boys: they are often undernourished, may have diseases and infections and/or injuries from the conflict. There is a high prevalence of HIV/AIDS in most fighting groups (Mazurana et al. 2002: 113; Uppard 2003; Wessells 2006: 121–122). Girls also have specific health concerns that result from the sexual violence perpetrated against them, such as genital injuries and infections (Kamya 2012: 72). They may have serious injuries from difficult pregnancies and childbirth in the bush or from self-inflicted or forced abortions.

Returning to civilian life often means not only the extra stigmatization based on their victimization and inferior status as 'damaged', but also more limited aid in the reintegration process compared to males (McKay et al. 2011). While there is an inadequate servicing of demobilized child soldiers of both sexes by disarmament, demobilization, and reintegration (DDR) programmes, in some contexts, girls, although not excluded, are unlikely or less likely to participate in DDR. One reason is that some DDR programmes require that a former fighter relinquish a gun to benefit from the programme. More males than females have personal guns that they can exchange for programme benefits (McKay 2004: 23). Even though this predicament of female soldiers has been identified and some adjustments have been made to some DDR schemes so that females and others without guns can meet the criteria to participate in DDR schemes, females are still underrepresented (Coalition to Stop the Use of Child Soldiers 2008: 29). Another reason that females are less likely to participate in DDR schemes is that the DDR programmes are often not welcoming for females due to the insecurity and violence that exist at some DDR facilities. Still another is that 'girls themselves may not wish to be identified as child soldiers for fear of rejection by families and communities, having been deemed to have "lost value" through involvement in sexual activity' (Coalition to Stop the Use of Child Soldiers 2008: 29). Additionally, some girls – as well as boys – do not see the value in participating in DDR schemes, or see more negative than positive aspects to participating in them, and bypass them to spontaneously demobilize (Denov 2010: 147–149). Demobilized child soldiers of both sexes bypass the receptions centres for different reasons such as fear of being targeted by the government for participation in a rebel group, fear of stigmatization, and lack of interest (Denov 2010: 159–160), and in some places, rehabilitation centres do not exist or cannot meet the needs of those who require the assistance (Singer 2005: 186). More critical attention needs to be given to the underrepresentation of females in DDR schemes, as well as the shortage of DDR programmes and the underutilization of DDR programmes by child soldiers of both sexes.

In the reintegration process, many girls 'fare poorly, and face dismal futures' (McKay 2004: 20). Like males, demobilized female child soldiers can suffer from PTS and can find themselves ill-equipped to deal with the norms of civilian life. However, while many demobilized female child soldiers suffer from PTS, Jeannie Annan and her co-investigators challenge the more pessimistic theories of female psychosocial reintegration by arguing that 'by and large women and girls are psychologically resilient, and there is little evidence of aggression and violence' (Annan et al. 2010: 3). The resilience of child soldiers is often downplayed in the common child soldier narrative for both sexes. Nevertheless, for some demobilized female child soldiers it is difficult to contend with norms of civilian life that emphasize the need to get married and to adopt the role of wife and mother. Either unwanted because of their experiences or themselves not wanting to marry, female former child soldiers can remain unmarried in a society that disapproves of such a condition.

Girls often return with children who were born as a result of forced sexual relationships within the fighting group. These children can hinder a girl's reintegration in a number of ways. A child is an extra mouth to feed and is a burden to a family that already struggles with limited resources. Also, the paternity of the child is an issue, especially in cultures in which wives and children traditionally join the husband's/father's family and community (Aptel 2010: 95). A child fathered by a rebel soldier is itself often viewed as a rebel.[1] An unmarried female with a child can be a disgrace to her community and family, especially in cultures where virginity before marriage is paramount. An unmarried female who is not a virgin can, in many cultures, be viewed as damaged, leading to her inability to marry or to marry well. In northern Uganda, women also reported that those who did marry could expect abuses levelled at them and harassment of their husbands who might be questioned and possibly ridiculed for marrying a former rebel (Fisher 2013).[2] In cultures in which marriage is seen as an important element of well-adjusted social life, females who cannot or choose not to marry are viewed as deviations and may be judged to reject the social norms of their communities.

This section presents only some of the gender-specific challenges that female child soldiers face. Since female child soldiers are treated differently simply because of their physiology, gender-based challenges should be acknowledged and addressed as a part of the pursuit of transitional justice. Gender-based violence and gender-based challenges are receiving increased attention as studies reveal the unique experience of female child soldiers. Academic and policy work must continue to underline the need for this focus lest women be again sidelined in transitional justice processes. More, however, still needs to be done.

Addressing sexual violence

There is a long history of rape and sexual violence against women (and men) in conflict. Rape has historically been prohibited by the laws of war, but it is only relatively recently that rape and sexual violence have been given serious attention and have been expressly prohibited in public international law and incorporated into international criminal law. There has been a concerted effort on the part of international activists to bring rape and sexual violence to the forefront and to treat them as among the most serious crimes (Campanaro 2001; Siegrist 2010: 11). It is for these reasons that the sexual violence that female child soldiers experience should be addressed within the transitional instruments of accountability. Impunity for sexual violence should not be tolerated, and overlooking this particular brand of violence and crime threatens the advancements in recognizing sexual violence as a particularly serious international crime and also signals lack of particular respect for females in the aftermath of widespread violence.

Despite the legal proscription of sexual violence in the early days of international humanitarian law (IHL), the reality of the situation 'attested to the utter disregard of sexual assault prohibitions' (Sellers n.d.: 6). It was not until the late 19th and early 20th centuries that there was actual progress in the prohibition of sexual violence. Traditional prohibitions of rape according to the laws of war were interpreted rather than explicit. Article 36 of the Hague Convention of 1907 states that 'family honour and rights, the lives of persons, and private property, as well as religious convictions and practice, must be respected'. This Article has been read, but not employed, as a prohibition against rape (Meron 1993: 425). Similar protections of dignity (also interpreted prohibition against rape) are present in the Geneva Conventions. Common Article 3 (common to all four Geneva Conventions) applies to non-international armed conflicts (and to persons not taking part in hostilities) and prohibits 'outrages upon personal dignity, in particular humiliating and degrading treatment' (Geneva Convention 1949: Article 3(c)). By the end of the Second World War, international covenants prohibited rape more explicitly. Article 27 of the fourth Geneva Convention, dealing with the protection of civilians in time of war, states that 'women shall be especially protected against any attack on their honour, in particular rape, enforced prostitution, or any form of indecent assault' (Geneva Convention IV 1949: Article 27). The Additional Protocols of 1977 attach further prohibitions to the Conventions.

Article 75 of Additional Protocol I, relating to the protection of victims of international armed conflict, specifies that this prohibition includes 'humiliating and degrading treatment, enforced prostitution and any form of indecent assault', and Article 4 of Additional Protocol II, relating to internal armed conflict, explicitly adds 'rape' to this list.

Sexual violence, of the type experienced by female child soldiers, therefore, is prohibited under international humanitarian law, and subsequently international criminal law. When part of widespread and systematic practice, rape and sexual slavery are recognized under international criminal law as crimes against humanity and war crimes (Rome Statute 1998: Article 7.1(g) and Article 8.2(b)(xxii)). Article 7 of the Rome Statute of the ICC prohibits the following as part of a widespread or systematic attack: rape, sexual slavery, enforced prostitution, forced pregnancy, enforced sterilization, or any other form of sexual violence of comparable gravity. Forced pregnancy means 'the unlawful confinement of a woman forcibly made pregnant, with the intent of affecting the ethnic composition of any population or carrying out other grave violations of international law' (Rome Statute: Article 7 (2) (f)). Article 8 of the Rome Statute states that the category of war crimes includes: rape, sexual slavery, enforced prostitution, forced pregnancy, as defined in article 7, paragraph 2 (f), enforced sterilization, or any other form of sexual violence also constituting a grave breach of the Geneva Conventions. In 2008, the SCSL went further to codify forced marriage in armed conflict as itself a distinct crime against humanity with the Appeals Chamber ruling in the case of three former leaders of the Revolutionary United Front (RUF) that forced marriage was distinct from the crime of sexual slavery.[3]

For situations in which girl soldiers were victims of sexual crimes, this distinct violence should be afforded particular attention. As the United Nations Office of the Special Representative of the Secretary-General for Children and Armed Conflict confirms, 'children want perpetrators who committed serious offences during armed conflict to be held accountable' (United Nations 2011: 12). It may not be possible to 'succeed in building sustainable peace in conflict areas unless we give the issue of sexual violence the centrality it deserves' (UK Foreign and Commonwealth Office 2012). There are significant grounds to pursue accountability for the sexual violence experienced by female child soldiers. The 'consequences of impunity for violence against women is both the denial of justice to the individual victims, but also the reinforcement of unequal and inequitable gender relations' (Kagoro 2012: 46).

These sexual crimes against female child soldiers should be addressed by some process of accountability, but there are significant challenges to doing so. In light of the stigma associated with coming forward about sexual victimization, often girls who were victimized are unwilling to draw extra attention to themselves and participate in any public process. There is also the problem that many girls who were victimized come to view the men who abused them as their husbands, and these men are for many of the female victims the fathers of their children. Alcinda Honwana recounts the story of a female child soldier and her 'husband' in Mozambique. The girl, who had been abducted at the age of 16, was chosen by one of the RENAMO commanders as his 'wife'. They lived together during their time with the fighting force and together had three children. When the war ended in 1992,

> she asked her family and community to forgive her husband for the atrocities committed during the war and to accept him as one of them. As she explained to [Honwana] during [the] conversation, '[T]his was the man who took care of me during the war . . . the father of my children.' (Honwana 2006: 86).

Attempting to pursue accountability for the individual perpetrators of sexual violence in these contexts, then, is a thorny pursuit.

In most situations, however, there is not even an attempt to pursue or explore accountability. In most post-atrocity contexts to which child soldiers return, there is no recourse for female victims of sexual violence to bring to account the males who victimized them. In fact, it is even at times the case that they are socially forced or feel compelled or drawn to return to relationships with their abusers. Sometimes female returnees with children are pushed to join the families of the fathers of their children for reasons of cultural traditions or expectations (Baines 2005: 49; Carlson and Mazurana 2010: 249). Other times, girls are received so poorly that they choose to return to relationships they made in the fighting force.

> Some girls find that the relationships they formed during the conflict are stronger than those with their family or community, especially when communities do not readily accept them back. Some leave to return to people with whom they formed relationships while in the fighting force, including captor 'husbands'.
>
> (McKay 2004: 26).

Another, albeit strange, argument posits that these relationships must be maintained to avoid infringing on the rights of the 'husbands' who abused the girls. 'One official of Uganda's Amnesty Commission believes that the fathers of children born in captivity have a right of access to these children and that girls and young women who return from captivity with children become a "social problem" when they separate from these men' (Carlson and Mazurana 2010: 248).

Bringing perpetrators of violence to account for their crimes is a significant element of post-conflict justice. A critical question to be asked regarding the social reconstruction processes of these societies must be how to address the particularly devastating and 'shameful' widespread crimes of sexual violence. Khristopher Carlson and Dyan Mazurana attempt to answer questions regarding accountability for sexual violence of this kind in armed conflict. They argue that such violence is one of the most serious human rights violations of such conflict and that the formal judicial processes must be used to address it. They argue that 'while traditional justice methods have a role to play in dealing with some violations committed during the war, they are not appropriate for addressing the sexual and gender-related crimes committed against captive girls and women' (Carlson and Mazurana 2010: 236). They contend that the task of adjudicating the LRA's crimes against girls is more appropriately the job of the Ugandan High Court and international judicial authorities (Carlson and Mazurana 2010: 236). Calson and Mazurana regard sexual violence among the worst crimes, the gravity of which demands the greatest condemnation.

Bringing to account these perpetrators demands nuance. Carlson and Mazurana have the right idea, although arguably partly for the wrong reasons. They claim that

> in light of the inadequacies of traditional measures to address forced marriage, rape, forced pregnancy and other similar crimes of equal gravity, there are two acceptable and adequate remedies: first, forced marriage should be considered a crime within the mandate of the special division... within the [national high court system], not a lesser offense to be dealt with through traditional measures; and second, the special division should prosecute not only top... leaders but also the commanders responsible for forced marriages, rape, forced pregnancies and the other violent gender-based crimes they ordered.
>
> (Carlson and Mazurana 2010: 263)

The fact that gender-based crimes are not standard fare for traditional mechanisms, however, does not mean that traditional mechanisms could not be amended to deal effectively with such wrongdoing. A modified mediation process of the nature described in the previous chapter might rightly be able to combine traditional elements with necessary modifications for the seriousness and delicacy of addressing gender-based violence (at least for lesser perpetrators).

Carlson and Mazurana are right to highlight the egregious nature of sexual violence in conflict. Sexual violence is rightly considered among the crimes of interest to the global community and codified in international criminal law. Carlson and Mazurana are also right to demand that the atrocity leaders responsible be prosecuted. Because these crimes are atrocity crimes and because the architects of atrocity demand the proper condemnation of criminal prosecution, these prosecutions ought to be held. Lesser perpetrators of these gender-based crimes, men and boys who raped girls repeatedly in the group's camp for example, might also deserve condemnation and accountability of a different form. Modified mediation or neo-traditional mechanisms of the sort promoted in this book (and of the sort that Carlson and Mazurana suggest is not equipped to address these violations), however, could be quite suitable for these crimes and these perpetrators.

Carlson's and Mazurana's argument against using traditional mechanisms is three-fold, citing their current form, their need for compensation, and the fear that the traditional mechanisms cannot safeguard the needs of females. First, they argue, 'because customary practices have not previously had to deal with forced marriage and similar crimes, using them to address such crimes would require substantial modifications or an entirely new system' (Carlson and Mazurana 2010: 253). Arguably, however, overhauling the traditional mechanisms of justice in favour of creating a neo-traditional design does not seem to be out of the question if the neo-traditional process can satisfy the need for appropriate accountability. They also point to the lack of resources that undermines the ability of participants to pay compensation, citing the central role of compensation in these traditional mechanisms. And lastly, they point to the patriarchal social structure from which these traditional mechanisms developed and argue that 'it is difficult to imagine how such a system could address the rights of women and girls competently and fairly' (Carlson and Mazurana 2010: 253). Part of the strategy of designing the post-atrocity accountability mechanism, of modifying the traditional mechanisms or incorporating traditional aspects to more Western processes of accountability, must address these concerns. These concerns do not, however, do fundamental damage to the prospect of using such hybrid mechanisms.

Another issue that the process of accountability should address is the reluctance of victims of sexual violence, especially in these contexts, to participate and relive the humiliation and attract further attention to their victimization. Options for confidential participation should be considered, as should outreach programs that aim to emphasize the injustice of discrimination based on victimization. Allowing victims of sexual violence to pursue accountability is important. Not all victims are like Honwana's Mozambican female child soldier who wanted to help foster forgiveness for her 'husband'. Many desire that the wrongdoing of their victimizers are acknowledged and addressed (Carlson and Mazurana 2010: 250). Bringing to account the perpetrators of sexual violence can help victims 'regain their sense of humanity, to re-establish trust within their homes and to have a voice in reconciliation forums' (Carlson and Mazurana 2010: 263).

Although this discussion has focused on violence committed against female child soldiers, it is important to note that in conflict environments sexual violence is not only directed at females associated with a fighting force, but also male soldiers and female and male civilians targeted by parties to the conflict and by their fellow civilians. Rape and other acts of sexual violence are terribly common in some war affected communities where order has broken down, and is often overlooked for a variety of reasons (Akello et al. 2012: 48). Justice demands that these violent acts of violation be addressed as well.

Naturally, the justice needs of girls or women who have been victimized go well beyond the need for judicial remedy. As argued earlier, however, the value of accountability practices stems from the expressive significance of the process of examining, evaluating, and imposing penalty when appropriate. The discounting of sexual violence as warranting accountability further imbeds the sentiment that impunity follows these crimes and that the victims of these crimes do not warrant significant consideration. Under international criminal law, the ICTY and the ICTR have both prosecuted and convicted men 'on the grounds that rape and other forms of sexual and gender violence be recognized as among the most serious offenses over which' such tribunals have jurisdiction (Franke 2006: 817). Local mechanisms of transitional justice must be willing to communicate similar condemnation for gender-based violence.

Responsibility and accountability for female child soldiers

Females, typically characterized as victims if their existence in fighting forces is acknowledged at all, generally escape accountability. Stuck with the non-responsible child characterization, female child soldiers can be conceived of as even more the victim than boys (Annan et al. 2010); this is not necessarily because of the sexual violence that conceivably most boys are spared,[4] but because the general perception of the nature of girls makes it almost unimaginable for some to see them as violent soldiers. Gender, as a social construct that expresses what it means to be male or female, plays a significant role in discussions of war, conflict resolution, and post-conflict reconstruction. Men are the major players in war; they are seen as aggressive, strong, and prone to conflict. Women, on the other hand, are typically regarded as peaceful and cooperative, and are sometimes argued to be better suited than men to foster peace and reconciliation. This gendered conception of violence is not always reflected by members of the local population, however, who can stigmatize female former soldiers both for their perceived contribution to atrocity and their sexual victimization. Sarah Kamya reports that the girls in her study in northern Uganda claimed 'that they were hated by community members because they were viewed as ex-combatants who had participated in atrocities toward the community' (Kamya 2012: 76). Gender discrimination creates difficulty for females in some DDR processes, but it also makes it less likely that responsibility borne by some female soldiers and/or judged to exist by community members will be acknowledged, evaluated, and addressed.

Susan McKay writes extensively on this problem. She writes that female child soldiers are 'characterized as victims who lack agency although recent research indicates that girls in these forces, willingly or otherwise, also participate in terrorist acts' (McKay 2005: 386). 'Many girls – particularly the older ones – participate as fighters who loot, commit atrocities, and kill' (McKay 2004: 22).

> Despite recent and increasingly robust data detailing girls in fighting forces, the international community, governments, and militaries continue to ignore and deny the extent of girls' involvement and offer inaccurate and reductionistic explanations for their presence. Pervasive gender discrimination in war-affected countries such as that existing in northern Uganda and Sierra Leone, perpetuates the notion of girls solely as victims, most notably as 'sex slaves', and as having lesser agency in perpetrating violence and terror than boys.
>
> (McKay 2005: 393)

McKay highlights the two incompatible facts of this conundrum: females can be regarded only as victims and there exist data that reveal that females commit harmful actions.

There is no reason to judge female child soldiers less responsible than males for human rights violations committed by the fighting group. Girls can employ tactical agency in the same way as boys, making choices despite bad and restrictive conditions.

As Alcinda Honwana contends,

> [Re-examinations of] women and war are vitally important, because war is a field normally conceptualized in terms of male discourse and characteristics. Men are seen as the principal protagonists [and antagonists]. Women are usually featured as victims or as loyal supporters who keep the home fires burning and nurse the wounded. Yet, women's roles in war, as numerous studies have demonstrated, go far beyond these. They are complex and contradictory, and require careful analysis. We must break the silence about women in this context and reinterpret war in the light of women's involvement.
>
> (Honwana 2006: 76)

It is important, both for moral and for practical reasons, that females are recognized as equally capable of committing atrocities for which they can be responsible. It is also important that they be seen as suitable for participation in accountability processes as perpetrators of violence in the same way as their male counterparts. This recognition of female agency is essential partly to ensure that those who are responsible for wrongdoing do not avoid deserved condemnation. It is also important because discounting females as possible responsible perpetrators does a disservice to female citizens, regarding them as weaker, less agentic beings.

Human rights, women and girls, and transitional justice

The previous two sections have outlined how violence committed both against and by female child soldiers must be acknowledged and addressed out of respect for women's rights and to promote gender equality. Justice for the victims of gender-based crimes and recognition of female community members as strong, moral agents is important to advance the rights of women in transitional societies and lay the foundation for peace and justice. Violence against women and girls is a significant and pervasive problem around the world, an obstacle to peace, equality, and justice in many regions. Gender-based discrimination 'impedes full development of women's capabilities' (Kagoro 2012: 45). Meeting the human rights of females and advancing equality within the transitioning society should be among the goals of transitional justice processes. A specific goal should be the empowerment of all persons, including women, in the post-transition society (Manea 2013).

Recent developments in international law on gender-based violence demonstrate the growing acknowledgement of the international community of the need to combat these crimes (United Nations Security Council Resolution 1325; United Nations Security Council Resolution 1888). However, despite these advances, gender-based issues are insufficiently addressed in transitional communities (Franke 2006; Nagy 2008). Questions of transitional justice are at once backward-looking and forward-looking. Transitional justice aims to address a legacy of conflict and widespread human rights violations and to rebuild social trust, promote reconciliation, advance democracy and peaceful conflict resolution, and communicate support and respect for human rights and a just society. To the forward-looking goals of transitional justice, addressing particular acts of gender-based violence is not sufficient to meet these goals, but not addressing acts of gender-based violence goes a long way to diminishing other attempts to meet them. Currently, far from enough is being done. Even when gender issues are addressed in transitional justice mechanisms, there is little effort to truly bring about equality and respect for women's human rights in the future iteration of the society. Partly, this is because 'women have been largely absent from forums that settle on the nature and design of transitional justice mechanisms' (Bell and O'Rourke 2007: 23). Transitional justice mechanisms, for the most part, emerge as consequences of negotiations to bring violent conflict to an end, and since women have less powerful roles in societies, they and their concerns are often not satisfactorily addressed.

Elham Menea argues that 'the concept of transitional justice has to be widened to include restoring "gender justice and equality" in states that systematically discriminate against women' (Manea 2013). Transitional justice processes must focus on targeting the systemic gender discrimination engrained in the culture. Gender-based violence can originate from a combination of cultural features. In exploring gender-based violence in the conflict in Sierra Leone, the Truth and Reconciliation Commission asked:

> Did the origins lie in the cultural and traditional history of Sierra Leone, where women were afforded a subservient status to men?

> Did the low status of women in socio-political life make them easy targets? Or is it because men still perceive women to be chattels, possessions belonging to them, symbols of their honour, making them the deliberate targets of an enemy determined to destroy the honour of the other? The answers probably lie somewhere in a combination between all of these factors.
>
> (Sierra Leone Truth and Reconciliation Commission 2004: Vol. Three B, 87)

To truly address a legacy of human rights abuses, the culture that supports gender discrimination and gives rise to gender-based violence must be addressed.

In virtually all societies around the world, even in liberal industrial democracies of the West, women still face significant disadvantages but, as mentioned above, many countries in which transitional justice is needed have serious histories of disregard for women's rights. In these countries, social, familial, and political relationships and roles are defined according to gender inequalities. Manea shows that in many countries in which great transitions occurred, women were often great advocates for change and workers for establishing peace, but were eliminated from the new social and political structures that arose from the transitions (Manea 2013). In disregarding the needs and agency of women in the transitional society, the emerging society is again one of inequality and human rights abuses, and ripe for civil strife.[5] Disregarding the systemic abuses of women is not compatible with establishing positive peace.

In Sierra Leone, strides were made to address gender inequalities and usher in a more just society. The final Report of the Sierra Leone Truth and Reconciliation Commission dedicated a chapter to women and to the question of why such extraordinary violence was perpetrated against women. The final report expresses the belief that 'it is only when the legal, social and political system treats women equally that they will realise their full potential' and that an evolution in addressing gender-based crimes is necessary 'in order to ensure that women are never again dehumanised the moment the rules of society break down' (Sierra Leone Truth and Reconciliation Commission 2004: Vol. Three B, 87).

The report recognized also that 'many women took on the role of perpetrators and/or collaborators, out of personal conviction or simply in order to survive' (Sierra Leone Truth and Reconciliation Commission 2004: Vol. Three B, 87). As is the case with all child soldiers, accountability mechanisms that address the harmful acts committed by female child soldiers must examine the context and specific influences, pressures, motivations, and intentions that led to the acts. Females should participate in transitional justice practices in the same way as their male counterparts, neither being sidelined from recognition as victims or as responsible perpetrators when applicable.

Conclusion

This final substantive chapter of the book has argued that promoting gender equality and women's rights is a necessary condition for transitional justice and the prospect of positive peace. Transitional justice must both address gender-based crimes committed against female child soldiers and it must address crimes committed by female child soldiers as a way to acknowledge the equal agency of females. Girls, as is the case with male child soldiers, can occupy a unique position on the responsibility continuum. They are victims who can also be perpetrators of serious brutality and other human rights violations. The particular victimization that is sexual violence must have a place in the accountability process necessary to address actions of the past and move forward. It must be acknowledged and its perpetrators must be acknowledged. So must the harmful acts committed by female soldiers be acknowledged. To appropriately address the wrongdoing committed by and against female child soldiers, there must be a way for them to participate fully in accountability mechanisms – as both victims and perpetrators, and as some complex combination of the two.

It is important to keep at the forefront of discussions regarding DDR and social reconstruction programmes concern for how persons of both genders are represented. Equality of treatment of the genders will denote the right foundation for the transitional society to come, one that is attentive to issues of gender and equality. A just recognition of the identification of women as useful targets and the agency of females in conflict establishes an arena in which females can be a strong and positive force in the transitional aspirations of the society. They can play integral roles, but often need to defy social stereotypes and the constraints of their traditional roles in society. In some fighting groups especially, girls have been given the opportunity to cast off the roles of the diminutive and repressed to sample the roles of the powerful. Females sometimes adopt leadership roles: directing other soldiers, making decisions, and devising strategy (McKay 2005). It is not beneficial to the females that they are relegated again in civilian life to be dominated according to their gender. It is also obstructive to the aim of establishing a just and prosperous post-transition society.

It is important to recognize that girls have special needs in the reintegration process. A high priority should be put on meeting the primary health needs, especially reproductive health needs, of former female child soldiers. They, like the boys, need opportunities to attend formal school or skills training to increase their prospects for financial independence and becoming contributing members of society. Many former female soldiers also require special social help to meet the needs of their children so that these children are well taken care of and can grow up to be productive and contributing members of the society. And, transitional justice must reach further, this chapter argued, than simply addressing particular acts of harm or particular needs of individuals affected by the conflict. Transitional justice must acknowledge and address systemic gender discrimination that, left untouched, would not be conducive to positive peace.

Strong females are both a resource for processes of transitional justice and also to a great extent dependant on the processes. Females, perhaps more so than males, return with more-or-less healthy feelings and characteristics that are considered contrary to the social norms of the society. The fact that female soldiers take on leadership roles in the fighting forces presents particular challenges for their reintegration. In these roles, they can develop strong senses of power, independence, and authority. These identities do not accord with the gender norms of many of the societies to which these female soldiers return. Therefore, 'to reintegrate successfully, they may have to renounce feelings of independence and power gained in conflict, although this varies by gender, age, status and roles within a force, and the nature of the force itself' (McKay 2004: 25). Females who return with a sense of power and independence incongruent with the gender norms of their society can either be ostracized or further empowered. It is also not uncommon that former female child soldiers, because of their wartime experiences – especially if they were subjected to sexual violence – may not wish to marry, a decision that in some cultures is frowned upon as diverging from cultural norms. Neither a sense of identity that originates from strength and autonomy nor a desire to be single is, on its own, a sign of post traumatic stress, aggression, or other emotional affliction.

These girls and women should have the opportunity to retain their independence and power. These qualities should also be harnessed for the benefit of post-conflict reconstruction initiatives. And, social reconstruction processes can help to support these individuals in their retention of identities that may not conform to conventional gender norms. This support is essential for the wellbeing of these former female soldiers themselves, but also for the society that can benefit from strong women helping to steer the transitional society to come.

Conclusion

As the many examples in this book suggest, where gross human rights violations have been committed by young persons who have themselves likely been victimized, complex questions arise about individual criminal and moral responsibility and how the actions of these child soldiers ought to be addressed. This book has questioned the best approach to understanding and addressing harmful acts committed by child soldiers to support positive peace and social reconstruction in the aftermath of mass atrocity. As a general moral principle, it is right that those who commit gross human rights violations and international crimes such as war crimes, crimes against humanity, and genocide should be held accountable for their acts. Holding individuals accountable for wrongdoing is expressively significant as a means of upholding, respecting, and confirming rights and social values. However, there are good reasons to view children in a very different light than adult perpetrators.

Most importantly, we need to envision and work towards a world that does not see children as 'weapons of war' (Machel 1996: v). Children are vulnerable and many of the world's children are subject to the effects of war as affected bystanders, targets, and fighters. Great and important strides forward have been attained for the universal protection of children, including the renouncement of the use of children in armed conflict. Strengthening international legal frameworks and norms enhance protection by denying impunity for crimes committed against children in times of war and political violence. Significantly more is needed until children are protected from the worst degradations of war.

In the meantime, yet, when children do participate in violent conflict, societies must work to address the harms committed by them in ways that are sensitive to their vulnerability and potential victimization and respectful of the rights of the child and also in ways that communicate respect and concern for all victims and understanding of the agency of young persons. This book has examined whether it makes sense, from the perspective of both moral and practical considerations, that child members of armed groups or forces can be attributed responsibility for acts of atrocity that they commit in war. It has also considered how, if some children can be said to bear some responsibility, they should be held accountable to properly address their personal responsibility, respect their vulnerability and likely victimization, and help the children and the post-conflict society move forward in a healthy manner.

Within the category of child soldier are individuals under the age of 18 who can genuinely be said to bear no moral responsibility for any wrongdoing either because their time with the fighting group did not constitute the commission or support of acts of international crime or because they have defences that absolve them of responsibility. Other child soldiers bear some diminished responsibility for harms that they inflicted on others. Others are youths who delight in the task of killing, brutalizing, and terrorizing. Some instigated operations, took up leadership roles, and employed appalling tactics to meet the goals of the group or for personal enjoyment or advancement. In light of the range of ages, characters, and experiences of child soldiers, this book examined the justice of the international strict 18 policy that views all persons under the age of 18 as non-responsible agents where crimes that 'shock the conscience of humanity' are concerned. After analysis, it would seem that a transitional justice strategy that respects the strict 18 policy is hazardous both morally and practically. An understanding of the agency of persons under the age of 18 that characterizes the whole group as non-responsible agents is neither accurate nor helpful.

There is no legal prohibition under international criminal law or an easy answer to how to address the agentic wrongdoing of persons under the age of 18, and international and national responses to harms committed by individuals under the age of 18 consist currently of a not-so-comedic inconsistency in treatments. Under most domestic criminal justice systems, child perpetrators of criminal actions face accountability under juvenile justice systems. There is no one correct answer to questions of transitional justice, especially when policies must address the particularly sensitive and complex challenges of dealing with child perpetrators of atrocity. However, there must be consistency in respect for the rights of children. It seems proper that persons of a certain immaturity who are in conflict with the law or who are causal agents of serious harm ought to be dealt with differently from adults. However, no recognized culture in the world views all children under the age of 18 as incapable of any critical assessment necessary to be held responsible for their actions. Persons under the age of 18 in all recognized cultures can be considered moral agents by those cultures. It is important to locate universal standards of human rights, juvenile protections, and transitional processes that can admit agents under the age of 18.

What is needed in post-conflict contexts is a more nuanced way of looking at child soldiers that admits the possibility of responsibility and even the possibility of prosecuting persons under the age of 18 within a juvenile justice system, if the individuals' actions and *mens rea* warrant it, in situations in which adults can be prosecuted, providing that there are appropriate protections and safeguards for juvenile defendants and ensuring that the prosecutions consider the youthfulness of the defendant. Interpretations of international law that deny the examination of responsibility for certain segments of the population block important nuanced discussions about accountability, and about transitional justice in general. The possible trend leading post-atrocity transitional justice towards a prohibition of attributing any responsibility to persons under the age of 18 is, arguably, not particularly useful and potentially dangerous to social reconstruction.

Sonja Grover, however, argues that 'this illogic is similar in a key aspect to that long since abandoned "blaming the victim" approach applied to rape victims in North America both by the courts and society in general' (Grover 2012: 8). The problem with the analogy she draws between child soldiers and rape victims, though, is that victims of rape, *qua* victims of rape, cause no harm to others. Grover argues that the state has a fundamental *a priori* duty to prevent the victimization of these children and claims that positions that suggest that child soldiers bear any responsibility for their actions are attempts to deflect attention away from the fact that the state did not provide protection in the form of a 'safe haven for children in the midst of armed conflict and mass atrocity' (Grover 2012: 8). Grover is right that the state has a fundamental obligation to protect children from recruitment into fighting forces. Nevertheless, there is a problem in conflating two distinct issues, each of which deserves adequate attention: a state's duty to its citizens, particularly its children; and the best way to understand and address the agency of a wide variety of returnees for a smooth and durable transition and to advance a strong and cohesive society.

The position that this book has advanced is one that promotes the importance of accountability, in its many forms. It endorses criminal prosecutions for perpetrators (adults and juveniles) whose suspected crimes and mental conditions (*mens rea*) invite such serious condemnation as valuable communicative tools. For most young causal perpetrators of acts of atrocity under the harsh conditions of child soldiering, however, means of accountability other than trials are more appropriate – means that allow for dialogue about actions and their results, for consideration of circumstances, for agents to accept responsibility when appropriate or convey experiences. Traditional reconciliation ceremonies are usually viewed by those who practice them as not above the law, but as complementary means of addressing wrongdoing (Baines 2005: 3; Mato Oput Project 2009: 33). Transitional justice schemes should use a variety of accountability mechanisms to properly address a wide range of responsibility for a multitude of wrongful actions. With creativity and flexibility there is the possibility for context-specific solutions tailored to the needs, priorities, and concerns of the affected population.

The proposal of this book, then, is multi-faceted. It supports the prosecution and punishment of those responsible for recruiting children into military service. It also promotes the possibility of prosecution under juvenile systems for some child soldiers (persons under the age of 18 at the time of the commission of the alleged crime), and different accountability mechanisms for others accused of grave human rights violations. This plan aims to balance competing needs and reflects an appreciation of 'the complexity of balancing culpability, a community's sense of justice and the "best interests of the child"' (Machel 1996: para. 250). Prosecution of children for crimes arising from their active participation in hostilities should be a matter of absolute last resort, reserved for individuals who bear significant responsibility for planning, orchestrating, and/or leading atrocity schemes. Other persons under the age of 18 who committed acts of harm in violation of international standards of legitimate warfare should be addressed by other means, for their own sake, for the sake of their victims, and for the sake of the wellbeing of the community.

Other transitional justice mechanisms that do not prioritize accountability should also be employed. Truth commissions are a great way to explore the broader causes, policies, and impact of the conflict. They can provide a forum for victims and perpetrators to convey their experiences and allow them to together establish a coherent record that spans more than the private encounters of individuals.

> Survivors' desire to know the details of their loved ones' deaths – the identity of the killers, the methods and motives of the murderers, the location of victims' bodies – drives their participation in [transitional

> justice mechanisms]. While the knowledge of these facts may prove crucial for identifying and punishing those guilty of committing crimes, it is also vital for people's personal understanding of events and for their catharsis.
>
> (Clark 2011: 264)

A truth and reconciliation commission (TRC) can memorialize events. Other memorialization projects should also be pursued.

It is also essential that accountability be paired with programmes of reconciliation – genuine attempts to foster goodwill and common interests between members of the post-conflict society. To address a legacy of violent conflict and mass violations of human rights, there is no one solution that must be used in all post conflict-contexts or one solution that can solve all problems in any one environment. Each situation is unique and the needs of individual victims and the requirements of the society reflect distinct situations. The challenge is to identify mechanisms that will be most appropriate for any particular context. What is important is that transitional justice processes strive to ensure accountability, and reflect and promote respect for victims, including child perpetrators of human rights violations, and an environment that fosters 'the health, self-respect and dignity of the child' (CRC: Art. 39).

Analysis to determine which mechanisms to employ must try to balance international standards and trying to meet local needs by culturally relevant means. 'One of the challenges – or dilemmas – encountered when addressing child rights within a transitional justice framework is the need to adapt justice, accountability and truth-seeking mechanisms in local contexts, while at the same time upholding international human rights standards' (Siegrist 2010: 10). Cultural differences should be recognized and attempts should be made to ensure that transitional justice is culturally relevant to the post-conflict society. If accountability is to be meaningful to the communities and children most affected, it must take into account cultural values. It is also important to acknowledge, appreciate, and demonstrate sensitivity towards local belief systems, especially those regarding age, agency, and post-atrocity afflictions. There is a difficult balance that must be struck between protecting children from cultural practices and judicial traditions that violate the rights of the child and forcing upon fragile societies in the throes of post-atrocity reconstruction notions of child agency (or lack thereof) that are not recognized or adhered to the world over.

Significant community outreach should be exercised to explain transitional justice objectives and capabilities (and to manage the expectations of community members concerning judicial and non-judicial accountability), but most important are community consultation, input, direction, and ownership of the mechanisms. This outreach and community consultation must be child-sensitive, recognizing that children have a right to be heard and that their voices are important to the post-conflict society (Ramirez-Barat 2012). The proposal of this book does not encourage or defend top-down, externally imposed solutions to social rebuilding problems. Community ownership is important for a number of reasons, not the least of which is that for a process to be expressively significant to its intended audience, it must be accompanied by local buy-in. Kagoro laments that

> regrettably, the bulk of present approaches to transitional justice in Africa are largely Eurocentric and even when they purport to promote indigenous mechanisms, these mechanisms are viewed mostly through a European-American lens – a lens that focuses on the functional utility of such mechanisms to handle large volumes of cases as opposed to their normative and cognitive value in creating new knowledge about being, becoming and belonging to a reality called 'Africa'.
>
> (Kagoro 2012: 16)

The approach to questions of transitional justice and social reconstruction must not be arrogantly dismissive of other ways of addressing, healing, and moving beyond harms or the philosophies and culture that underpin the local understanding of and need for justice. Academics and practitioners in the field of transitional justice must work to balance knowledge and beliefs acquired and filtered through their own experiences and education with the particularities of unique post-atrocity contexts.

This does not mean, however, that confidence in home-bred solutions is obligatory or paramount. Even Kagoro acknowledges that traditional mechanisms need some help and that

> most traditional mechanisms were designed to deal with personalised individual conflicts and are hardly suited to address large-scale human rights violations that include crimes which were either taboo or had complex redress mechanisms such as heterosexual rape, sodomy rape, and incineration and mass murder of the unborn while in the womb.
>
> (Kagoro 2012: 9)

As David Kaulemu argues, cultural traditions can be particularly productive in transitions, but there needs to be self-conscious handling of the relationship between tradition and justice. He argues that we 'sometimes forget that the rules of what we do are developed as responses to human needs, aspirations and strategies for solving concrete social problems' (Kaulemu 2012: 81). Doing so can trap us in customs that have outlived their usefulness.

The proposal to employ a modified mediation process, then, would be most effective when suited and adapted to incorporate and reflect locally meaningful customs and values. And, a modified mediation process to deal with harms committed by child soldiers, with the exception that special cases can be referred to a criminal justice system, could also help to rehabilitate former soldiers who had learned violence as a reasonable means of influencing others to act as they wish and as a way to penalize those with whom they have a disagreement. Employing a modified mediation process can help to cultivate new appreciation for respectful communication and negotiation. As Phil Clark writes in regards to Rwanda's gacaca, 'Within the concept of positive peace, gacaca plays an important *educative* role by inculcating in the population ideas and methods of future cooperation and conflict resolution' (Clark 2011: 221 emphasis original). Consultation, open deliberation, and negotiation help to provide for both negative and positive peace, where negative peace is the absence of violent conflict and positive peace is the long-term condition of social reconstruction where there is trust and peaceful co-existence between previously antagonistic parties.

Its denial of a culture of impunity is a way in which a policy of accountability promotes positive peace. Accountability acts to support respect of all members of the society and reinforce the post-conflict social norms and order. Awareness of the rule of law can be educative regarding the evident distinctions between norms of life as a soldier and the social norms of civilian life. That accountability justly follows harms committed is an important lesson for child soldiers to learn; many had experienced an environment that exhibited arbitrary punishment and lack of proportionality, and that rewarded violence. The objective, then, is to reintegrate former child soldiers into civilian life in a way that respects justice and also the needs of these former soldiers and the needs of the broader society.

Accountability and respect for victims of atrocity are important, but accountability-seeking alone will not secure justice for victims (Machel 2010: xiii). The effects of widespread violence and mass atrocity live on long past the end of the conflict. Dealing with the past and rebuilding for the future are extensive projects. Years after the 'end' of the conflict in northern Uganda, questions regarding transitional justice remain (Mato Oput Project 2009: 5; Odoi-Musoke Ajok 2013). For two decades, innocents were slaughtered and maimed, and children and young adults were abducted to participate in the brutality. Although the last version of the Juba Peace Accord of 2008 was not signed, the conflict-affected areas have enjoyed a high degree of security for some years now. People have returned home from the internally displaced persons (IDP) camps and are trying to rebuild their lives. They have many immediate problems, many stemming from economic concerns. As Brian Kagoro argues in his contribution to a recent book on transitional justice in Africa, accountability is only part of the story; 'Peace and justice will remain elusive as long as transitional justice remains disconnected from development questions (the creation of inclusive wealth and the eradication of poverty and inequality)' (Kagoro 2012: 14). For the victims of the widespread violence, justice includes support for rebuilding lives affected by the conflict so that they can move into the future with prospects of wellbeing and prosperity.

Children ought to play significant roles in the design of transitional justice and reconstruction schemes. It is not enough that adults consider their interests; children's voices must be heard (Machel 2010: x). Children have unique experiences and unique insight. They are also the foundation of the future society. The promotion of child participation in deliberation about design must be met with ensuring their protection and comfort in the processes. Children want to be involved in bringing about a stable and more just society (Green 2013). With children's input, and the help of international actors, post-conflict societies should be able to devise innovative responses that can help community members move beyond the past and establish a foundation for a strong, just, and prosperous post-conflict society.

Notes

Introduction

1. Prosecutor v. Charles Ghankay Taylor, Case No. SCSL-03-01-I-001; SCSL-03-01-I-003 Indictment.
2. Prosecutor v. Charles Ghankay Taylor. Case. No. SCSL-03-01-T. Sentencing Judgement. IV.
3. Prosecutor v. Thomas Lubanga Dyilo. Case No. ICC-01/04 -01/06.
4. Prosecutor v. Thomas Lubanga Dyilo. Case No. ICC-01/04-01/06-2842.
5. Prosecutor v. Thomas Lubanga Dyilo. Case No. ICC-01/04-01/06.
6. One in particular, Omar Khadr, unlike some other youths who were detained at Guantánamo Bay, was housed with adult detainees and had no access to education or other rehabilitation assistance (Human Rights Watch 2008).
7. Under International Humanitarian Law (IHL), an armed force is a state's military force including its organized groups and units; an armed group is a non-state entity such as a rebel group.

1 Child Soldiering

1. Interview with Formerly Abducted Soldier, Kampala. 27 February 2011.
2. See Introduction, page 3.
3. Myriam Denov discusses representations of militarized children and claims the media generally portrays child soldiers in extreme and largely contrastive ways, as dangerous and disorderly, as hapless victims or heroes. (Denov 2010: 5–14). Mark Drumbl speaks to the reductionist 'faultless passive victim' child soldier narrative (Drumbl 2012: 6–11). Brandon Kohrt and his co-investigators also point to the 'Hollywood image' of child soldiers (Kohrt et al. 2010: 91).
4. These states include Colombia, the Netherlands, Spain, and Uruguay.
5. This debate is given attention later in this chapter. See the section on the principle of non-voluntary recruitment, pages 32–35.
6. Myriam Denov illustrates this inconsistency and overlap:

   > To complicate matters further, constructed and formalized definitions of 'child', 'youth', adolescent' or 'young people' differ between international organizations and, in some cases, overlap. While the UN Convention on the Rights of the Child considers a child to be anyone under the age of 18, the UN's World Programme of Action for Youth identifies 'youth' as 15–24 years old (United Nations 2010). Moreover, the World Health Organization and the United Nations Children's Fund (UNICEF) differentiate between 'adolescents' (15–19 years old), 'youths' (15–24 years old), and 'young people' (10–24 years old).
   >
   > (Denov 2010: 3).

7. Shelly Whitman highlights the fact that the Canadian government, under Prime Minister Stephen Harper, has deemed the term 'child soldier' inappropriate, preferring instead 'children in armed conflict' to reflect the multiple roles that children can play in fighting forces and the fact that children cannot legally be soldiers. The preference is also, in part, Whitman argues, because of the politicization of certain cases involving children in conflict, particularly the Omar Khadr case (Whitman 2012: 153).
8. Christine Ryan writes that, although the participation of children in conflict is not restricted to Africa, it is seen as an area of the world that holds a higher risk of continuing and possibly increasing the use of child soldiers (Ryan 2012: 3).
9. Interview with Paul Omach, Department of Political Science and Public Administration, Makerere University (Kampala), 2 November 2011.

2 The Difficult Reintegration

1. See Chapter 6 for a more comprehensive examination of the issue of trauma and psychological health.
2. Interview: Moses C. Okello, Head of Research and Advocacy Department, Refugee Law Project, Faculty of Law, Makerere University, Kampala. 23 January 2007. Also see Lamony 2007: 3.
3. Despite there being no statistics on the current practice of Mato Oput, Acholi clan leaders assert that very few returnees participate in such accountability and reconciliation mechanisms (Fisher 2013).
4. The radio announcements were mentioned in a number of interviews conducted at part of qualitative research in northern Uganda in 2013, including an interview with William Odur, Senior Psychiatric Clinical Officer, Gulu Regional Referral Hospital, 29 January 2013.
5. See Introduction.
6. The Paris Principles also, however, state that children should not be prosecuted by an international court or tribunal (Article 8.6).
7. For a fine and succinct discussion of youth and domestic criminal law, see: Drumble 2012: 104–106.
8. In establishing the SCSL and defining its jurisdiction, two opposing views emerged: the government of Sierra Leone and representatives of Sierra Leone civil society wanted a process of judicial accountability for child soldiers; international child rights organizations opposed the criminal prosecution of children (Aptel 2010: 103–104).
9. Thomas Kwoyelo alias Latoni v. Uganda. Constitutional Petition No. 036/2011 (Reference)
10. Warrant for Arrest of Dominic Ongwen. International Criminal Court. Situation in Uganda. ICC-02/04–01/05–57 13–10–2005.
11. Such stories were related by former child soldier interviewees in qualitative research conducted by author in Uganda in 2011 and 2013.
12. In Ishmeal Beah's account of his time in the UNICEF rehabilitation centre he reports feelings of anger towards being told 'It's not your fault' (Beah 2007: 160).

3 Moral and Legal Responsibility of Child Soldiers

1. The common law principle of *doli incapax* legally embeds the presumption that an individual can be incapable of criminal intention or malice, not of the age of discretion, or not possessed of sufficient discretion and intelligence to distinguish between right and wrong to the extent of being criminally responsible for his or her actions.
2. Prosecutor v. Dražen Erdemović, ICTY, Indictment, Case No. IT-96–22, 22/05/1996.
3. T and V v. United Kingdom (1999) 7 B.H.R.C. 659.
4. The Child Rights International Network (CRIN) advocates for distinguishing between responsibility and criminalizing.
5. One need not agree that collectively running air conditioners contributes to dangerous air conditions or that contributing in such a way to bad environmental conditions should necessarily be judged morally wrong to grasp Isaacs' point that it might reasonably be the case that actions performed as part of a greater scheme or contributing (intentionally or not) to a significant harm are of a worse character than the same act performed in isolation.
6. For a similar argument, see Sloane (2007: 59–62).

4 The Expressive Value of Post-Atrocity Accountability

1. Both of these cases are referred to elsewhere in this book, including the Introduction and again later briefly in this chapter.
2. This amnesty act applies to Ugandans over the age of 12 because this is the age of majority in Uganda.
3. Uganda's Amnesty Act (enacted in 2000) was quietly allowed to expire in May 2012 (Schenkel 2012).
4. International crime narrowly and precisely defined refers to criminal conduct that is international, constituting an offence against the global community. In its broadest interpretation, the category of international crime can also refer to any international law that deals with criminal activity, and includes law that is transnational, including, for example, extradition, transborder organized criminal activity, counterfeiting and treaties on drug trafficking or genocide. Transnational crime affects the interests of more than one state. The narrower construal, however, represents a unique category of activity and it is this narrower interpretation that is applied in this discussion. It includes wrongdoing such as the commission of crimes against humanity, genocide, and war crimes.
5. As Anthony Lang explains succinctly, 'If it is specific, it is an attempt to deter a particular agent from violating the same norm again. If it is general, it is an attempt to deter others from violating the law by using the individual case as an example' (Lang 2007:12).
6. Some theorists, such as Jean Hampton, separate out what can be called the moral education theory of punishment, distinguishing it from the expressive theory. However, the education can be viewed as a possible by-product (a reasonable, but not necessary, outcome) of the message conveyed by punishment. Hampton, although she sees punishment as educative,

maintains that persons are autonomous beings who may choose to accept and internalize the lesson or not (Hampton 1984).

7. The retributive complement to the expressive theory, as proposed here, must be distinguished from what R.A. Duff labels 'side constraints and "negative" retribution' that are not absolute and that merely argue that punishing innocents or punishing wrongdoers too harshly is wrong (Duff 2001: 11–13). The retributive-expressive theory offered here justifies punishment based partly on the fact that perpetrators deserve punishment and the intrinsic wrongness of the action.
8. This assertion is based primarily on a liberal political philosophical stance and common contemporary intuition. Liberal political philosophy begins with the premise of moral egalitarianism, which advocates the equal wellbeing or potential for equal wellbeing of all members of society.
9. This comment was made in relation to the work of truth commissions in replacement for any criminal prosecutions; however, the message remains salient in cases in which restorative justice mechanisms can be employed to deal with individuals for whom criminal trials would not be appropriate.
10. Of course, as discussed in Chapter 1, the category of 'child soldier' is not a uniform one. There are great differences in the types of armed force in which they participate (government or opposition/rebel), their recruitment, and their roles and experiences in the conflict. Nevertheless, certain overlapping similarities suggest a range of responsibility that is greatly diminished by the characteristics of the agents and the conditions in which they operate.
11. These are questions attributed by Zehr to retributive justice approaches.
12. These are questions attributed by Zehr to restorative justice approaches.

5 Accountability and Social Reconstruction

1. There is no reason, however, to believe that a question concerning how atrocity architects under the age of 18 should be addressed is simply part of an academic pursuit with no real-world application. The Interahamwe, the Hutu paramilitary organization that carried out acts of the Rwandan Genocide against the Tutsis, was a militia of armed youth supporters of the Mouvement Republicain National pour la Démocratie et le Développement (MRND) and Coalition pour la Défense de la République (CDR) parties (Wallis 2007). The Tamil Tigers were created out of youth movements, with some of the founding members in their late teens and 20s (Jordan and Denov 2007: 44–45). There is no reason to believe that if young adults can devise and lead acts of genocide and terrorism, teenagers in another context cannot or would not.
2. Nevertheless, even though trials may not be the optimal instrument for discovering and recording history, some of the greatest accounts of German history and the atrocities that occurred before and during the Second World War can be found in the legal transcripts of the Nuremberg trials.
3. Arguably, this communal attitude is rapidly changing in Uganda, becoming more individualistic, but the basic communal values are still valid, for now. Interview with Jessica Nalwoga, Acting Program Officer for Peace and Human Rights, Church of Uganda – PDR. Kampala. 15 February 2007.

4. The research supporting the arguments in this chapter consists mainly of qualitative interviews primarily of the Acholi, Langi, Iteso, Baganda, and Banyankole peoples who are spread across the country and represent a cross-section of the different tribal cultures. These interviews, conducted mainly in 2007 (of field research conducted between 2007 and 2013), are supplemented by literature research. Throughout this chapter reference to a few other tribal cultures is made.
5. Interview with Moses C. Okello, Head of Research and Advocacy Department, Refugee Law Project, Faculty of Law, Makerere University, Kampala, 23 January 2007.
6. Interviews with Karamajang man, 29 January 2007; Banyankole elders, Biharwe village, just outside of Mbarara, 4 February 2007.
7. Interview with Acholi elders (Amuru District, Gulu), 31 January 2007.
8. Interviews with Baganda man, Kampala, 23 January 2007; Banyankole man, Kampala, 9 February 2007; Iteso elders, Kampala, 10 February 2007.
9. In the last product of the Juba Peace Talks, *The Agreement on Accountability and Reconciliation*, in the definitions section, the definition of each of the traditional mechanisms includes the words 'after full accountability.' (2). At no point in the *Agreement* or the later composed *Annexure to the Agreement on Accountability and Reconciliation* (2008) is 'accountability' defined or explained. See: Between the Government of the Republic of Uganda and the Lord's Resistance Army/Movement. 2007, and Between the Government of the Republic of Uganda and the Lord's Resistance Army/Movement 2008.
10. Interview with Godman Okonye, Language Institute, Makerere University, Kampala, 13 February 2007.
11. For an intra-clan murder, compensation was usually excluded.
12. Interview with Iteso elders, 10 February 2007.
13. Interview with Iteso elders, 10 February 2007
14. Interview with Banyankole elders, Biharwe village, 4 February 2007.
15. Interview with Banyankole elders, Biharwe village, 4 February 2007.
16. Interview with Banyankole man, Kampala, 9 February 2007.
17. Interview with Banyankole elders, Biharwe village, 4 February 2007.
18. Interview with Okot Constantine Ngom Loko-Coo (Paicho) Acholi Clan Chief, Gulu city, Gulu, 3 February 2013.
19. Interview with Acholi elders, Amuru District, Gulu, 31 January 2007.
20. Interview with Acholi elders, Amuru District, Gulu, 31 January 2007.
21. Interview with Jessica Nalwoga, Acting Program Officer for Peace and Human Rights, Church of Uganda – PDR. Kampala, 15 February 2007.

6 Trauma, Truth-Telling, and Post-Atrocity Justice

1. The fourth edition of the Manual, DSM-IV-TR, includes in the definition of a traumatic event that the person's response involved intense fear, helplessness, or horror. The fourth edition claims that in children the response may be disorganized or agitated behaviour. This criterion (A2) is eliminated from the fifth edition of the Manual (DSM-5) (Freidman et al. 2011: 755–756).
2. Christopher Blattman claims that 'psychologists consistently find that victims of violence are in general resilient, and a growing psychological literature

finds that experiences of personal growth are more common than distress in the aftermath of violent trauma' (Blattman 2009: 231). The effectiveness of rehabilitation centres in facilitating healing is also debatable. Some studies show that child soldiers who self-demobilize and bypass the reception centres are no worse off than those who complete programmes at the centres (See: Wessells 2006: 155).

7 Accountability for Child Soldiers

1. For a more elaborate argument supporting this statement, refer to Fisher 2012: 78–102.
2. Interview with Okot Constaintine Ngom Loko-Coo, Paicho Clan Chief, Chairman of Customary Chiefs of the Executive Committee, 3 February 2013.
3. Interview with Stephen Kisembo, Ugandan Joint Christian Council, 23 January 2007.

8 Distinctly Girl Soldiers

1. The stigmatization of children of rebels was voiced as a significant problem for children born in the bush of northern Uganda (Fisher 2013).
2. William Odur, Senior Psychiatric Clinical Officer at Gulu Regional Referral Hospital, confirmed what individual female interviewees suggested by their individual stories was the general attitude of the communities about men marrying former girl soldiers. Interview with William Odur, Senior Psychiatric Clinical Officer, Gulu Regional Referral Hospital, 29 January 2013.
3. *Prosecutor v. Alex Brima, Brima Bazzy Kamara and Santigie Kanu*, SCSL Trial Chamber, Judgement, Case No. SCSL-04-16-A, 03/03/2008.
4. There are also often underreported acts of sexual violence committed against boys and men (Siegrist 2010: 9).
5. Erik Melander argues that more equal societies are associated with lower levels of intrastate armed conflict (Melander 2005).

Bibliography

Achilles, Mary and Howard Zehr. (2001) 'Restorative Justice for Crime Victims: The Promise and the Challenge.' In Gordon Bazemore and Mara Schiff (eds) *Restorative Community Justice: Repairing Harm and Transforming Communities*. Cincinnati, OH Anderson Publishing Co. 87–99.

African Charter on the Rights and Welfare of the Child. OAU Doc. CAB/LEG/24.9/49 (1990), entered into force Nov. 29, 1999.

Aikins, Deane E., D.C. Johnson, J.L. Borelli, D.H. Klemanski, P.M. Morrissey, T.L. Benham, S.M. Southwick, and D.F. Tolin. (2009) 'Thought Suppression Failures in Combat PTSD: A Cognitive Load Hypothesis." *Behaviour Research and Therapy*. 47(9): 744–751.

Akello, Grace, Annemiek Richters and Ria Reis. (2006) 'Reintegration of Former Child Soldiers in Northern Uganda: Coming to Terms with Children's Agency and Accountability.' *Intervention*. 4(3): 229–243.

Akello, Grace. (2012) Notes Contributing to Draft Article. Private Communication with Author. 28 November 2012. (Notes on file with Author.)

Akello, Grace, Annemiek Richters, Ria Reis and Charles B. Rwabukwali. (2012) 'Children's Psychological Distress and Needs in Northern Uganda's Conflict Zone: An Assessment of Stakeholders' conflicting Engagements.' In E. Alvarez and A. Escobar (eds) *Psychology of War*. New York: Nova Publishers. 33–61.

Akhavan, Payam. (2005) 'The Lord's Resistance Army Case: Uganda's Submission of the First State Referral to the International Criminal Court.' *American Journal of International Law*. 99: 403–421.

Allan, Alfred. (2000) 'Truth and Reconciliation: A Psycholegal Perspective.' *Ethnicity and Health*. 5(3–4): 191–204.

Allen, Tim. (2006) *Trial Justice: The International Criminal Court and the Lord's Resistance Army*. London: Zed Books.

Allen, Tim and Koen Vlassenroot (eds). (2010) *The Lord's Resistance Army: Myth and Reality*. London: Zed Books.

Amann, Diane Marie. (2001) 'Calling Children to Account: The Proposal for a Juvenile Chamber in the Special Court for Sierra Leone.' *Pepperdine Law Review*. 20(1): 167–186.

American Psychiatric Association. (2000/2013) *Diagnostic and Statistical Manual of Mental Disorders* (Revised 4th ed./Revised 5th ed.). Washington, DC: American Psychiatric Association.

Amnesty Act (2000) (Uganda). Kampala: Parliament of Uganda. http://www.beyondjuba.org/BJP1/policy_documents/Amnesty_ACT_Chapter_294.pdf

Amnesty International. (2000) 'Child Soldiers: Criminals or Victims?' *AI Index: IOR 50/02/00*

Amnesty International. (2002) *Sri Lanka: Rape in Custody* (28 January 2002). ASA 37/001/2002. http://www.unhcr.org/refworld/docid/3c552e584.html

Amstutz, Lorraine Stutzman. (2009) *The Little Book of Victim Offender Conferencing*. Intercourse, PA: Good Books.

Angucia, Margaret. (2009) 'Children and War in Africa: The Crisis Continues in Northern Uganda.' *International Journal on World Peace*. 26(3): 77–95.

Annan, Kofi. (1997) *International Criminal Court Promises Universal Justice, Secretary-General Tells International Bar Association*. United Nations. Department of Public Information. 12 June 1997. Press Release. SG/SM/6257.

Annan, Jeannie, Christopher Blattman and Roger Horton. (2006) *The State of Youth and Youth Protection in Northern Uganda: Findings from the Survey of War Affected Youth*. Uganda: UNICEF

Annan, Jeannie, Christopher Blattman, Dyan Mazurana, and Khristopher Carlson. (2010) *Civil War, Reintegration, and Gender in northern Uganda*. http://www.chrisblattman.com/documents/research/2010.CivilWar ReintegrationGender.pdf

Aptel, Cécile. (2010) 'International Criminal Justice and Child Protection.' In Sharanjeet Parmar, Mindy Jane Roseman, Saudamini Siegreist, and Theo Sowa (eds) *Children and Transitional Justice: Truth-Telling, Accountability and Reconciliation*. Cambridge, MA: Human Rights Program at Harvard Law School. 67–113.

Aptel, Cécile and Virginie Ladisch. (2011) *Through a New Lens: A Child-Sensitive Approach to Transitional Justice*. New York: International Center for Transitional Justice.

Arendt, Hannah. (1994) *Eichmann in Jerusalem: A Report on the Banality of Evil*. New York: Penguin.

Ashworth, Andrew. (2002) 'Responsibilities, Rights and Restorative Justice.' *British Journal of Criminology*. 43: 578–95.

Bachmann, Klaus. (2013) 'The Invisible Cost of Retribution.' (Draft of Forthcoming Chapter) In Kirsten J. Fisher and Robert Stewart (eds) *Transitional Justice and the Arab Spring*. London: Routledge. (Draft Chapter on File with Author)

Baines, Erin. (2003) *The Peace Process in Northern Uganda*. Vancouver: Liu Institute for Global Issues, University of British Columbia.

Baines, Erin K. (2005) *Roco Wat I Acholi/Restoring Relationships in Acholiland: Traditional Approaches to Justice and Reconciliation*. Vancouver: Liu Institute for Global Issues, University of British Columbia.

Baines, Erin K. (2007) 'The Haunting of Alice: Local Approaches to Justice and Reconciliation.' *International Journal of Transitional Justice*. 1: 91–114.

Baines, Erin K. (2009) 'Complex Political Perpetrators: Reflections on Dominic Ongwen.' *Journal of Modern African Studies*. 47(2): 163–191.

Baines, Erin. (2010) 'Spirits and Social Reconstruction After Mass Violence: Rethinking Transitional Justice.' *African Affairs*. 109(436): 409–430.

Baines, Erin and Beth Stewart. (2011) 'I Cannot Accept What I Have Not Done: Storytelling, Gender and Transitional Justice.' *Journal of Human Rights Practice*. 3(3): 245–263.

Barber, Brian K. (2009) 'Glimpsing the Complexity of Youth and Political Violence.' In Brian K. Barber (ed.) *Adolescents and War: How Youth Deal with Political Violence*. Oxford: Oxford University Press[0]. 3–32.

Bayles, Michael D. (1982) 'Character, Purpose and Criminal Responsibility.' *Law and Philosophy*. 1: 5–20.

BBC. (2011) 'Ugandan LRA Rebel Thomas Kwoyelo Granted Amnesty.' (22 September 2011) http://www.bbc.co.uk/news/world-africa-15019883

Beah, Ishmael. (2007) *A Long Way Gone: Memoirs of a Boy Soldier*. Toronto: Douglas and McIntyre.

Bedau, Hugo Adam. (1978) 'Retribution and the Theory of Punishment.' *Journal of Philosophy*. 75: 601–620.

Beijing Rules. (1985) United Nations Standard Minimum Rules for the Administration of Juvenile Justice. United Nations General Assembly. G.A. Res 40/33, U.N. Doc. A/RES/40/33 (29 November 1985).

Bell, Christine and Catherine O'Rourke. (2007) 'Does Feminism Need a Theory of Transitional Justice? An Introductory Essay.' *International Journal of Transitional Justice*. 1: 23–44.

Bentham, Jeremy. (1962) 'Principles of Penal Law.' In John Bowring (ed.) *The Works of Jeremy Bentham*. New York: Russell and Russell.

Bercovitch, Jacob. (2011) *Theory and Practice of International Mediation*. New York: Routledge.

Betancourt, Theresa S., Jessica Agnew-Blais, Stephen E. Gilman, David R. Williams and B. Heidi Ellis. (2010) 'Past Horrors, Present Struggles: The Role of Stigma in the Association Between War Experiences and Psychosocial Adjustment Among Former Child Soldiers in Sierra Leone.' *Social Science and Medicine*. 70: 17–26.

Between the Government of the Republic of Uganda and the Lord's Resistance Army/Movement' (2007) *Agreement on Accountability and Reconciliation*. Juba, Sudan. 29 June 2007.

Between the Government of the Republic of Uganda and the Lord's Resistance Army/Movement. (2008) *Annexure to the Agreement on Accountability and Reconciliation*. Juba, Sudan. 19 February 2008.

Biderman, Seth. (2012) 'From Child Soldier to Civilian: A Tough Transition in Columbia.' *New Internationalist*. 449 (1 January) http://www.newint.org/features/2012/01/01/columbia-child-soldiers/

Bjørkhaug, Ingunn. (2010) *Child Soldiers in Colombia: The Recruitment of Children into Non-State Violent Armed Groups*. MICROCON Research Working Paper 27. Brighton: MICROCON.

Blake, Michael. (2008) 'International Justice.' *The Stanford Encyclopedia of Philosophy* (Winter 2008 Edition) In Edward N. Zalta (ed.) http://plato.stanford.edu/archives/win2008/entries/international-justice/.

Blattman, Christopher. (2009) 'From Violence to Voting: War and Political Participation in Uganda.' *The American Political Science Review*. 103(2) (May): 231–247.

Blattman, Christopher and Jeannie Annan. (2010) 'The Consequences of Child Soldiering.' *The Review of Economics and Statistics*. 92(4): 882–898.

Boothby, N., J. Crawford and J. Halperin. (2006) 'Mozambique Child Soldier Life Outcome Study: Lessons Learned in Rehabilitation and Reintegration Efforts.' *Global Public Health*. 1(1): 87–107.

Boraine, Alexander L. (2006) 'Transitional Justice: A Holistic Interpretation.' *Journal of International Affairs*. 60(1): 17–27.

Branch, Adam. (2007) 'Uganda's Civil War and the Politics of ICC Intervention.' *Ethics and International Affairs*. 21(2): 179–198.

Branch, Adam. (2010) 'Exploring the Roots of LRA Violence: Political Crisis and Ethnic Politics in Acholiland.' In Tim Allen and Koen Vlassenroot (eds) *The Lord's Resistance Army: Myth and Reality*. New York: Zed Books. 25–44.

Brett, Rachel. (2004) 'Girl Soldiers: Denial of Rights and Responsibilities.' *Refugee Survey Quarterly*. 23(2): 30–37.

Briggs, Jimmie. (2005) *Innocents Lost: When Child Soldiers Go To War*. New York: Basic Books.

Brounéus, Karen. (2010) 'The Trauma of Truth Telling: Effects of Witnessing in the Rwandan Gacaca Courts on Psychological Health.' *Journal of Conflict Resolution*. 54(3): 408–437.

Brudholm, Thomas. (2006) 'Revisiting Resentments: Jean Amery and the Dark Side of Forgiveness and Reconciliation.' *Journal of Human Rights*. 5: 7–26.

Bryant, Richard A., T. Sackville, S.T. Dang, M. Moulds, and R. Guthrie. (1999) 'Treating Acute Stress Disorder: An Evaluation of Cognitive Behavior Therapy and Supportive Counseling Techniques.' *American Journal of Psychiatry*. 156(11): 1780–1786.

Campanaro, Jocelyn. (2001) 'Women, War, and International Law: The Historical Treatment of Gender-Based War Crimes.' *Georgetown Law Journal*. 89: 2557–2592.

Cape Town Principles and Best Practices (27–30 April 1977) Available at: http://www.unicef.org/emerg/files/Cape_Town_Principles%281%29.pdf.

Carlson, Khristopher and Dyan Mazurana. (2010) 'Accountability and Reconciliation in Northern Uganda.' In Sharanjeet Parmar, Mindy Jane Roseman, Saudamini Siegreist, and Theo Sowa (eds) *Children and Transitional Justice: Truth-Telling, Accountability and Reconciliation*. Cambridge, MA: Human Rights Program at Harvard Law School. 235–265.

Carr, Craig L. (1991) 'Duress and Criminal Responsibility.' *Law and Philosophy*. 10(2): 161–188.

Casey, B.J., Rebecca M. Jones, and Todd A. Hare. (2008) 'The Adolescent Brain.' *Annals of the New York Academy of Science*. 1124: 111–126.

Cassese, Antonio. (1999) 'The Statute of the International Criminal Court: Some Preliminary Reflections.' *European Journal of International Law*. 10: 144–171.

Child Rights International Network. (2012) 'Stop Making Children Criminals.' *Policy Paper*. (08-March-2012). http://www.crin.org/resources/infodetail.asp?id=27829#asserting

Chinapen, Rhiana and Richard Vernon. (2006) 'Justice in Transition.' *Canadian Journal of Political Science*. 39: 117–134

Ciocchetti, Christopher. (2003) 'Wrongdoing and Relationships: An Expressive Justification of Punishment.' *Social Theory and Practice*. 29: 74–79.

Clark, Phil. (2011) *The Gacaca Courts, Post-Genocide Justice and Reconciliation in Rwanda: Justice without Lawyers*. Cambridge: Cambridge University Press.

Coalition to Stop the Use of Child Soldiers (2004) *Child Soldiers Global Report 2004*. http://www.child-soldiers.org/document_get.php?id=966

Coalition to Stop the Use of Child Soldiers. (2008) *Child Soldiers Global Report 2008*.

Cohen, Judith A., Robin F. Goodman, Elissa J. Brown, and Anthony Mannarino (2004). "Treatment of Childhood Traumatic Grief: Contributing to a New Emerging Condition in the Wake of Community Trauma." *Harvard Review of Psychiatry* 12(4): 213–216.

Convention on the Prevention and Punishment of the Crime of Genocide, 9 December 1948. UN General Assembly. 1948, A/RES/260

Convention on the Rights of the Child, General Comment 10. Children's rights in juvenile justice, 25 April 2007, CRC/C/GC/10, Forty-fourth session, Geneva.

Cooper, David E. (2001) 'Collective Responsibility, "Moral Luck", and Reconciliation.' In Alesandar Jokic (ed.) *War Crimes and Collective Wrongdoing: A Reader.* Oxford: Blackwell. 205–215.

Corbin, Joanne N. (2008) "Returning Home: Resettlement of Formerly Abducted Children in Northern Uganda." *Disasters.* 32(2): 316-335.

Cortes, Liliana and Marla Jean Buchanan. (2007) 'The Experience of Columbian Child Soldiers from a Resilience Perspective.' *International Journal for the Advancement of Counselling.* 29: 43–55.

Cottingham, John. (1979) 'Varieties of Retribution' *Philosophical Quarterly,* 29: 238–246.

Coundouriotis, Eleni. (2010) 'The Child Soldier Narrative and the Problem of Arrested Historicization.' *Journal of Human Rights.* 9: 191–206.

Crane, David. (2008) 'Prosecuting Children in Times of Conflict: The West African Experience.' *Human Rights Brief.* 15(3): 11–17.

CRC. Convention on the Rights of the Child, 20 November 1989, United Nations, adopted and opened for signature, ratification and accession by General Assembly resolution 44/25 of 20 November 1989, entered into force on 2 September 1990, in accordance with article 49.

Creighton Backpack Journalism. (2012) *Mato Oput.* Video Documentary. http://vimeo.com/33414929

Crocker, David A. (2000) 'Truth Commissions, Transitional Justice, and Civil Society.' In Robert I. Rotberg and Dennis Thompson (eds) *Truth V. Justice.* Princeton, NJ: Princeton University Press. 99–121.

Cushman, Fiery. (2008) 'Crime and Punishment: Distinguishing the Roles of Causal and Intentional Analyses in Moral Judgment.' *Cognition.* 108: 353–380.

Dallaire, Roméo. (2010) *They Fight Like Soldiers, They Die Like Children.* Toronto: Random House of Canada.

Davis, Michael. (1983) 'How to Make the Punishment Fit the Crime.' *Ethics.* 93: 726–752.

de Greiff, Pablo. (2002) 'Deliberative Democracy and Punishment.' *Buffalo Criminal Law Review.* 5: 373–403.

Declaration of the Rights of the Child. (1959) UN General Assembly, Adopted by the General Assembly on 20 November 1959 (Resolution 1386 (XIV).

Denov, Myriam. (2010) *Child Soldiers: Sierra Leone's Revolutionary United Front.* Cambridge: Cambridge University Press.

Denov, Myriam and Richard McLure (2007) 'Turnings and Epiphanies: Militarization, Life Histories, and the Making and Unmaking of Two Child Soldiers in Sierra Leone.' *Jouranl of Youth Studies.* 10(2): 243–261.

Department of Justice, Canada. (n.d.) 'The Act of 1908.' In The Evolution of Juvenile Justice in Canada. http://www.justice.gc.ca/eng/pi/icg-gci/jj2-jm2/sec02.html

Derluyn, Ilse, Eric Broekaert, Gilberte Schuyten, Els De Temmerman. (2004) 'Post-Traumatic Stress in Former Ugandan Child Soldiers.' *The Lancet.* 363(9412) (13 March) 861–863.

de Soyza, Niromi. (2011) *Tamil Tigress.* Sydney: Allen and Unwin.

Dickson-Gomez, Julia. (2003) 'Growing Up in Guerrilla Camp: The Long-Term Impact of Being a Child Soldier in El Salvador's Civil War.' *Ethos.* 30(4): 327–356.

DiMeglio, Richard P. (2006) 'The Evolution of the Just War Tradition: Defining *Jus Post Bellum*.' *Military Law Review*. 186: 116–163.

Dore, Christopher L. (2008) 'What to Do with Omar Khadr: Putting a Child Soldier on Trial: Questions of International Law, Juvenile Justice, and Moral Culpability.' *John Marshall Law Review*. 41: 1281–1307.

Driberg, J.H. (1923) *The Lango: A Nilotic Tribe of Uganda*. London: T. Fisher Unwin.

Drumbl, Mark. (2007) *Atrocity, Punishment, and International Law*. Cambridge: Cambridge University Press.

Drumbl, Mark. (2012) *Reimagining Child Soldiers: In International Law and Policy*. Oxford: Oxford University Press.

Duff, R.A. (2001) *Punishment, Communication, and Community*. New York: Oxford University Press.

Du Toit, André. (2000) 'The Moral Foundations of the South African TRC: Truth as Acknowledgment and Justice as Recognition.' In Robert I. Rotberg and Dennis Thompson *Truth V. Justice*. Princeton, NJ: Princeton University Press. 122–140.

Eichstaedt, Peter. (2009) *First Kill Your Family: Child Soldiers of Uganda and the Lord's Resistance Army*. Chicago, IL: Laurence Hill Books.

Esuruku, Robert Senath. (2012) 'The Peace, Recovery and Development Plan for Northern Uganda.' In Moses Chispus Okello, Chris Dolan, Undine Whande, Nokukhanya Mncwabe, Levis Onegi and Stephen Oola (eds) *Where Law Meets Reality: Forging African Transitional Justice*. Dakar: Pambazuka Press. 144–166.

Faltas, Sami. (2005) *DDR without Camps: The Need for Decentralized Approaches*. Topical Chapter for the Conversion Survey. Bonn International Center for Conversion. http://www.government.se/content/1/c6/06/54/02/5d16fcf2.pdf

Fegley, Randall (2008) 'Comparative Perspectives on the Rehabilitation of Ex-Slaves and Former Child Soliders with Special Reference to Sudan.' *African Studies Quarterly*. 10(1) (Spring): 35–69.

Feinberg, Joel. (1965) 'The Expressive Function of Punishment.' *The Monist*. 49: 397–423.

Finnström, Sverker. (2008) *Living With Bad Surroundings: War, History and Everyday Moments in Northern Uganda*. Durham: Duke University Press.

Fisher, Kirsten J. (2012) *Moral Accountability and International Criminal Law: Holding Agents of Atrocity Accountable to the World*. London: Routledge.

Fisher, Kirsten J. (2013) Unpublished results of field research conducted in January and February 2013. Interviews are saved in digital recording format and on file with author.

Fitzgerald, Caitlin. (2009) 'Juveniles Charged as Adults.' *Children's Legal Rights Journal*. 29: 80–81.

Flock, Elizabeth. (2012) 'Child Soldiers Still Used in More than 25 Countries Around the World.' *The Washington Post*. (14 March 2012).

Franke, Katherine. (2006) 'Gendered Subjects of Transitional Justice.' *Columbia Journal of Gender and Law*. 15(3): 813–828.

Freidman, Matthew J., Patricia A. Resick, Richard A. Bryant, and Chris R. Brewin. (2011) 'Considering PTSD for DSM-5.' *Depression and Anxiety*. 28: 750–769.

Friscolanti, Michael. (2012) 'The Secret Omar Khadr File.' *McLean's*. (27 September 2012). http://www2.macleans.ca/2012/09/27/the-secret-khadr-file/

Galvan, A., T. Hare, H. Voss, G. Glover and B.J. Casey. (2007) 'Risk-Taking and the Adolescent Brain: Who is at Risk?' *Developmental Science*. 10(2): F8-F14.

Gardner, Thomas J. and Terry M. Anderson. (2011) *Criminal Law.* Belmont: Wadsworth Publishing.

Gates, Scott and Simon Reich. (2010) "Introduction." In Scott Gates and Simon Reich (eds) *Child Soldiers in the Age of Fractured States.* Pittsburgh: University of Pittsburgh Press. 3–23.

Geneva Declaration of the Rights of the Child. (1924) League of Nations. 26 September 1924.

Getz, Lindsey. (2012) "Trauma-Focused Cognitive-Behavioral Therapy: Hope for Abused Children." *Social Work Today.* 12(3): 22.

Ghetti, Simona and Allison D. Redlich. (2001) 'Reactions to Youth Crime: Perceptions of Accountability and Competency.' *Behavioral Sciences and the Law.* 19: 33–52.

Gibson, James L. (2002) 'Truth, Justice, and Reconciliation: Judging the Fairness of Amnesty in South Africa.' *American Journal of Political Science.* 46(3): 540–556.

Golash, Deirdre. (2010) 'The Justification of Punishment in the International Context.' In Larry May and Zachary Hoskins (eds) *International Criminal Law and Philosophy.* Cambridge: Cambridge University Press. 201–223.

Goldhagen, Daniel Jonah. (1996) *Hitler's Willing Executioners.* New York: Vintage

Goldstone, Richard. (1998) 'Foreword.' in Martha Minow (ed.) *Between Vengeance and Forgiveness.* Boston, MA: Beacon Press. ix–xiii.

Green, Andrew. (2013) 'South Sudan's Red Army Comes of Age.' *The Guardian.* 27 March 2013. http://m.guardian.co.uk/global-development/2013/mar/27/south-sudan-red-army-comes-age

Green, Matthew. (2008) *The Wizard of the Nile: The Hunt for Africa's Most Wanted.* London: Portobello Books.

Greenawalt, Kent. (2000) 'Amnesty's Justice.' In Robert I. Rotberg and Dennis Thompson (eds) *Truth V. Justice.* Princeton, NJ: Princeton University Press. 189–210.

Grover, Sonja. (2008) "'Child Soldiers" as "Non-Combatants": The Inapplicability of the Refugee Convention Exclusion Clause.' *International Journal of Human Rights.* 12(1): 53–65.

Grover, Sonja C. (2012) *Child Soldier Victims of Genocidal Forcible Transfer: Exonerating Child Soldiers Charged with Grave Conflict-Related International Crimes.* Berlin: Springer.

Gruber, Staci A. and Deborah A. Yurgelun-Todd. (2005) 'Neurobiology and the Law: A Role in Juvenile Justice?.' *Ohio State Journal of Criminal Law.* 3: 321–340.

Gutmann, Amy and Dennis Thompson. (2000) 'The Moral Foundations of Truth Commissions.' In Robert I. Rotberg and Dennis Thompson (eds) *Truth V. Justice.* Princeton, NJ: Princeton University Press. 22–44.

Hague Convention (IV) Respecting the Laws and Customs of War on Land and Its Annex: Regulations Concerning the Laws and Customs of War on Land, 18 October 1907.

Hampton, Jean. (1984) 'The Moral Education Theory of Punishment.' *Philosophy and Public Affairs.* 13: 208–238.

Happold, Matthew. (2006) 'The Age of Criminal Responsibility for International Crimes Under International Law.' In Karin Arts and Vaasselin Popovski (eds) *International Criminal Accountability and the Rights of Children.* The Hague: Hague Academic Press.

Harbour, Frances V. (2003) 'Collective Moral Agency and the Political Process' In Toni Erskine (ed.) *Can Institutions Have Responsibilities?*. New York: Palgrave Macmillan. 69–83.

Harlacher, Thomas, Francis Xavier Okot, Caroline Aloyo Obonyo, Mychelle Bathazard and Ronald Atkinson. (2006) *Traditional Ways of Coping in Acholi: Cultural Provisions for Reconciliation and Healing from War*. Kampala: Caritus Gulu Archdiocese.

Hart, Henry M. Jr. (1958) 'The Aims of the Criminal Law.' *Law and Contemporary Problems*. 23(3): 401–441.

Harvey, Allison G., R.A. Bryant, and N. Tarrier. (2003) 'Cognitive Behaviour Therapy for Posttraumatic Stress Disorder. *Clinical Psychology Review*. 23(3): 501–522.

Hayner, Priscilla B. (2011) *Unspeakable Truths: Transitional Justice and the Challenge of Truth Commissions*. (Second Edition; First Edition Printed in 2001) New York: Routledge.

Held, Virginia. (1970) 'Can a Random Collection of Individuals Be Morally Responsible?.' *Journal of Philosophy*. 67: 471–481.

Herman, Judith Lewis. (1997) *Trauma and Recovery: The Aftermath of Violence – from Domestic Abuse to Political Terror*. New York: Basic Books.

Honwana, Alcinda. (1997) 'Healing for Peace: Traditional Healers and Post-War Reconstruction in Southern Mozambique.' *Peace and Conflict: Journal of Peace Psychology*. 3(3): 293–305.

Honwana, Alcinda. (2002) 'Negotiating Postwar Identities: Child Soldiers in Mozambique and Angola.' In George Bond and Nigel Gibson (eds) *Contested Terrains and Constructed Categories*. New York: Westview Press.

Honwana, Alcinda. (2006) *Child Soldiers in Africa*. Philadelphia, PA: University of Pennsylvania Press.

Honwana, Alcinda (2009) 'Children in War: Reintegrating Child Soldiers.' *IDS Bulletin*. 40(1): (January) 63–68.

Hovil, Lucy and Zachary Lomo. (2005) *Whose Justice: Perceptions of Uganda's Amnesty Act 2000: The Potential for Conflict Resolution and Long-Term Reconciliation*. Working Paper Series, working paper no. 15. Kampala: Refugee Law Project.

Hovil, Lucy and Joanna Quinn. (2005) *Peace First, Justice Later: Traditional Justice in Northern Uganda*. Working Paper Series, working paper no. 17. Kampala: Refugee Law Project.

Human Rights Watch. (2003) *You'll Learn Not to Cry: Child Soldiers in Colombia*. New York: Human Rights Watch.

Human Rights Watch. (2004) 'Living in Fear: Child Soldiers and the Tamil Tigers in Sri Lanka.' *Human Rights Watch*. 16(13). http://www.hrw.org/sites/default/files/reports/srilanka1104.pdf

Human Rights Watch. (2008) 'US: Stop Unfair Trial of Guantanamo Youth.' (February 1) http://www.hrw.org/news/2008/02/01/us-stop-unfair-trial-guantanamo-youth

Human Rights Watch. (2009) 'Uganda: Drop Treason Charges Against Abducted Child.' (January 6) http://www.hrw.org/news/2009/01/06/uganda-drop-treason-charges-against-abducted-child

Human Rights Watch. (2012) 'Country Summary: Colombia.' (January) http://www.hrw.org/sites/default/files/related_material/colombia_2012_0.pdf

ICRC. (1977a) International Committee of the Red Cross. Protocol Additional to the Geneva Conventions of 12 August 1949, and relating to the Protection of Victims of International Armed Conflicts (Protocol I), 8 June 1977.

ICRC. (1977b) International Committee of the Red Cross. Protocol Additional to the Geneva Conventions of 12 August 1949, and relating to the Protection of Victims of Non-International Armed Conflicts (Protocol II), 8 June 1977.

International Center for Transitional Justice. (n.d.) 'What is Transitional Justice?' http://ictj.org/about/transitional-justice

International Center for Transitional Justice. (2005) *Forgotten Voices: A Population-based Survey on Attitudes about Peace and Justice in Northern Uganda*. New York: ICTJ.

IRIN. (2008) 'Rwanda: Turning Ex-child Soldiers into Able Citizens' (September 30). http://www.irinnews.org/Report.aspx?ReportId= 80668

Isaacs, Tracy. (2006) 'Individual Responsibility for Collective Wrongs' in Joanna Harrington, Michael Milde and Richard Vernon (eds) *Bringing Power to Justice?* Montreal: McGill-Queen's University Press.

Jamison, Melissa A. (2008) "The Sins of the Father: Punishing Children in the War on Terror." *University of La Verne Law Review*. 29: 88–151.

Johnson, Kirsten, Gillian Morantz, Helen Seignior, Tanya Zayed and Shelly Whitman. (2012) 'From Youth Affected by War to Advocates of Peace, Round Table Discussions with Former Child Combatants from Sudan, Sierra Leone and Cambodia.' *Journal of International Peacekeeping*. 16(1–2): 152–174.

Jones, Lynne. (2002) 'Adolescent Understandings of Political Violence and Psychological Well-being: A Qualitative Study from Bosnia Herzegovina.' *Social Science and Medicine*. 55(8): 1351–1371.

Jordan, Kim and Myriam Denov. (2007) 'Birds of Freedom? Perspectives on Female Emancipation and Sri Lanka's Liberation Tigers of Tamil Eelam.' *Journal of International Women's Studies*. 9(1): 42–62.

Justice and Reconciliation Project. (2007) *The Cooling of Hearts: Community Truth-Telling in Acholi-land*. Gulu District NGO Forum, Liu Institute for Global Issues.

Kagoro, Brian. (2012) 'The Paradox of Alien Knowledge, Narrative and Praxis: Transitional Justice and the Politics of Agenda Setting in Africa.' In Moses Chispus Okello, Chris Dolan, Undine Whande, Nokukhanya Mncwabe, Levis Onegi and Stephen Oola (eds) *Where Law Meets Reality: Forging African Transitional Justice*. Dakar: Pambazuka Press. 4–52.

Kamya, Sarah. (2012) 'Resettlement of Abducted Girls in Northern Uganda: The Case of Gulu District.' *Africa Peace and Conflict Journal*. 5(2): 67–78.

Kant, Immanuel. (1996) [1797] *The Metaphysics of Morals*. Edited by Mary Gregor. Cambridge: Cambridge University Press.

Kar, Nilamadhab. (2011) 'Cognitive Behavioural Therapy for the Treatment of Post-Traumatic Stress Disorder: A Review.' *Neuropsychiatric Disease and Treatment*. 7: 167–181.

Karekezi, Urusaro Alice, Alphonse Nshimiyimana, and Beth Mutamba. (2004) 'Localizing Justice: Gacaca Courts in Post-Genocide Rwanda.' In Eric Stover and Harvey M. Weinstein (eds) *My Neighbor, My Enemy*. Cambridge: Cambridge University Press. 69–84.

Kaulemu, David. (2012) 'Culture, Customs, Traditions and Transitional Justice.' In Moses Chispus Okello, Chris Dolan, Undine Whande, Nokukhanya Mncwabe, Levis Onegi and Stephen Oola (eds) *Where Law Meets Reality: Forging African Transitional Justice*. Dakar: Pambazuka Press. 80–98.

Kearins, Yvonne E. (2002) *The Voices of Girl Soldiers*. New York: Quaker United Nations Office.

Keairns, Yvonne E. (2003) *The Voices of Girl Soldiers: Sri Lanka*. New York: Quaker United Nations Office.

Ker Kwaro Acholi. *Law to Declare the Acholi Customary Law*. J.B. Enterprises. (Booklet of customary law used by Acholi chiefs. Limited publication run. Author was able to photocopy a booklet owned by a clan chief in Gulu. Photocopied booklet on file with Author.)

Key Principles for Children and Transitional Justice. (2010) Outcome of Children and Transitional Justice Conference., Cambridge, MA: Harvard Law School. 27–29 April 2009. Found as Annex to *Children and Transitional Justice: Truth-telling, Accountability and Reconciliation*. Sharanjeet Parmar, Mindy Jane Roseman, Saudamini Siegrist, and Theo Sowa (eds.) Cambridge, MA: Human Rights Program at Harvard Law School.

Kimmel, Carrie E. and Jini L. Roby. (2007) 'Institutionalized Child Abuse: The Use of Child Soldiers.' *International Social Work*. 50(6): 740–754.

Kisige, Abou. (2012) 'Issue Ex-LRA Commander Kwoyelo Amnesty Certificate, Court Rules.' *New Vision*. (25 January 2012) http://www.newvision.co.ug/news/628591-issue-ex-lra-commander-kwoyelo-amnesty-certificate-court-rules.html

Kiss, Elizabeth. (2000) 'Moral Ambition Within and Beyond Political Constraints.' In Robert I. Rotberg and Dennis Thompson (eds) *Truth V. Justice*. Princeton, NJ: Princeton University Press. 68–98.

Klabbers, Jan. (2001) 'Just Revenge? The Deterrence Argument in International Criminal Law.' *Finnish Yearbook of International Law*. 12: 249–267.

Klimchuk, Dennis. (2001) 'Retribution, Restitution and Revenge.' *Law and Philosophy*. 20: 81–101.

Kohrt, Brandon A., Mark J.D. Jordans, Weitse A. Tol, Rebecca A. Speckman, Sujen M. Maharjan, Carol M. Worthman, and Ivan H. Komproe. (2008) 'Comparison of Mental Health Between Former Child Soldiers and Children Never Conscripted by Armed Groups in Nepal.' *Journal of American Medical Association*. 300(6): (August) 691–702.

Kohrt, Brandon A., Wietse A. Tol, Judith Pettigrew, and Rohit Karki. (2010) 'Children and Revolution: Mental Health and Psychosocial Well-being of Child Soldiers in Nepal.' In Merrill Singer and G. Derrick Hodge (eds) *The War Machine and Global Health*. New York: Altamira. 89–116.

Komakech, Lyandro. (2012) 'Traditional Justice as a Form of Adjudication in Uganda.' In Moses Chrispus Okello, Chris Dolan, Undine Whande, Nokukhanya Mncwabe, Levis Onegi and Stephen Oola (eds.) *Where Law Meets Reality: Forging African Transitional Justice*. Dakar: Pambazuka Press. 64–79.

Koskenniemi, Martti. (2002) 'Between Impunity and Show Trials.' *Max Planck Yearbook of United Nations Law*. 6: 1–32.

Krishnan, Sonny Inbaraj. (2011) 'The Transition of Teenage Girls and Young Women from Ex-Combatants to Civilian Life: A Case Study in Sri Lanka.' *Intervention*. 9(2): 137–144.

Lamont, Julian and Christi Favor. (2008) 'Distributive Justice.' In Edward N. Zalta (ed.) *The Stanford Encyclopedia of Philosophy (Fall 2008 Edition)*. http://plato.stanford.edu/archives/fall2008/entries/justice-distributive

Lamony, Stephen Arthur. (2007) 'Alternative Forms of Traditional Justice in Uganda.' *Draft Manuscript*. Kampala: Uganda Coalition for the ICC (Draft manuscript on file with author).

Lang, Anthony. (2007) 'Crime and Punishment: Holding States Accountable.' *Ethics and International Affairs*. 21: 239–257.

Lansdown, Gerison. (2005) 'The Evolving Capacities of the Child.' *Innocenti Research Centre*. UNICEF/Save the Children: Florence.

Latimer, Jeff. (2005) 'The Effectiveness of Restorative Justice Practices: A Meta-Analysis.' *Prison Journal*. 85: 127–144.

Levitt, Jeremy I. (2012) *Illegal Peace in Africa: An Inquiry into the Legality of Power-Sharing with Warlords, Rebels and Junta*. Cambridge: Cambridge University Press.

Litvak, Olga. (2006) *Conscription and the Search for Modern Russian Jewry*. Bloomington: Indiana University Press. Lomo, Zachary and Lucy Hovil. (2004) *Behind the Violence: The War in Northern Uganda*. Monograph No. 99. Pretoria: Institute for Security Studies.

Longman, Timothy, Phuong Pham, and Harvey M. Weinstein. (2004) 'Connecting Justice to Human Experience: Attitudes Toward Accountability and Reconciliation in Rwanda.' In Eric Stover and Harvey M. Weinstein (eds) *My Neighbor, My Enemy*. Cambridge: Cambridge University Press. 206–225.

Ludwig, Frederick J. (1949) 'Rationale of Responsibility for Young Offenders.' *Nebraska Law Review*. 29: 521–546.

Machel, Graça. (1996) *Impact of Armed Conflict on Children: Report of the Expert of the Secretary-General*. U.N. Doc. A/51/306 (26 August 1996). Report of the expert of the Secretary-General, Ms. Graca Machel, submitted pursuant to General Assembly resolution 48/157.

Machel, Graça. (2010) 'Foreword.' In Sharanjeet Parmar, Mindy Jane Roseman, Saudamini Siegrist, and Theo Sowa (eds) *Children and Transitional Justice: Truth-telling, Accountability and Reconciliation*. Cambridge, MA: Human Rights Program at Harvard Law School. ix–xiv.

Maepa, Traggy. (2005) 'The Truth and Reconciliation Commission as a Model of Restorative Justice.' In Traggy Maepa (ed.) *Beyond Retribution: Prospects for Restorative Justice in South Africa*. Monograph no. 111, February. Pretoria: Institute for Security Studies, with the Restorative Justice Centre.

Makumbi, Cissy, and James Eriku. (2011) 'Clergy Demand Truth and Reconciliation Commission for Northern Uganda.' *Sunday Monitor*. 12 September 2011. http://www.monitor.co.ug/News/National/-/688334/1234760/-/bj9w0gz/-/index.html

Mallinder, Louise. (2009) 'The Role of Amnesties in Conflict Transformation.' In Cedric Ryngaert (ed.) *The Effectiveness of International Criminal Justice*. Cambridge: Intersentia.

Manea, Elham. (2013) 'Transitional Justice and the Arab Spring from a Gender Perspective.' (Draft of Forthcoming Chapter) In Kirsten J. Fisher and Robert Stewart (eds) *Transitional Justice and the Arab Spring*. London: Routledge. (Draft version of chapter on file with author.)

Manirakiza, Pacifique (2009) 'Les enfants face au système international de justice: à la recherche d'un modèle de justice pénale internationale pour les délinquants mineurs.' *Queen's Law Journal*. 34: 719–768.

Mann, Howard. (1987) 'International Law and the Child Soldier.' *International and Comparative Law Quarterly*. 36: 32–57.

Mantle, Greg, Darrell Fox and Mandeep K. Dhami. (2005) 'Restorative Justice and Three Individual Theories of Crime.' *Internet Journal of Criminology*. http://www.crim.cam.ac.uk/people/academic_research/mandeep_dhami/12.pdf

Mapp, Susan. (2011) *Global Child Welfare and Well-being*. Oxford: Oxford University Press.

Maroney, Terry A. (2010) 'The False Promise of Adolescent Brain Science in Juvenile Justice.' *Notre Dame Law Review*. 85: 89–176.

Martins, Catarina. (2011) 'The Dangers of the Single Story: Child-Soldiers in Literary Fiction and Film.' *Childhood*. 18(4): 434–446.

Masten, Ann S. and Jenifer L. Powell. (2003) 'A Resilience Framework for Research, Policy, and Practice.' In Suniya S. Luthar (ed) *Resilience and Vulnerability: Adaption in the Context of Childhood*. Cambridge: Cambridge University Press. 1–26.

Mato Oput Project (2009) *Community Perspectives on The Mato Oput Process*. The Mato Oput Project Report. Gulu University.

May, Larry. (1987) *The Morality of Groups*. Notre Dame, IN: University of Notre Dame Press.

May, Anika. (2005) *Dealing with the Past: Experiences of Transitional Justice, Truth and Reconciliation Processes after Periods of Violent Conflict in Africa*. London: Conciliation Resources.

May, Larry. (2012) *After War Ends: A Philosophical Perspective*. Cambridge: Cambridge University Press.

May, Larry and Andrew Forcehimes (eds). (2012) *Morality, Jus Post Bellum, and International Law*. Cambridge: Cambridge University Press.

Maynard, Kimberly. (1997) 'Rebuilding Community: Psycho-Social Healing, Reintegration, and Reconciliation at the Grassroots.' In K. Kumar (ed.) *Rebuilding Societies After Civil War: Critical Roles for International Assistance*. Boulder, CO: Lynne Rienner. 203–226.

Mazurana, Dyan E., Susan McKay, Khristopher Carlson and Janel Kasper. (2002) 'Girls in Fighting Forces and Groups: Their Recruitment, Participation, Demobilization, and Reintegration.' *Peace and Conflict: Journal of Peace Psychology*. 8(2): 97–123.

McDiarmid, Claire. (2006) 'What Do They Know? Child Defendants and the Age of Criminal Responsibility: A National Law Perspective.' In Karin Arts and Vesselin Popovski (eds) *International Criminal Accountability and the Rights of Children*. The Hague: Hague Academic Press.

McDonnell, Faith J. H. and Grace Akallo. (2007) *Girl Soldier: A Story of Hope for Northern Uganda's Children*. Grand Rapids, MI: Chosen Books.

McKay, Susan. (2004) 'Reconstructing Fragile Lives: Girls' Social Reintegration in Northern Uganda and Sierra Leone.' *Gender and Development*. 12(3): 19–30.

McKay, Susan. (2005) 'Girls as "Weapons of Terror" in Northern Uganda and Sierra Leonean Rebel Fighting Forces.' *Studies in Conflict and Terrorism*. 28: 385–397.

McKay, Susan, Angela Veale, Miranda Worthen and Michael Wessells. (2011) 'Building Meaningful Participation in Reintegration Among War-Affected Young Mothers in Liberia, Sierra Leone and Northern Uganda.' *Intervention*. 9(2): 108–124.

McMahan, Jeff. (2010) 'An Ethical Perspective of Child Soldiers.' In Scott Gates and Simon Reich (eds) *Child Soldiers in the Age of Fractured States*. Pittsburgh, PA: University of Pittsburgh Press. 27–36.

Melander, Erik. (2005) 'Gender Equality and Intrastate Conflict.' *International Studies Quarterly*. 49(4): 695–714.

Mendeloff, David. (2009) 'Trauma and Vengeance: Assessing the Psychological and Emotional Effects of Post-Conflict Justice.' *Human Rights Quarterly*. 31(3): 592–623.

Mennecke, Martin. (2007) 'Punishing Genocidaires: A Deterrent Effect or Not?'. *Human Rights Review*. 8(4): 319–339.

Meron, Theodor. (1993) 'Rape as a Crime Under International Humanitarian Law.' *American Journal of International Law*. 87(3): 424–428.

Michels, An. (2006) 'Supporting Vulnerable Witnesses in Sierra Leone.' In Karin Arts and Vaasselin Popovski (eds) *International Criminal Accountability and the Rights of Children*. The Hague: Hague Academic Press.

Milgram, Stanley. (1963) 'Behavioral Study of Obedience.' *Journal of Abnormal Social Psychology*. 67: 371–378.

Minow, Martha. (1998) *Between Vengeance and Forgiveness*. Boston: Beacon Press.

Minow, Martha. (2000) 'The Hope For Healing: What Can Truth Commissions Do?.' In Robert I. Rotberg and Dennis Thompson (eds) *Truth V. Justice*. Princeton, NJ: Princeton University Press. 235–260.

Model Penal Code and Commentaries. (official draft and revised comments). (1985) *With text of model penal code as adopted at the 1962 annual meeting of the American Law Institute*. Washington, DC: American Law Institute.

Moloney, Anastasia. (2012) 'Colombia's Ex-child Soldiers Tell of Long Road Ahead.' *AlertNet*. (13 August 2012). http://www.trust.org/alertnet/news/colombias-ex-child-soldiers-tell-of-long-road-ahead

Moroz, Kathleen J. (2005) 'The Effects of Psychological Trauma on Children and Adolescents.' *Report Prepared for the Vermont Agency of Human Services, Department of Health, Division of Mental Health, Child Adolescent and Family Unit*. http://mentalhealth.vermont.gov/sites/dmh/files/report/cafu/DMH-CAFU_Psychological_Trauma_Moroz.pdf

Murphy, Jeffrie G. (1986) 'Marxism and Retribution.' In Joel Feinberg and Hyman Gross (eds) *Philosophy of Law*, 3rd edn. Wadsworth, CA: Wadsworth Publishing.

Murphy, Colleen. (2010) 'Political Reconciliation and International Criminal Trials.' In Larry May and Zachary Hoskins (eds) *International Criminal Law and Philosophy*. Cambridge: Cambridge University Press. 224–244.

Nagy, Rosemary. (2008) 'Transitional Justice as Global Project: Critical Reflections.' *Third World Quarterly*. 29(2): 275–289.

Nzita, Richard and Mbaga Niwampa. (1993) *Peoples and Cultures of Uganda*. Kampala: Fountain Publishing Inc.

Odoi-Musoke, Rachel and Margaret Ajok. (2013) 'JLOS Holds Transitional Justice Policy Consensus Building Workshop. ' Justice, Law and Order Sector, Report. Uganda. http://www.jlos.go.ug/index.php/component/k2/item/288-transitional-justice-policy-reviewed

OHCHR. (2007) *Making Peace Our Own: Victims' Perceptions of Accountability, Reconciliation and Transitional Justice in Northern Uganda*. (August 2007) UN Office of the High Commissioner for Human Rights.

Omar, Dullah. (n.d.) 'Introduction by the Minister of Justice.' Government of South Africa. http://www.justice.gov.za/trc/legal/justice.htm

Oola, Stephen. (2012) 'A Conflict-Sensitive Justice: Adjudicating Traditional Justice in Transitional Contexts.' In Moses Chrispus Okello, Chris Dolan, Undine Whande, Nokukhanya Mncwabe, Levis Onegi and Stephen Oola (eds) *Where*

Law Meets Reality: Forging African Transitional Justice. Cape Town: Pambazuka Press. 53–63.

Orend, Brian. (2002) 'Justice After War.' *Ethics and International Affairs*. 16(1): 43–56.

Osiel, Mark J. (2005) 'Modes of Participation in Mass Atrocity. *Cornell International Law Journal*. 38: 793–822.

Otunnu, Olara A. (2005) *'Era of Application': Instituting a Compliance and Enforcement Regime for CAAC*. Statement before the Security Council. Under-Secretary-General Special Representative of the Secretary-General for Children and Armed Conflict. https://www.essex.ac.uk/armedcon/story_id/eraofapplication.pdf

Pagnanelli, Enrico. (2007) 'Children as Adults: The Transfer of Juveniles to Adult Courts and the Potential Impact of Roper v. Simmons.' *American Criminal Law Review*. 44: 175–194.

Pain, Dennis. (1997) *The Bending of the Spears: Producing Consensus for Peace and Development in Northern Uganda*. London: International Alert and Kacoke Madit.

Pal, Radhabinod. (1953) *Military Tribunal for the Far East: Dissentient Judgment of Justice R.B. Pal, MA LLD*. Calcutta: Sanyal and Co.

Pape, Robert A. (2003) 'The Strategic Logic of Suicide Terrorism.' *American Political Science Review*. 97(3): 1–19.

Paris Principles. (2007) Principles and Guidelines on Children Associated with Armed Forces or Armed Groups. February. 2007. UN Children's Fund (UNICEF)

Parman, Sharanjeet, Mindy Jane Roseman, Saudamini Siegrist, and Theo Sowa. (eds) (2010) *Children and Transitional Justice: Truth-Telling, Accountability and Reconciliation*. Cambridge, MA: Human Rights Program at Harvard Law School.

Pavlich, George. (1996) 'The Power of Community Mediation: Government and Formation of Self.' *Law and Society Review*. 30: 101–127.

Penney, Stephanie R. and Marlene M. Moretti. (2005) 'The Transfer of Juveniles to Adult Court in Canada and the United States: Confused Agendas and Compromised Assessment Procedures.' *International Journal of Forensic Mental Health*. 4(1): 19–37.

Perrot, Sandrine. (2010) 'Northern Uganda: A "Forgotten Conflict", Again? The Impact of the Internationalization of the Resolution Package.' In Tim Allen and Koen Vlassenroot (eds.) *The Lord's Resistance Army: Myth and Reality*. London: Zed Books. 187–204.

Pickert, Kate. (2009) 'A Brief History of the Tamil Tigers.' *Time*. (4 January 2009). http://www.time.com/time/world/article/0,8599,1869501,00.html

Pillai, Priya. (2008) 'A "Call to Arms": A Gender Sensitive Approach to the Plight of Female Child Soldiers in International Law.' *Human Rights Brief*. 15(2): 23–27.

Purdon, Christine. (1999) 'Thought Suppression and Psychopathology.' *Behaviour Research and Therapy*. 37(11): 1029–1054.

Ramirez-Barat, Clara. (2012) *Engaging Children and Youth in Transitional Justice Processes: Guidance for Outreach Programs*. New York: International Center for Transitional Justice.

Rawls, John. (1999) *A Theory of Justice*. Boston, MA: Harvard University Press.

Reis, Chen. (1997) 'Trying the Future, Avenging the Past: The Implications of Prosecuting Children for Participation in Internal Armed Conflict.' *Columbia Human Rights Law Review:* 28: 629–655.

Rice, Cecil A. (2004) *Group Interventions for Treatment of Psychological Trauma. Module 6: The Later Stage: The Role of Group Interventions in Coping with the Aftermath of Traumatic Events*. American Group Psychotherapy Association. http://www.agpa.org/pubs/6-later-stage.pdf

Rikhof, Joseph. (2009) 'Child Soldiers: Should They be Punished?.' *Sword and Scale*. (May) 1–9.

Roberts, Paul. (2003) 'Restoration and Retribution in International Criminal Justice: An Exploratory Analysis.' In Andrew von Hirsch et al. (eds) *Restorative Justice and Criminal Justice: Competing or Reconcilable Paradigms?* Oxford: Hart Publishing. 115–134.

Robinson, Darryl. (2003) 'Serving the Interests of Justice: Amnesties, Truth Commissions and the International Criminal Court.' *European Journal of International Law*. 14(3): 481–505.

Rome Statute of the International Criminal Court, A/CONF.183/9, 17 July 1998, entered into force 1 July 2002.

Rosen, David M. (2005) *Armies of the Young: Child Soldiers in War and Terrorism*. London: Rutgers University Press.

Rossner, Meredith. (2011) 'Emotions and Interaction Ritual: A Micro Analysis of Restorative Justice.' *British Journal of Criminology*. 51: 95–119.

Rotberg, Robert I. (2000) 'Truth Commisions and the Provision of Truth, Justice, and Reconciliation.' In Robert I. Rotberg and Dennis Thompson (eds) *Truth V. Justice*. Princeton, NJ: Princeton University Press. 3–21.

Ryan, Christine. (2012) *Children of War: Child Soldiers as Victims and Participants in the Sudan Civil War*. New York: I.B. Taurus.

Scanlon, Helen and Kelli Muddell. (2009) 'Gender and Transitional Justice in Africa: Progress and Prospects.' *African Journal on Conflict Resolution*. 9(2): 9–28.

Schabas, William. (2011) 'Transitional Justice and the Norms of International Law.' Conference Paper, Annual Meeting of the Japanese Society of International Law. (Kwansei Gakuim University, 8 October 2011).

Schenkel, Mark. (2012) 'Uganda: Amnesty Act without Amnesty.' *Radio Netherlands Worldwide*. 3 June 2012. http://m.rnw.nl/international-justice/node/141206

Schmidt, Alice (2007) 'Volunteer Child Soldiers as Reality: A Development Issue for Africa.' *New School Economic Review*. 2(1): 49–76.

Schomerus, Mareike. (2010) 'Chasing the Kony Story.' In Tim Allen and Koen Vlassenroot (eds.) *The Lord's Resistance Army: Myth and Reality*. London: Zed Books. 93–112.

Scott, Elizabeth, N. Dickon Reppucci, Jennifer L. Woolard. (1995) 'Evaluating Adolescent Decision Making in Legal Contexts.' *Law and Human Behavior*. 19(3): 221–244.

SCSL (2007) 'Guilty Verdicts in the trial of AFRC Accused.' Press Release: Press and Public Affairs Office, Freetown, Sierra Leone: Special Court for Sierra Leone. 20 June 2007. http://www.sc-sl.org/LinkClick.aspx?fileticket=XOv%2F79UMaiY%3D&tabid=110

Sendabo, Teferi. (2004) *Child Soldiers: Rehabilitation and Social Reintegration in Liberia*. Uppsala: Life and Peace Institute.

Shaw, Rosalind. (2005) *Rethinking Truth and Reconciliation Commissions: Lessons from Sierra Leone*. Special Report. Washington, DC: United States Institute of Peace.

Shepler, Susan. (2005) 'The Rites of the Child: Global Discourses of Youth and Reintegrating Child Soldiers in Sierra Leone.' *Journal of Human Rights*. 4(2): 197–211.

Shnabel, Nurit and Arie Nadler. (2008) 'A Needs-Based Model of Reconciliation: Satisfying the Differential Emotional Needs of Victim and Perpetrator as a Key to Promoting Reconciliation.' *Journal of Personality and Social Psychology*. 94(1): 116–132.

Siegrist, Saudamini. (2010) 'Child Rights and Transitional Justice.' In Sharanjeet Parmar, Mindy Jane Roseman, Saudamini Siegreist, and Theo Sowa (eds) *Children and Transitional Justice: Truth-Telling, Accountability and Reconciliation*. Cambridge, MA: Human Rights Program at Harvard Law School. 1–30.

Sierra Leone Truth and Reconciliation Commission. (2004) *Witness to Truth: Final Report of the Sierra Leone Truth and Reconciliation Commission*. Freetown: Sierra Leone Truth and Reconciliation Commission.

Silverman, Wendy K., Claudio D. Oritz, Chockalingham Viswesvaran, Barbara J. Burns, David J. Kolko, Frank W. Putnam and Lisa Amaya-Jackson. (2008) 'Evidence-Based Psychosocial Treatment for Children and Adolescents Exposed to Traumatic Events.' *Journal of Clinical Child and Adolescent Psychology*. 37(1): 156–183.

Singer, P.W. (2004) 'Talk is Cheap: Getting Serious About Preventing Child Soldiers.' *Cornell International Law Journal*. 37: 561–586.

Singer, P.W. (2005) *Children at War*. New York: Pantheon Books.

Sloane, Robert D. (2007) 'The Expressive Capacity of International Punishment: The Limits 'of the National Law Analogy and the Potential of International Criminal Law." *Stanford Journal of International Law*. 43: 39–94.

Slye, Ronald C. (2000) 'Amnesty, Truth, and Reconciliation: Reflections on the South African Amnesty Process.' In Robert I. Rotberg and Dennis Thompson (eds) *Truth V. Justice*. Princeton, NJ: Princeton University Press. 170–188.

Smith, Alison. (2010) 'Basic Assumptions of Transitional Justice and Children.' In Sharanjeet Parmar, Mindy Jane Roseman, Saudamini Siegreist, and Theo Sowa (eds) *Children and Transitional Justice: Truth-Telling, Accountability and Reconciliation*. Cambridge, MA: Human Rights Program at Harvard Law School. 31–66.

Somasundaram, Daya. (2002) 'Child Soldiers: Understanding the Context.' *BMJ*. 324: 1268–1271.

Stahn, Carsten and Jann Kleffner (eds). (2008) *Jus Post Bellum: Towards a Law of Transition from Conflict to Peace*. Den Haag: T.M.C. Asser Press.

Statute of the Special Court for Sierra Leone, UN Security Council, 16 January 2002, established pursuant to Security Council resolution 1315.

Stauffer, Carl and Brandon Hamber (1996) 'Putting a Face on the Past: Survivor-Offender Mediation and the Truth and Reconciliation Commission.' *Centre for the Study of Violence and Reconciliation*. http://www.csvr.org.za/wits/papers/papbhcs.htm#note1

Stearns, Jason K. (2012) *Dancing in the Glory of Monsters: The Collapse of the Congo and The Great War of Africa*. New York: Public Affairs.

Steinberg, Laurence. (2007) 'Risk Taking in Adolescence: New Perspectives From Brain and Behavioural Science.' *Current Directions in Psychological Science*. 16(2): 055–59.

Steinberg, Laurence and Elizabeth S. Scott. (2003) 'Less Guilty by Reason of Adolescence: Developmental Immaturity, Diminished Responsibility, and the Juvenile Death Penalty.' *American Psychologist.* December. 58(12): 1009–1018.

Summerfield, Derek. (1996) *The Impact of War and Atrocity on Civilian Populations: Basic Principles for NGO Interventions and a Critique of Psychosocial Trauma Projects.* Network Paper 14. London: Relief and Rehabilitation Network.

Summerfield, Derek. (2001) 'The Invention of Post-Traumatic Stress Disorder and the Social Usefulness of a Psychiatric Category.' *British Medical Journal.* 322: 95–98.

Summerfield, Derek. (2004) 'Cross-Cultural Perspectives on the Medicalisation of Human Suffering.' In G.M. Rosen (ed.) *Posttraumatic Stress Disorder: Issues and Controversies.* Chichester: Wiley. 233–246.

Suzman, Jonathan and John Cottingham. (1987) 'Just Punishment.' *Proceedings of the Aristotelian Society.* 61: 41–55.

Tallgren, Immi. (2002) 'The Sensibility and Sense of International Criminal Law.' *European Journal of International Law.* 13: 561–595.

Teitel, Ruti G. (2003) 'Transitional Justice Genealogy.' *Harvard Human Rights Journal.* 16: 69–94.

Theidon, Kimberly. (2007) 'Transitional Subjects: The Disarmament, Demobilization and Reintegration of Former Combatants in Colombia.' *International Journal of Transitional Justice.* 1: 66–90.

Tobach, Ethel. (2004) 'Peace Rebuilding Needs Social Justice.' *Peace and Conflict: Journal of Peace Psychology.* 10(3): 305–307.

Tonheim, Milfrid. (2012) '"Who will comfort me?" Stigmatization of Girls Formerly Associated with Armed Forces and Groups in Eastern Congo.' *The International Journal of Human Rights.* 16(2): 278–297.

Transitional Justice Working Group. (2012) *The Amnesty Law (2000) Issues Paper* (April 2012) Uganda: Justice Law and Order Sector.

Truth and Reconciliation Commission Act 2000 (Sierra Leone). In Line with the Lomé Peace Agreement. 10 February 2000.

Truth and Reconciliation Report, Sierra Leone. (2003) *Truth and Reconciliation Commission Report for the Children of Sierra Leone: Child-Friendly Version.* Freetown: Truth and Reconciliation Commission. http://www.unicef.org/wcaro/WCARO_SL_Pub_TruthReconciliationRpt.pdf

Tutu, Archbishop Desmond. (1999) *No Future Without Forgiveness.* Toronto: Doubleday.

UK Foreign and Commonwealth Office. (2012). 'Foreign Secretary Launches New Government Initiative to Prevent Sexual Violence in Conflict.' Speech by Foreign Secretary William Hague. 29 May 2012. https://www.gov.uk/government/speeches/foreign-secretary-launches-new-government-initiative-to-prevent-sexual-violence-in-conflict

Umbreit, Mark S. (2001) *The Handbook of Victim Offender Mediation: An Essential Guide to Research and Practice.* San Francisco, CA: Jossey-Bass Inc. http://media.johnwiley.com.au/product_data/excerpt/18/07879549/0787954918.pdf

Umbreit, Mark S., Robert B. Coates and Betty Vos. (2004) 'Victim-Offender Mediation: Three Decades of Practice and Research.' *Conflict Resolution Quarterly.* 22(1–2): 279–303.

UNDP (2004) United Nations Development Program, "' Access to Justice, ' Practice Note (9/3/2004)

http://www.undp.org/content/dam/aplaws/publication/en/publications/democratic-governance/dg-publications-for-website/access-to-justice-practice-note/Justice_PN_En.pdf

UNICEF (2002) *International Criminal Justice and Children*. http://www.unicef.org/emerg/files/ICJC.pdf

United Nations. (1996) Preparatory Committee on the Establishment of an International Criminal Court. 25 March-12 April 1996. A/AC.249/1 17 (7 May 1996)

United Nations. (2002) Optional Protocol to the Convention on the Rights of the Child on the involvement of children in armed conflict. Adopted and opened for signature, ratification and accession by General Assembly resolution A/RES/54/263 of 25 May 2000. Entered into force on 12 February 2002.

United Nations. (2010). World Programme of Action for Youth. New York: United Nations. http://www.un.org/esa/socdev/unyin/documents/wpay2010.pdf

United Nations. (2011) *Children and Justice During and in the Aftermath of Armed Conflict*. United Nations Office of the Special Representative of the Secretary-General for Children and Armed Conflict. Working Paper. (September 2011).

UN Office of the High Commissioner for Human Rights. (2007) *Making Peace Our Own: Victims' Perceptions of Accountability, Reconciliation and Transitional Justice in Northern Uganda* (August 2007). http://www.unhcr.org/refworld/docid/46cc4a690.html [accessed 10 May 2012]

United States Institute of Peace. (n.d.) 'Social Reconstruction.' http://www.usip.org/guiding-principles-stabilization-and-reconstruction-the-web-version/social-well-being/social-reconst

UN Secretary-General (UNSG) (2011) *Report of the Secretary-General's Panel of Experts on Accountability in Sri Lanka*. (31 March 2011). United Nations.

United Nations Security Council Resolution 1325. (2000) Adopted by the Security Council at its 4213th meeting on 31 October 2000. UNSC S/RES/1325.

United Nations Security Council Resolution 1888. (2009) Adopted by the Security Council at its 6195th meeting on 30 September 2009. UNSC S/RES/1888.

Uppard, Sarah. (2003) 'Child Soldiers and Children Associated with the Fighting Forces.' *Medicine, Conflict and Survival*. 19(2): 121–127.

Van der Kolk, B. A., Pelcovitz, D., Roth, S., Mandel, F., MacFarlane, A., Herman, J.L. (1996) 'Dissociation, Affect Regulation and Somatization: The Complex Nature of Adaptation to Trauma.' http://www.trauma-pages.com/a/vanderk5.php

Veale, Angela. (2006) 'The Criminal Responsibility of Former Child Soldiers: Contributions from Psychology.' In Karin Arts and Vesselin Popovski (eds) *International Criminal Accountability and the Rights of Children*. The Hague: Hague Academic Press.

Veale, Angela and Aki Stavrou. (2007) 'Former Lord's Resistance Army Child Soldier Abductees: Explorations of Identity in Reintegration and Reconciliation.' *Peace and Conflict: Journal of Peace Psychology*. 13(3): 273–292.

Vernon, Richard. (2002) 'What is Crime against Humanity.' *Journal of Political Philosophy*. 10: 231–249.

Vinci, Anthony. (2005) 'The Strategic Use of Fear by the Lord's Resistance Army.' *Small Wars and Insurgencies*. 16(3): 360–381.

Wall, I. R. (2006) 'Duress, International Criminal Law, and Literature.' *Journal of International Criminal Justice*. 4(4): 724–744.

Waller, James. (2007) *Becoming Evil: How Ordinary People Commit Genocide and Mass Killing* (Second edition). New York: Oxford University Press.

Wallis, Andrew. (2007) *Silent Accomplice: The Untold Story of France's Role in the Rwandan Genocide*. London: I.B. Tauris.

Wang, Peng. (2011) 'Women in the LTTE: Birds of Freedom or Cogs in the Wheel?.' *Journal of Politics and Law*. 4(1): 100–108.

War Child. (n.d.) 'Child Soldiers.' http://www.warchild.org.uk/issues/child-soldiers

Webster, Timothy. (2007) 'Babes with Arms: International Law and Child Soldiers.' *George Washington International Law Review*. 39: 227–254.

Wenzlaff, Richard M. and Daniel M. Wegner. (2000) 'Thought Suppression.' *Annual Review of Psychology*. 51: 59–91.

Wessells, Michael, and Carlinda Monteiro. (2001) 'Psychosocial Intervention and Post-War Reconstruction in Angola: Interweaving Western and Traditional Approaches.' In Christie, D. J., Wagner, R. V., & Winter, D. A. (eds) *Peace, Conflict, and Violence: Peace Psychology for the 21st Century*. New Jersey: Prentice-Hall.

Wessells, Michael. (2006) *Child Soldiers: From Violence to Protection*. Cambridge, MA: Harvard University Press.

Wessells, Michael and Kathleen Kostelny. (2009) 'Youth Soldiering: An Integrated Framework for Understanding Psychosocial Impact.' In Brian K. Barber (ed.) *Adolescents and War: How Youth Deal with Political Violence*. Oxford: Oxford University Press. 105–122.

Whitman, Shelly. (n.d.) *Preventing the Use of Child Soldiers: The Role of the International Criminal Court*. Dalhousie University: Child Soldiers Initiative. http://childsoldiersinitiative.org/pdfs/whitman-preventing.pdf

Whitman, Shelly. (2012) 'The Responsibility to Protect and Child Soldiers.' In Andy Knight and Fraser Egerton (eds) *The Routledge Handbook on the Responsibility to Protect*. London: Routledge. 152–165.

Wilson, Stuart. (2001) 'The Myth of Restorative Justice: Truth, Reconciliation and the Ethics of Amnesty.' *South African Journal on Human Rights*. 17: 531–562.

Wilson, Fionna, Gabriele Oettingen, Judith Daniels, Manuela Post, Catrin Hoyer, and Hubertus Adam. (2010) 'Posttraumatic Resilience in Former Ugandan Child Soldiers.' *Child Development*. 81(4): 1096–1113.

Wood, Elizabeth Jean. (2009) 'Armed Groups and Sexual Violence: When Is Wartime Rape Rare?' *Politics and Society*. 37: 131–161.

World Health Organization. (2003) *Mental Health in Emergencies: Mental and Social Aspects of Health and Populations Exposed to Extreme Stressor*. Geneva: Department of Mental Health and Substance Dependence, World Health Organization.

Zarowsky, Christina and Duncan Pedersen. (2000) 'Rethinking Trauma in a Transnational World.' *Transcultural Psychology*. 37(3): 291–293.

Zehr, Howard (2002) *The Little Book of Restorative Justice*. Intercourse, PA: Good Books.

Zehr, Howard. (2005) *Changing Lenses: A New Focus for Crime and Justice*. Scottdale, PA: Herald Press.

Zernova, Margarita. (2007) *Restorative Justice: Ideals and Realities*. Abingdon: Ashgate Publishing Group.

Cases

International Courts

Prosecutor v. Alex Brima, Brima Bazzy Kamara and Santigie Kanu, Case No. SCSL-04–16-A (SCSL Trial Chamber).

Prosecutor v. Charles Ghankay Taylor, Case No. SCSL-03–01-T (SCSL Trial Chamber).

Prosecutor v. Dražen Erdemović, Case No. IT-96–22 (ICTY Trial Chamber).

Prosecutor v. Thomas Lubanga Dyilo, Case No. ICC-01/04–01/06 (ICC Trial Chamber).

Warrant for Arrest of Dominic Ongwen, Case No. ICC-02/04–01/05–57, Situation in Uganda (13 October 2005).

National Courts

Uganda

Prosecution v. Thomas Kwoyelo alias Latoni, HCT-00-ICD Case No. 02/10 (Uganda's High Court, International Crimes Division).

Thomas Kwoyelo alias Latoni v. Uganda, Constitutional Petition No. 036/2011 (Reference).

United Kingdom

T and V v. United Kingdom (1999) 7 B.H.R.C. 659.

United States

United States of America v. Omar Ahmed Khadr. MC Form 458 Jan 2007, Block VI Referral.

Interviews Cited

Acholi elders. Interview by author, 31 January 2007. Amuru District, Uganda. Tape recording.

Baganda man. Interview by author, 23 January 2007. Kampala, Uganda. Tape recording.

Banyankole elders. Interview by author, 4 February 2007. Biharwe village, Uganda. Tape recording.

Banyankole man. Interview by author, 9 February 2007. Kampala, Uganda. Tape recording.

Formerly Abducted Soldier, Uganda. Confidential Reporter 27021101. Interview by author, 27 February 2011. Kampala, Uganda. Digital recording.

Iteso elders. Interview by author, 10 February 2007. Kampala, Uganda. Tape recording.

Kakwa man. Interview by author, 23 January 2007. Kampala, Uganda. Tape recording.

Karamajang man, Interview by author, 29 January 2007. Kampala, Uganda. Tape recording.

Kisembo, Stephen, Uganda Joint Christian Council. Interview by author, 23 January 2007. Kampala, Uganda. Tape Recording.

Loko-Coo, Okot Constantine Ngom, Paicho Clan Chief, Chairman of Customary Chiefs of the Executive Committee. Interview by author, 3 February 2013. Digital Recording.

Nalwoga, Jessica, Acting Program Officer for Peace and Human Rights, Church of Uganda – PDR. Interview by author, 15 February 2007. Kampala, Uganda. Tape recording.

Odur, William, Senior Psychiatric Clinical Officer, Gulu Regional Referral Hospital. Interview by author, 29 January 2013. Gulu, Uganda. Digital Recording.

Okello, Moses C., Head of Research and Advocacy Department, Refugee Law Project, Faculty of Law, Makerere University. Interview by author, 23 January 2007. Tape recording.

Okonye, Godman, Language Institute, Makerere University. Interview by author, 13 February 2007. Tape recording.

Omach, Paul, Department of Political Science and Public Administration, Makerere University. Interview by author, 2 November 2011. Digital Recording.

Index

Printed and bound in the United States of America